Performance Interventions

Series Editors: **Elaine Aston**, University of Lancaster, and Bryan Reynolds, University of California, Irvine

Performance Interventions is a series of monographs and essay collections on theatre, performance, and visual culture that share an underlying commitment to the radical and political potential of the arts in our contemporary moment, or give consideration to performance and to visual culture from the past deemed crucial to a social and political present. *Performance Interventions* moves transversally across artistic and ideological boundaries to publish work that promotes dialogue between practitioners and academics, and interactions between performance communities, educational institutions, and academic disciplines.

Titles include:

Alan Ackerman and Martin Puchner (*editors*)
AGAINST THEATRE
Creative Destructions on the Modernist Stage

Elaine Aston and Geraldine Harris (*editors*)
FEMINIST FUTURES?
Theatre, Performance, Theory

Elaine Aston and Geraldine Harris
A GOOD NIGHT OUT FOR THE GIRLS
Popular Feminisms in Contemporary Theatre and Performance

Anna Birch and Joanne Tompkins (*editors*)
PERFORMING SITE-SPECIFIC THEATRE
Politics, Place, Practice

Maaike Bleeker
VISUALITY IN THE THEATRE
The Locus of Looking

Sara Brady
PERFORMANCE, POLITICS AND THE WAR ON TERROR
'Whatever it Takes'

Clare Finburgh and Carl Lavery (*editors*)
CONTEMPORARY FRENCH THEATRE AND PERFORMANCE

James Frieze
NAMING THEATRE
Demonstrative Diagnosis in Performance

Lynette Goddard
STAGING BLACK FEMINISMS
Identity, Politics, Performance

Alison Forsyth and Chris Megson (*editors*)
GET REAL: DOCUMENTARY THEATRE PAST AND PRESENT

D1142901

Leslie Hill and Helen Paris (*editors*)
PERFORMANCE AND PLACE

D.J. Hopkins, Shelley Orr and Kim Solga (*editors*)
PERFORMANCE AND THE CITY

Amelia Howe Kritzer
POLITICAL THEATRE IN POST-THATCHER BRITAIN
New Writing: 1995–2005

Alison Jeffers
REFUGEES, THEATRE AND CRISIS
Performing Global Identities

Stephen Greer
CONTEMPORARY BRITISH QUEER PERFORMANCE

Marcela Kostihová
SHAKESPEARE IN TRANSITION
Political Appropriations in the Post-Communist Czech Republic

Jon McKenzie, Heike Roms and C.J W.-L. Wee (*editors*)
CONTESTING PERFORMANCE
Emerging Sites of Research

Jennifer Parker-Starbuck
CYBORG THEATRE
Corporeal/Technological Intersections in Multimedia Performance

Ramón H. Rivera-Servera and Harvey Young
PERFORMANCE IN THE BORDERLANDS

Mike Sell (*editor*)
AVANT-GARDE PERFORMANCE AND MATERIAL EXCHANGE
Vectors of the Radical

Melissa Sihra (*editor*)
WOMEN IN IRISH DRAMA
A Century of Authorship and Representation

Brian Singleton
MASCULINITIES AND THE CONTEMPORARY IRISH THEATRE

Performance Interventions
Series Standing Order ISBN 978–1–403–94443–6 Hardback
978–1–403–94444–3 Paperback
(*outside North America only*)

You can receive future titles in this series as they are published by placing a standing order. Please contact your bookseller or, in case of difficulty, write to us at the address below with your name and address, the title of the series and the ISBN quoted above.

Customer Services Department, Macmillan Distribution Ltd, Houndmills, Basingstoke, Hampshire RG21 6XS, England

Performing Site-Specific Theatre

Politics, Place, Practice

Edited by

Anna Birch
Lecturer in Research, Royal Conservatoire of Scotland, UK

and

Joanne Tompkins
Professor of Drama, School of English, Media Studies and Art History, University of Queensland, Australia

palgrave
macmillan

First published 2012 by
PALGRAVE MACMILLAN

Palgrave Macmillan in the UK is an imprint of Macmillan Publishers Limited,
registered in England, company number 785998, of Houndmills, Basingstoke,
Hampshire RG21 6XS.

Palgrave Macmillan in the US is a division of St Martin's Press LLC,
175 Fifth Avenue, New York, NY 10010.

Palgrave Macmillan is the global academic imprint of the above companies
and has companies and representatives throughout the world.

Palgrave® and Macmillan® are registered trademarks in the United States,
the United Kingdom, Europe and other countries.

ISBN 978–0–230–36405–9 hardback
ISBN 978–0–230–36406–6 paperback

This book is printed on paper suitable for recycling and made from fully
managed and sustained forest sources. Logging, pulping and manufacturing
processes are expected to conform to the environmental regulations of the
country of origin.

A catalogue record for this book is available from the British Library.

A catalog record for this book is available from the Library of Congress.

10   9   8   7   6   5   4   3   2   1
21 20 19 18 17 16 15 14 13 12

Printed and bound in Great Britain by
CPI Antony Rowe, Chippenham and Eastbourne

Contents

Illustrations

Cover image: *Wollstonecraft Live!* Written by Kaethe Fine, produced and directed by Anna Birch, Fragments & Monuments film and performance company on Newington Green, London N16, UK

Maps

Images

Figure

Acknowledgements

Thanks to the contributors of the chapters in this volume with whom it has been a pleasure to work. We are only sorry that word limits precluded many others from also contributing. Thanks to the two anonymous readers whose advice was extremely helpful in the shaping of this book. Paula Kennedy and Ben Doyle from Palgrave Macmillan have been very supportive throughout the process.

We could not have completed this book without the assistance of Sarah Thomasson, who has been invaluable in collating, standardizing, and assembling the manuscript; we thank her not only for her time and formatting skills, but also for her valuable insight. Thanks too to Alan Lawrence for proofreading and preparing the index.

Contributors

Bruce Barton is a creator/scholar who teaches playmaking, dramaturgy, and intermedial performance at the University of Toronto, Canada. He has published in a wide range of scholarly and practical periodicals, as well as several national and international essay collections. His book publications include *At the Intersection Between Art and Research* (2010), *Developing Nation: New Play Creation in English-Speaking Canada* (2009), *Collective Creation, Collaboration and Devising* (2008), and *Reluctant Texts from Exuberant Performance: Canadian Devised Theatre* (2008). He is the co-editor of the recent issues of *Canadian Theatre Review* on 'Theatrical Devising' (2009) and 'Memory' (2011) and the forthcoming issue of *Theatre Research in Canada* on 'Theatre and Intermediality' (2011). Current funded research includes a study on physical dramaturgies in devised and intermedial performance. His stage plays have been produced on stages across Canada, and he also works extensively as a director and dramaturge with physically based, devising, and intermedial performance companies.

Susan Bennett is University Professor in the Department of English at the University of Calgary in Canada. Author of the well-known *Theatre Audiences* (1997), she is widely published across a variety of theatre and performance studies topics. Her current research projects are concerned with ideas of place in both early modern and contemporary performance settings.

Anna Birch is a lecturer in research at the Royal Conservatoire of Scotland, Scotland. Her practice-based research interests focus on gender and performance, site-specific theatre, film and new writing. Since 2000 she produced and directed a series of performance and film projects. Her recent publications include the 2012 special issue, 'Site-Specificity and Mobility' in *Contemporary Theatre Review* (with Joanne Tompkins), 'Performing Research: Cite, Sight, Site' in *On Making*, edited by Leora Farber, and *The Wollstonecraft Live Experience!* (with Taey Iohe). Her work is found in libraries, museums, and specialist archive holdings as evidence of the hidden histories of women's achievement. Most recently she directed the performance and film of A *Pageant of Great Women* by Cicely Hamilton to celebrate the centenary of the original performance, directed by Edith Craig. She is Artistic Director of Fragments & Monuments performance and film company, based in Hackney, UK. (www.fragmentsandmonuments.com). Currently she co-convenes the Performance as Research Working Group at the annual International Federation of Theatre Research Conference.

Jane Collins is a professor of theatre and performance at Wimbledon College of Art, University of the Arts, London. She is a writer, director, and theatre maker. For the Royal Court, in partnership with the National Theatre of Uganda, she co-directed *Maama Nalukalala Ne'zzadde Lye* (*Mother Courage and Her Children*) by Bertolt Brecht, with a Ugandan cast in Kampala. The production toured to America and South Africa. *The Story of the African Choir,* which she researched, wrote, and directed, examined the reception of performances by a group of black South African singers in nineteenth-century England. It was staged at the Grahamstown International Festival in 2007. In 2010, Collins created the audio component of *Space and Light*, an exhibition on the life and work of Edward Gordon Craig, at the Victoria and Albert Museum. She is co-editor of *Theatre and Performance Design: a Reader in Scenography.*

Lesley Ferris, Arts and Humanities Distinguished Professor of Theatre at the Ohio State University, USA, currently serves as Director of OSU/Royal Shakespeare Company Programs. Her research interests focus on gender and performance, carnival, and the use of masks. Her books include *Acting Women: Images of Women in Theatre* and *Crossing the Stage: Controversies on Cross Dressing.* She co-curated (with Adela Ruth Tompsett, London) the exhibition *Midnight Robbers: The Artists of Notting Hill Carnival* (London, 2007). She was guest co-editor (with Penny Farfan, University of Calgary) for a special issue of *Theatre Journal* entitled 'Contemporary Women Playwrights' (December 2010). Ferris has directed more than 50 productions in Britain, South Africa, and the USA; the most recent was *The Camouflage Project*, a devised work that focused on the role of women agents in Britain's undercover activity in German occupied France in World War II (2011).

Susan Haedicke is an associate professor in the School of Theatre, Performance, and Cultural Policy Studies at the University of Warwick in the UK. She received her MA and PhD in theatre from the University of Michigan/Ann Arbor. She has published extensively on European street arts, including *Contemporary European Street Arts: Aesthetics and Politics*

(2012). She co-edited *Political Performances: Theory and Practice* (2009) and *Performing Democracy: International Perspectives on Urban Community-Based Performance* (2001). She also works as a professional dramaturge in France and the USA. Her current practice-as-research project 'Hope is a Wooded Time' is a multi-stage project that seeks to play a role in preserving biodiversity by using art to increase public awareness and knowledge of its importance to the survival of the planet.

Helen Iball teaches at the University of Leeds, UK, in the Workshop Theatre, part of the School of English. Her current project, 'Theatre Personal: Audiences with Intimacy', explores contemporary 'audience participation' using research methods that include interdisciplinary workshops and conversations with makers and participants. The project website (theatrepersonal.co.uk) houses archive documentation and an up-to-date list of *Theatre Personal* publications. Iball is the author of *Sarah Kane's Blasted* (2008) for Continuum Modern Theatre Guides and a contributor to *Bobby Baker: Redeeming Features of Daily Life* (2007), and has published widely on contemporary British theatre, particularly in the contexts of scenography, gender, and performance. She is currently preparing an article on the ethics of the intimate audience, and is exploring Bobby Baker's *Diary Drawings* in a chapter arising from her interest in the comparative study of autobiography across sequential drawing and performance.

Kathleen Irwin is a professional scenographer, writer, and educator whose practical and theoretical research focuses on site-specific practice, alternative performative spaces, and Internet performativity. As co-artistic director of *Knowhere Productions*, she has produced large-scale performances in an abandoned mental hospital and a brick factory. She is Head of the Theatre Department, University of Regina, Canada. Her research is published in Canadian and international journals and anthologies. She is Canadian Education Commissioner and Co-chair of the History and Theory Commission for the International Organization for Scenographers, Theatre Architects and Technicians. She is a tutor with the graduate-level Summer Academy for Practice-Based Research at Aalto University. Her publications include *Sighting/Citing/Sighting* (2009) and *The Ambit of Performativity* (2007).

Michael McKinnie is a senior lecturer in drama at Queen Mary, University of London, UK. His research focuses on theatre and space, and the cultural economics of performance. He is the author of *City Stages:*

Theatre and Urban Space in a Global City (2007), which was awarded the Ann Saddlemyer Prize for an outstanding book by the Canadian Association for Theatre Research. He is also the editor of *Space and the Geographies of Theatre* (2007). Additional publications include articles in *Theatre Journal, Modern Drama, Contemporary Theatre Review, Essays on Canadian Writing, Theatre Research in Canada,* and *Canadian Theatre Review.* He is currently working on a book about performance and the cultural politics of place.

Sophie Nield teaches theatre and film in the Department of Drama and Theatre at Royal Holloway, University of London, UK. She works on questions of space, theatricality, and representation in political life and the law, and on the performance of 'borders' of various kinds. She recently co-edited, with Marett Leiboff of the Faculty of Law, University of Wollongong, a special issue of *Law Text Culture* on the relationships between theatricality and law, entitled *Law's Theatrical Presence.* She is a member of the board of directors of the research organisation Performance Studies International, and of the executive committee of the Theatre and Performance Research Association. Between 2003 and 2006, she was Director of the AHRC-funded Mander and Mitchenson Theatre Collection Access for Research Project. She is a regular contributor to the *Guardian's* stage blog, and is on the editorial board of the journal *About Performance.*

Louise Owen is a lecturer in theatre and performance at Birkbeck College, University of London, UK. Her research examines the relationship between contemporary theatre and performance, political economy, and modes of governance. Her writing has been published in *Performance Research, Drama: the Journal for National Drama, Contemporary Theatre Review* and *RiDE: the Journal of Applied Theatre and Performance.* She is currently working on a monograph exploring cultural work and neoliberalization in Britain, and essays examining post-feminism, precarity, and performance, and alternative theatre in London since 1972. She currently co-convenes the London Theatre Seminar and the annual ATHE Performance Studies Focus Group Pre-Conference.

Mike Pearson trained as an archaeologist. He was a member of RAT Theatre (1972–3) and an artistic director of Cardiff Laboratory Theatre (1973–80) and Brith Gof (1981–97). He continues to make performance as a solo artist and in collaboration with artist/designer Mike Brookes as Pearson/Brookes (1997–present). He is co-author with

Michael Shanks of *Theatre/Archaeology* (2001) and author of '*In Comes I': Performance, Memory and Landscape* (2006), *Site-Specific Performance* (2010), and *The Mickery Theater: An Imperfect Archaeology* (2011). He is currently a professor of performance studies in the Department of Theatre, Film and Television Studies, Aberystwyth University, UK.

Julie Sanders is a professor of English literature and drama at the University of Nottingham, UK. She is the author of several books and articles on the subject of seventeenth-century literature and on adaptation theory, including *Ben Jonson's Theatrical Republics* (1998) and *Adaptation and Appropriation* (2006). She edited *Ben Jonson in Context* (2010) and has edited plays by Ben Jonson, James Shirley, and Richard Brome. Her most recent monograph, *The Cultural Geography of Early Modern Drama, 1620–1650*, was published in 2011. She is currently working on an Arts and Humanities Research Council-funded project with Dr James Loxley on Ben Jonson's walk to Scotland.

Joanne Tompkins has taught drama in the School of English, Media Studies and Art History at UQ since 1996. She is currently Head of School. She is the (co-)author of *Post-Colonial Drama* (with Helen Gilbert) and of *Women's Intercultural Performance* (with Julie Holledge). She is the author of *Unsettling Space: Contestations in Contemporary Australian Theatre* (2006), which explores the politics of contemporary Australian theatre and argues that theatre regularly stages the nation's anxieties about space/place/landscape and settlement. She co-edited *Modern Drama* for five years with Ric Knowles and W.B. Worthen, during which time they produced the volume *Modern Drama: Defining the Field*. In addition to conventional research, she has produced an innovative research tool to enable the analysis of theatre space through virtual reality. This interdisciplinary and collaborative project, Ortelia, analyses and archives art gallery, museum, and theatre spaces, exhibitions, and performances.

Richard Windeyer is a digital media creative, audio artist, composer, musician, and educator. He is a member of the core creative team behind the internationally acclaimed bluemouth inc presents, a theatre company that creates uniquely immersive and participatory experiences that challenge conventional audience–performer relationships. He thrives on working and thinking across disciplines. His main area of interest is the impact of digital technologies and generative systems on creative process, live performance, and user experience. He currently teaches courses in music technology and electroacoustic music at Wilfrid Laurier University in Waterloo, Canada.

Keren Zaiontz is a lecturer in drama, theatre, and performance at Roehampton University. She is co-editor of *Reluctant Texts from Exuberant Performance: Canadian Devised Theatre* (2008) and *Performing Adaptations: Essays and Conversations on the Theory and Practice of Adaptation* (2009). Her current research examines the role that arts festivals play in the creative promotion of place, and assesses how citizens are scripted as 'place patriots' in large-scale celebrations like the Cultural Olympiad.

1
The 'Place' and Practice of Site-Specific Theatre and Performance

Joanne Tompkins

Performing Site-Specific Theatre engages with theatre and performance that is grounded in an in-depth exploration and expression of spatial practice. This volume emerged from the editors' fascination with how different types of spatial arrangements affect our understanding of and relationships with performance: specifically, the particularities of 'place' and its capacity to recontextualize performance, just as performance can reformulate how we perceive and experience space and place.[1] The form continues to provoke questions about what both performance and site convey; in response, this volume investigates how the genre operates now and into the future, when space, place, site, landscape, and location are regularly characterized by ambiguity, contingency, and unsettlement.

The rise of performance studies as a discipline has seen the expansion and active problematizing of what constitutes contemporary performance; it has also afforded a resurgence of interest in site-specific performance. The specific nature of this increasingly popular genre is not as easy to isolate as many other forms of performance for several reasons, the most significant being the propensity for the boundaries of both 'site' and 'performance' to slip. For Nick Kaye, this slippage is inherent to the form: 'site-specificity arises precisely in uncertainties over the borders and limits of work and site' (2000, p.215). While such slippages are a central, significant trope of site-specific work, they complicate simple definitions of even the components of the genre, let alone the form as a whole. This collection attempts to articulate the aesthetic, cultural, and political effects of such a generic 'instability'. The volume's response to the complexity of the genre is twofold. First, it aims to augment the account of productive theatrical and theoretical work of and about site-specific performance. Second, it provides a forum to re-assess the form: many of the chapters herein argue the case for producing and interpreting more critically nuanced versions of the performance of site-specificity.

Nevertheless, a study of the effects of site-specific performance calls for at least some awareness of the nature of the form, regardless of its complexity. Mike Pearson and Michael Shanks's 2001 definition of site-specific theatre continues to be a benchmark:

> Site-specific performances are conceived for, mounted within and conditioned by the particulars of found spaces, existing social situations or locations, both used and disused [...]. They rely, for their conception and their interpretation, upon the complex coexistence, superimposition and interpenetration of a number of narratives and architectures, historical and contemporary, of two basic orders: that which is of the site, its fixtures and fittings, and that which is brought to the site, the performance and its scenography: of that which pre-exists the work and that which is of the work: of the past and of the present. They are inseparable from their sites, the only contexts within which they are intelligible. Performance recontextualises such sites: it is the latest occupation of a location at which other occupations – their material traces and histories – are still apparent: site is not just an interesting, and disinterested, backdrop. [...] The multiple meanings and readings of performance and site intermingle, amending and compromising one another.
>
> (2001, p.23)

Pearson and Shanks (2001) explain that simply setting 'site' and 'performance' side by side is insufficient because a foundational intersection of the components is required wherein both 'performance' and 'site' inform each other so that an active relationship between them remains fluid. The relationship between the two core concepts clearly remains the most contested – and contestable – territory, to the point that Kaye maintains, from a different perspective, that a form of friction between these elements underpins site-specific performance rather than an inherent mutuality. Kaye asserts that 'site-specific art frequently works to *trouble* the oppositions between the site and the work' (2000, p.11; original emphasis). He stresses that this troubling means that 'the site functions as a text perpetually in the process of being written and being read, [...so] the site-specific work's very attempt to establish its place will be subject to the process of slippage, deferral and indeterminacy in which its signs are constituted' (Kaye, 2000, p.183). Both Pearson and Shanks's and Kaye's versions privilege the interrelationship between site and performance; they are intended to assist readers new to the field but, as many of the chapters in this volume explore, what may or may not be deemed 'site-specific' transforms as the nature of a performance and/or a site itself alters. Many of the contributors challenge the genre in such a way that definitions of site-specific performance must remain contingent.

Susan Bennett and Julie Sanders take this argument well outside 'just' the contemporary moment. Their chapter in this volume investigates how Milton's 1634 play, *A Masque Presented at Ludlow Castle*, might be valuably re-read as site-specific in order to bolster the temporal reach of the form but, more importantly, to provide the form with the critical weight that its exposure to another historical (and performance) context can offer. From a different perspective, the genre of site-specific performance is increasingly being ascribed simply to a production that takes place outside a conventional theatre venue, rather than to performances that have been developed in the context of a particular location. This skews a conventional understanding of the genre, presenting quite a few difficulties that Michael McKinnie raises in his chapter, through the example of a production of Beth Steel's *Ditch*, relocated from its original site to a tunnel under London's Waterloo Station. Both of these chapters address the expansion of the genre's parameters, arguing for an investigation of what the field might mean, and the implications of such expansion.

Performing Site-Specific Theatre aims to outline key questions for the form, beyond simply itemizing the innumerable ways to address different sites and to create different examples of performance. The form is currently robust enough to promote new versions of how one might perceive the relationship between site and performance, and additional spatial contexts will continue to challenge both 'site' and 'performance'. Two such challenges which emerge in this book are multimedia and cyberspace. Critics and performers alike might wish to consider how these and other performance traditions and historical eras intersect with, and contribute to, the genre (if at all). How might the ambiguity, contingency, and unsettlement that we perceive to be characterizing site-specific performance be explored productively? Finally, how might cultural politics – whether expressed through urban regeneration, the economics of culture, or even an ethics of performance (among other possibilities) – be enhanced through the generation and performance of site-specific work? And how might the critique of such work contribute not just to the development of a critical praxis, but also to the articulation of cultural activity as crucial to social well-being. Anna Birch and Louise Owen discuss in their chapters that where public spaces are taken over by performance, encouraging different modes of participation is key to the success of the events. Sophie Nield, on the other hand, shows what happens when no agreement has been reached for that participation to take place. Cultural activity as a central aspect of social well-being depends on public space to support it.

The next two sections – Place and Practice – highlight aspects that contribute to a nuanced understanding of the form, while also allowing for the contingency that it continues to require.

Place

Just as site-specific performance itself is difficult to define, attempts to pin down a mutually agreed-upon understanding of 'place' – in either precise physical or metaphorical terms – is fraught with dangers. Rather than defining 'place', 'space', or 'site' here, I suggest just three critical contexts for 'place': place as geographical site, place which situates social or historical position, and the place or location of performance. These metaphoric interpretations of the term contextualize this volume.

The scholarship on geographical place and space is extensive, with spatial studies expanding considerably in the late twentieth century. Place as geographical site has been widely theorized by philosophers, cultural geographers, and historians, among others.[2] Theorists such as Edward Casey (2009), Michel de Certeau (1984), Michel Foucault (1986), David Harvey (2000), Henri Lefebvre (1991), Doreen Massey (1997), and Yi-Fu Tuan (1977) have made valuable contributions to how we understand place and space, both with and against time. To select just a few of the positions they advance, Harvey notes the power of space by arguing the primacy of geography in social interaction: 'spatial form controls temporality, [such that] an imagined geography controls the possibility of social change and history' (2000, p.160). For Lefebvre, culture emerges from and is determined by a 'hypercomplexity of social space' (1991, p.88). More specifically, he asserts that '[s]ocial relations, which are concrete abstractions, have no real existence save in and through space. *Their underpinning is spatial*' (Lefebvre, 1991, p.404; original emphasis). De Certeau similarly argues the centrality of space, albeit from a different perspective: 'spatial practices,' he maintains, 'secretly structure the determining conditions of social life' (1984, p.96). These theorists insist on multifaceted, mutable interpretations of space and place which are predicated on – and contribute to – an understanding of social, political, gender, and economic factors that in turn determine form and function.

Studying site requires an understanding of politics and social production, since the control of place is determined by power structures well beyond topography. Edward Said even argues that 'none of us is completely free from the struggle over geography. That struggle is complex and interesting because it is not only about soldiers and cannons but also about ideas, about forms, about images and imaginings' (1993, p.7). That struggle is made all the more significant because space and place are fundamentally always still in process; as they continue to change, these mutations continue to force a re-assessment of 'place'. Doreen Massey maintains that:

> If you really *were* to take a slice [of space or place] through time it would be full of holes, of disconnections, of tentative half-formed first encounters, littered with a myriad of loose ends, a geological map (if you must) of fault-lines and discontinuities, bringing different temporalities hard up against each other. A discourse of closure it ain't.
>
> (1997, p.222; original emphasis)

Engaging with 'site', then, must accommodate different aspects of place and space through time. In addition, site becomes part of a 'cultural landscape' that accounts for human interaction in, through, and around geographical space (Blair and Truscott, 1989, p.3). The study of place thus requires more than a compass or a map.

A second way of describing place is the 'location' of the form of site-specific performance as a discrete discipline with its own history. The form's current popularity is evidenced by its increasing presence in tertiary courses in the English-speaking world: the publication of Mike Pearson's *Site-Specific Performance* (2010), designed for university students, illustrates an awareness that the form has potential for students both in and beyond theatre departments. In *Site-Specific Performance*, Pearson notes how the nature of site has transformed, and he identifies 'new kinds of site, more or less stable, within which performance might be enacted' (2010, p.14).[3]

The critical history of this form is only several decades old. Mutability is such a characteristic of the form that even its origins differ, depending on the version of history to which one subscribes.[4] Nick Kaye and Miwon Kwon both chart the history of the form as emerging from visual art and then being co-opted by theatre in their core texts. By contrast, in his chapter in this volume, Michael McKinnie marks its emergence in theatre from 1960s environmental performance and 'happenings'. Whatever its origins, site-specific performance was a significant form of theatre internationally in the 1990s, prompting a flurry of publications in the first few years of the twenty-first century, including Nick Kaye's *Site-Specific Art: Performance, Place and Documentation* (2000), Mike Pearson and Michael Shanks's *Theatre/Archaeology* (2001), and Miwon Kwon's *One Place after Another: Site-specific Art and Locational Identity* (2002). Kwon investigates the ways in which site-specificity of the very early twenty-first century both looked back to and away from the work of the 1960s. 'On the one hand', she argues,

> this phenomenon indicates a return of sorts: an attempt to rehabilitate the critically associated with the anti-idealist, anticommercial site specific-practices of the late 1960s and early 1970s, which incorporated the physical conditions of a particular location as integral to the production, presentation, and reception of art. On the other hand, it signals a desire to *distinguish* current practices from those of the past.
>
> (2002, p.1; original emphasis)

Performing Site-Specific Theatre reflects Kwon's interpretation of the phenomenon in 2002; a decade later, it marks the ways in which the form continues the line of history in some regards, while deviating from past practices in others.

Cutting across the historicizing of place in terms of position is a third interpretation of 'place', one in which a 'place' – or venue – is an essential requirement of the performance. In a theatrical experience, of course, one witnesses the construction and reconstruction of sites (or the settings required for a performance), next to and often on top of each other, depending on a performance's diegesis. Una Chaudhuri has addressed the issue of what 'place' on stage comes to mean through her focus on 'the double-edged problem of place and place as problem' (2002, p.53). In analysing performance in conventional theatre venues, she recognizes that 'place' in the context of performance carries with it a central ambiguity arising only partly out of the fictional frame often ascribed to performance.

While Chaudhuri is one of the few theatre critics who combines an understanding of theatricality with place in the performance of conventional theatre, these issues do change when one moves outside traditional performance venues. Given that site-specific performance seeks a social activity in a social place, the theatre building can, for many reasons, sever the relationship between the idea of a specific social activity and a performance. Site-specific performance can provide a more appropriate forum for reflecting on and interpreting the relationship between performance, specific places in our worlds, and social contexts than theatre that takes place in conventional theatre venues. In the late 1990s, some critics interpreted the value of site-specificity in political terms: for Baz Kershaw, 'performances in theatre buildings are deeply embedded in theatre as a *disciplinary system*' (1999, p.31; original emphasis), reflecting hegemonic values that are likely to be at odds with the values of the performers. His articulation of radical performance outside theatre venues offered the opportunity to resist socio-political and theatrical disciplinary systems. At roughly the same time, the Kenyan novelist and playwright Ngugi wa Thiong'o argued that 'the struggle for performance space is integral to the struggle for democratic space and social justice' (1997, p.29). Ngugi characterizes theatre venues associated with the state as standing for 'confinement' (1997, p.28). Certainly not all performances that take place in traditional theatres comply with Ngugi's strict terms, but it is more likely that those performances that take place outside theatre venues will be able to explore a more flexible range of performance codes and strategies.[5]

There are, of course, numerous other ways to read 'place' – increasingly, in terms of markets and globalization – that are productive to such a study. The commodification (even the branding of space in what Anna Klingmann (2007) calls 'brandscapes') of land, ownership, and spatiality requires continued investigation.

It is through the 'practice' of site-specific performance that such interrogation of the control of spatiality is possible. The next section points to ways in which the chapters in this collection help to rethink the significance of place through the practice of contemporary performance.

Practice

The practice of site-specific performance has the potential to (re-)invigorate both 'place'/'site' and 'performance'. I outline some of the particular features of a site-specific performance model, where site and performance intertwine to seek meaning in both the intersections and frictions between them. Of the many issues that emerge from the chapters herein, I highlight three: the host/ghost relationship, audience interactivity, and the significance of affect. These factors influence not just the production of site-specific performance, but also its reception and interpretation, and even its place in cultural and social landscapes.

In this collection, Mike Pearson refers to the host/ghost connection, one of the many contributions to site-specific performance made by Cliff McLucas, who was the designer and co-artistic director (with Pearson) of the Welsh theatre company Brith Gof. As Pearson outlines in this volume, McLucas understood

> site-specific performance as the coexistence and overlay of two basic sets of architectures: those of the extant building or what he called the *host*, that which is *at* site – and those of the constructed scenography and performance or the *ghost*, that which is temporarily brought *to* site. The site itself became an active component in the creation of performative meaning, rather than a neutral space of exposition or scenic backdrop for dramatic action.
>
> (p.70; original emphasis)

This relationship between host and ghost has supported and structured a particular form of site-specific performance. In his chapter on *The Persians*, Pearson investigates how this concept is more complicated than McLucas allowed, since there are forms of ghosting that can predate the relationship between the site and what is brought to the site. This rethinking emerges from both the site (host) and from the performance (ghost), and not only in consideration of Marvin Carlson's (2001) description of the haunting that almost automatically takes place in theatre, regardless of its type of venue.[6] For Pearson, the ghosting that predates the production materializes from a text with its own history (*The Persians*), as well as a site that is itself ghostly (the Skills House positioned on the edge of Cilienni – a replica village on the Sennybridge Training Area near Brecon Beacons National Park in Wales). Sophie Nield's chapter in this volume also takes issue with this palimpsest form of host/ghost,[7] arguing, like Pearson, that both the site and the performance have the potential to introduce hosting and ghosting. Nield's object of analysis, London's Parliament Square, extends the questions of hosting and ghosting well beyond 'just' performance to argue for looser borders between the two terms that create site-specific performance.

There are several other ways in which this host/ghost concept – central to late twentieth-century site-specific performance – can be rethought for twenty-first-century versions of the form. The re-performance of historical texts certainly provides a different order of ghosting as original productions and/or subsequent productions of a well-known text are echoed in a site-specific context.[8] Perhaps a more significant intervention in the host/ghost practice is the increasingly prominent use of multimedia in site-specific performance. Just as multimedia is becoming a standard aspect of theatrical performance within theatre buildings, it also features in site-specific performance. While multimedia (whether presented through film/video or other intermedial forms) does not replace 'site', it can significantly challenge the ways in which 'site' is configured, including introducing further ways in which the host can itself be echoed, replicated, or 'ghosted'. Extending a site through film certainly recontextualizes space: its tactility (or lack thereof), its representation, its fixity, and its interpretation. Of course film deals with location very differently, and Louise Owen explores this in ' "Places, like property prices, go up and down": site-specificity, regeneration and *The Margate Exodus*', in this volume. She assesses the place of the video project that forms one part of *The Margate Exodus*, which finds itself at odds with other forms of performance in their depictions of site.

Not all such experiments necessarily conclude with this disjunction, since multimedia can also reconfigure productively the dimensions of 'live' performance and place. Pearson's analysis of *The Persians* introduces the ways in which multimedia and the actual function of a site complicate the interrogation of politics, temporality, and geo-history. In 'Embodied presence and dislocated spaces: playing the audience in *Ten Thousand Several Doors* in a promenade, site-specific performance of John Webster's *The Duchess of Malfi*', Jane Collins explores video's extension of performance out of the 'frame' of the production, raising the question of what is hidden versus what is deliberately left apparent, and proposing expanded parameters for what 'site' might mean via multimedia. This extension of the 'real' of the site – and the implications which that development provides – is also core to Susan Haedicke's exploration of site-specific performances which deal with climate change. In 'Beyond site-specificity: environmental heterocosms on the street', she addresses a production by the Cambridge, UK-based company Metis Arts. This production relies on an associated website, such that the 'extension' of 'site' continues well after the performance has been completed and involves a radical rethinking of what 'site' means, and, in this case, *where* the performance takes place. Cyberspace, or virtual space, becomes an additional geographical 'place' that increasingly affects and underpins site-specific performance. The exploration of virtual spaces (whether virtual environments or websites that augment existing locations or contexts) has the potential to expand the physical and metaphysical potential scope of site-specificity.

Anna Birch's 'Repetition and performativity: site-specific performance and film as living monument' investigates most extensively the deployment of multimedia, and the attendant rethinking of host/ghost. Film is the chief means by which Birch charts the performance of the site of Newington Green – with its reference to Mary Wollstonecraft's own life there in the eighteenth century – over time in the iterations of performances by her company, Fragments & Monuments. Rather than rendering 'place' static through film, this dynamic deployment of video looks to new ways of keeping the performance of this site alive, and, in effect, enlivens the form itself. Fragments & Monuments deploys multimedia so that audiences are immediately and repeatedly incorporated in the action: not only do they assist when required, their images, displayed on large screens, become part of the archive that is redeployed in subsequent iterations of performing Wollstonecraft in Newington Green.

The second point of this section (and a key feature of many of this book's chapters) is this augmented relationship with – and even the role of – the audience in site-specific performance. Audiences may find themselves having to participate in other, tangible ways, often acting as an actor 'substitute', or even an agent to propel the action forward. At one level this is unsurprising, given Sally Mackey's argument that '[p]lace-based performance [...] expects more from its participants' (2007, p.181). Several chapters explore the effects of this argument, particularly the deployment of the audience as an active agent which frequently *dis*locates audiences, their subjectivity and even continually recreates their very position within the site. Whether a site-specific performance is interactive or downright confronting, audiences are rarely able to participate passively. In 'Ambulatory audiences and animate sites: staging the spectator in site-specific performance', Keren Zaiontz discusses 'ambulatory audiences' who are, from the beginning of the productions she explores, on the move. A more active participation in both site and performance provides the opportunity to actually embody 'site'. Audience members may rub up against other audience members, making the reading of the performance experiential in multiple ways, rather than limited to the end-on approach prescribed by many forms of theatre architecture.

Affect, an increasingly significant consideration in contemporary site-specific performance, is the third factor in this section. Affect, or a heightened experience of feeling, is, according to Erin Hurley, 'an organism's autonomic reaction to an environmental change; this reaction is a subjective experience, meaning that only the person whose blood is rushing to his or her extremities can feel it' (2010, p.17). In 'My sites set on you: site-specificity and subjectivity in "intimate theatre" ', Helen Iball argues the role of affect in one-to-one performance or ambulatory performance that the audience experiences with the aid of an MP3 player. Affect offers an additional interpretational possibility to address an audience member's relationship with site and embodiment within that site. Such theatre alters the geographical location of the performance (which is determined by a specific area that the participant traverses), threatening to breach the boundaries of 'personal space', or that personal zone which is generally not invaded by strangers.

One aspect of affect that is particularly visceral in site-specific performance is the creation or augmentation of sound as 'place'; while seldom addressed critically, sound clearly changes with context, even creating its own location. Every 'site' has its own sound, and sound is increasingly forming a site in its own right in site-specific performance, as Iball's discussion of Rotozaza's *Wondermart* outlines. Bruce Barton and Richard Windeyer's contribution to this volume, 'Immersive negotiations: binaural perspectives on site-specific sound', investigates the ways in which the development of a 'soundscape' is as foundational to site-specific performance as a 'landscape'. Their performative chapter suggests that sound challenges how we consider both embodiment and affect when 'immersive sound' provides an additional 'site', one which is otherwise considered to be a part of the body itself.

The intersection (or friction) between 'site' and 'performance' has the potential to generate more than simply a performance and more than simply a focus on a particular site when, in Barton and Windeyer's example, site can also be the body of the audience member itself. A basic aim in site-specific work is to encourage audiences to see and experience more of their surroundings, and/or to see their surroundings differently; this volume rethinks not only what that might be but how they are experienced.

Performing site-specific theatre

This final part of the introduction clarifies the book's shape, before addressing some consideration of the field's future. The volume is segmented into five parts, beginning with Site-Specificity and Economics. The sole contribution in this part, McKinnie's 'Rethinking site-specificity: monopoly, urban space, and the cultural economics of site-specific performance' poses fundamental questions about the viability of site-specificity and troubling definitions about the relationship between performance and place. While other chapters, notably Owen's, probe economic issues, McKinnie's challenge to the form itself sets the tone for the volume.

The next four chapters appear under the heading Site-Specificity and the Narratives of History. They continue McKinnie's contestation of the form in different ways, perhaps best characterized by their further troubling of the nature of site. The chapters in this part each connect site and a different aspect of time. Bennett and Sanders interrogate the assumption that site-specific theatre is simply a contemporary phenomenon. Their reading of Milton's 1634 play, sometimes called *Comus*, as site-specific develops understandings of what contemporary site-specific performance might be: a site's appeal to a history or histories serves to renew the form now.

The remaining three chapters in this group also address history, but in the context of more contemporary performance. Both Collins and Pearson discuss contemporary productions based on classical texts. Collins analyses how the location of a site-specific performance of John Webster's *The Duchess of Malfi* in Brighton (both city-specific and building-specific) is firmly fixed in the past (indeed, in several orders of the past), but also in the 'present' of the moment of performance, recasting potential meanings for 'site'. Pearson's chapter intensifies this embeddedness of the history of site: the production of Aeschylus's *The Persians* in an army training ground layers experiences of wars upon wars, at the same time as it unearths previous iterations of meaning associated with this Welsh site. Kathleen Irwin's expression of history engages with the historical record of a particular rural location, that of Ponteix, Saskatchewan. In 'Toiling, tolling and telling: performing dissensus', she explores the relationship that her site-specific company, Knowhere Productions, had with the rural community that wished to explore its history through site-specificity. She argues for a careful articulation of 'the tension and the potential' in producing and analysing such work, raising the issue of ethics in storytelling and performance. For both Pearson and Irwin, 'site' incorporates perspectives of history, geography, and social politics. In each subsequent chapter, the authors also take issue with easy formulations of site, performance, and the nature of their intersections.

Part three, Site-Specificity and the Slippages of Place, focuses on urban productions to investigate different aspects of this form of site-specificity. While both Pearson and Irwin's chapters specifically operate outside urbanity, the urban 'site' is more often explored in site-specific performance than rural experiences. Forming a counterbalance to the chapters that introduce history (in its various forms) to site-specificity, Susan Haedicke explores performance that deals with the future, particularly the future of climate change. She discusses performances that fracture 'site' further, investigating how these examples pursue imagined and dystopic environments, while retaining still-located dimensions in recognizable sites of the present. While any form necessarily changes through time, Haedicke posits the potential for speculating about site in the future, in the context of its actuality in the present. Birch's chapter pursues this speculation about the future of 'site' in the repeated performance work of Fragments & Monuments. Her work with iterations of the role and 'place' of Mary Wollstonecraft in Newington Green rethinks both site-specificity and contemporary performance of a recycled, mediatized and distributed presence. This is complemented by 'Contemporary *ekkeklemas* in site-specific performance', in which Lesley Ferris analyses three urban productions from different points in the recent past of site-specificity (including Birch's work) to argue that site-specificity remains a 'nomadic' form.

The final chapter in this part focuses in a different way on the urban site to intersect with the economic regeneration agenda that is often associated with site-specific performance. Yet, as Owen argues, the economic issues raised by this performance encompass much more than simple associations of economics as being equivalent to property values: 'site' continues to be contingent on a range of factors beyond the mere reinvestment of financial value in a particular site.

The fourth part, Site-Specificity and Theatrical Intimacy, reduces the scale of performance to consider theatre designed for small audiences or for a more specifically personal engagement. Zaiontz's chapter compares to Owen's in that both isolate performances that force audiences to be on the move, but rather than pursuing Owen's interest in social regeneration, Zaiontz focuses on the specifics of location that the ambulatory audience encounters. Barton and Windeyer pursue this even more personally, exploring Windeyer's work as a sound artist through the productions of Bluemouth inc. presents, a company which foregrounds immersive theatre. They address a 'site' that is both personal (the body) and enhanced by technology (through augmented sound, among other factors). Iball's investigation of intimate theatre also incorporates both the technologically defined 'site' that headphones provide, in addition to a more conventional form of personal theatre, where one actor performs for one audience participant. While the scale is much more focused, the scope of this form of site-specificity resonates broadly.

From this attention to the personal, the volume concludes with a more public interrogation. Sophie Nield's chapter, 'Siting the people: power, protest, and public space', acts as the anchor of the book in a part called Site-Specificity and Politics. She pushes the physicality of 'site' into the realm of where and when a site is 'legally sanctioned' for specific activities and when it is not. While David Harvey argues that historically, '[t]he association between city life and personal freedoms, including the freedom to explore, invent, create, and define new ways of life, has a long and intricate history' (2000, p.158), Nield's piece demonstrates the stark limits to that wish for freedom that 'site' comes to represent in the context of Brian Haw's public 'performance' in London. Most crucially, the ability to rescind such freedoms – whether metaphoric or actual – has significant implications for site in the context of protest, both in and out of performance.

The specific resonances between the chapters as they are ordered here are reflected in the section headings; no doubt readers will discover additional ways in which the contributions create dialogues with each other and with the key issues. There remains plenty of room for further work – and opposing views. Rather than identifying what is and isn't site-specific or what the boundaries for the genre might be, the contributors push the form in different directions (and not always in agreement with each other) to argue for new and renewed approaches to site-specific performance. Some inclusions may seem surprising, but they investigate how broadly the genre may apply to other eras, 'places', and contexts.

Site-specific performance is no longer an alternative or fringe genre; it is symptomatic of an increasing diversity in art forms (incorporating multimedia and film, let alone social networking) and in how globalization is expressed through culture. Illustrating this point, the chapters in this book traverse a diversity of sites and pursue multiple aspects of theatricality and performativity to investigate how site-specific theatre operates as a social activity in a widely definable 'social' space. The chapters variously blend genres, contexts, knowing and unknowing audiences, and of course deconstructions and reconstructions of site. They raise questions that will inform the practice and critique of performance even in conventional contexts. Most also argue an interdisciplinarity that extends the debate beyond merely the interactions between location and performance; this is perhaps not a surprise when they have been authored by academics, performers, and, in several cases, practitioner-scholars. They also indicate a particular form of analytical practice: not only do many practitioners explore the experience and effects of their performative work, most of the book's contributors provide detailed descriptions of site-specific performances and/or events, which offers a form of performative reading, and is reflected in the contributions of each of the editors of this volume. The nature of site-specific work demands a detailed writing of site-specific performance's repertoire into the archive, to use Diana Taylor's terms (2003).

There will inevitably be absences in the 'archive' of any volume in which editors must select a limited number of chapters from a much greater number of possible projects. While this book charts a range of intersections with place, theory, theatricality, performativity, and history that site-specific performance encourages, there is still much to explore in this field. Among these absences are two which suggest some of the directions for further work on and with this genre: coverage of a broader geographical footprint, and the actual mechanics of making site-specific performance. Regarding the first, this volume was not able to address whether site-specificity operates significantly differently in a wider global context. Inevitably the form brings with it additional layers of meaning in Asia, the Asian Pacific, Africa, Latin America, and elsewhere. While there are no chapters from the non-English-speaking world (aside from Haedicke's treatment of a site-specific performance in France), the exploration of site-specificity in other parts of the world will no doubt encompass both cultural landscape and cultural politics, and enhance the study of the form in the English-speaking Western world.

In terms of the second significant absence, the practicalities of site-specific performance, there is more work to be done on the actual and mundane – but numerous and increasing – forms of cultural gatekeeping that exist now and which complicate urban site-specific work. The logistics of devising, producing, and performing site-specific theatre today must account for occupational health and safety, crowd control, rights of way, security, and other such civic concerns that inevitably affect such work and can, in part, limit its success and effect significantly. There is yet much room for a more practical assessment of the permits and permissions that are required to engage with the urban landscape in particular; the exploration of the possibilities for site-specific performance need to be balanced by better understandings of the practicalities and logistics of generating such work.

The form of site-specific performance as a whole relies on the inherent instabilities of both 'site' and 'performance': the (deliberate) absence of precise meaning and the multiplication of potential meanings. This form of performative social practice requires a complex interrelationship among and between 'site' and 'performance' (on their own and in conjunction with each other) such that each has some room for manoeuvre and for the nexus that these two component parts create. The experience of weaving this volume together has reinforced the understanding that the borders around each part should remain flexible so that the form can accommodate shifts and slippages while resisting becoming prescriptive or simplistic. No doubt the form and its critical interpretations will continue to develop as it persists in challenging our relationships with site, place, and location.

Notes

1. While this introduction is single-authored, the volume and its development emerges from discussions between both co-editors.
2. The interdisciplinarity that characterizes studies of space and place also tends to be associated with site-specific performance.
3. As if in response to this development, there are, at the time of writing, two special issues of journals that focus on site and performance in the context of one 'unstable' form of site, that of walking and/or mobility: a 2010 issue of *Performance Research* called *Fieldworks*, edited by Heike Roms, Mike Pearson, and Stephen Daniels; and a 2012 special issue of *Contemporary Theatre Review*, guest-edited by this volume's co-editors. In addition to many article-length analyses over the last few decades, there have been numerous culturally specific edited collections, including Andrew Houston's *Environmental and Site-specific Theatre* (2007) about site-specific theatre in Canada and, to a lesser extent, Gay McAuley's *Unstable Ground: Performance and the Politics of Place* (2006) regarding Australian performance.
4. Even the name of the genre fluctuates from site-specific to site-sensitive, in addition to the variants that Kwon notes: '[s]ite-determined, site-orientated, site-referenced, site-conscious, site-responsive, site-related' (2002, p.1).
5. Kershaw (1999) and Ngugi (1997) both present arguments for deploying public space in performance as a means of engaging political resistance, but their arguments assume, to some extent, that performers have access to such oppositional public space. For numerous reasons, access to public space may itself be inhibited, whether for political factors, or owing to the closure/demolition of locations in urban centres, or for reasons of personal safety. Neither argument raises the simple factor of cost: the expense of hiring a conventional theatre venue must also be factored into a resistance to performing in traditional theatre buildings. See also Birch (2004 and 2006) for an analysis of the semiotic shift of meanings achieved through the recontextualization of theatre from new writing based in the theatre building to site-specific performance. This process of recontextualization, from script-based performance staged in the conventional proscenium-arch theatre to site-based performance – and on to the projection and streaming over the Internet of the film of the site-based performance – is a process that she calls 'progressive exteriorisation' (Birch, 2004, p.24).
6. For Carlson, the theatre is 'deeply involved with memory and haunted by repetition' (2001, p.11). Of course, 'site' also produces a preoccupation with memory that is conducive to 'haunting'.

7. See also McKinnie in this volume, who asserts that this is one of the most common ways in which site-specific performance is characterized.

8. An additional ghostly 'presence' can emerge from the absence of original production practices. See, in this volume, Pearson's use of *The Persians* and Jane Collins's site-specific production of Webster's *The Duchess of Malfi*: while neither attempts to replicate original practices, both inevitably conjure an audience's knowledge of them.

Part I
Site-Specificity and Economics

2
Rethinking Site-Specificity: Monopoly, Urban Space, and the Cultural Economics of Site-Specific Performance

Michael McKinnie

During the past few years there has been a proliferation of site-specific performance in the UK.[1] As Susannah Clapp, theatre critic for *The Observer* newspaper, put it in her review of the 2010 production of Beth Steel's *Ditch* by High Tide Theatre and the Old Vic in London:

> This wouldn't have happened five years ago. Kevin Spacey's Old Vic – that place of gilt – has taken over a tunnel under Waterloo station, where Beth Steel's *Ditch* […] launches a series of plays. Those who thought that theatre outside purpose-built stages, theatre blending installation art with drama, was just a fad have been proved wrong. It has become a main strand in British theatre.
>
> (2010, p.39)

Site-specific work is not, as the work of a company such as Wales's Brith Gof during the 1980s and 1990s demonstrates, a new phenomenon in the UK. Nonetheless, Clapp's observation about the growth in the amount of site-specific work being produced in the UK in more recent years – of which *Ditch* is only one of a number of recent examples – is likely to be correct. Moreover, the extent to which this work now involves co-productions between small and very large theatre companies (such as High Tide and the Old Vic; Punchdrunk, Shunt and the National Theatre; and Blast Theory and the Barbican Centre) is notable. And the creation of site-specific performance also increasingly involves an extensive, and quite complex, network of theatrical, political, and economic agents. The production of site-specific work in London now often entails formal relationships between theatre companies and bodies outside the theatre sector (sometimes several at once). In recent years these have included quangos like the Creative Space Agency (a service, funded by the Arts Council England, London and the London Development Agency, that links arts organizations with owners of vacant properties), consultants like Futurecity (which aims to undertake urban regeneration through cultural projects), property managers like Network Rail Property (formerly Spacia, which manages property in and around Britain's railway network), and property developers like Ballymore (which specializes in high-end office and residential developments in city cores).[2] In London, as in other cities around the world, site-specific performance has become tied up with the political–economic management of the city.

There has also been a growing critical interest, both in the UK and internationally, in site-specific performance. Like the work itself, this interest is not without precedent (after all, Richard Schechner's pioneering analysis, '6 Axioms for Environmental Theatre', was published in 1968), but the growth in scholarship about site-specific performance during the past decade is readily apparent. This quantitative increase in scholarship is less interesting, however, than the tropes that critics have predominantly employed to represent the relationship between performance and place in site-specific performance. Critics have tended to figure the relationship between performance and place in site-specific work in three main ways: as heterotopic, dialogic, or palimpsestic (with its corollary, the spectral – more than most people, performance scholars see a lot of ghosts). When framing the relationship as heterotopic, critics commonly draw on Michel Foucault's (1986) discussion of heterotopias, which operate through the simultaneous invocation of multiple but differentiated places, both physical and imaginary (Bryant-Bertail, 2000; Meerzon, 2007; Tompkins, 2009; Wiles, 2003, pp.7–8; Wilkie, 2002a).[3] Site-specific performance, then, is heterotopic because it self-consciously puts actual and imaginary places into play at the same time.[4] Dialogic accounts of the relationship between performance and place highlight the extent to which site-specific performance might enable theatrical material (performers, texts, scenographies, and so on) to enter into productive 'dialogue' with place – often places that theatre has commonly elided (Babb, 2008; Bennett, 2008; Somdahl-Sands, 2008; Stephenson, 2010). In palimpsestic or spectral accounts, site-specific performance negotiates an environment's past use (Hunter, 2005; Kaye, 2000; Kloetzel, 2010; Lavery, 2005; McEvoy, 2006; Pearson and Shanks, 2001; Turner, 2004). This results in what Cathy Turner, drawing on Mike Pearson, calls 'the rewriting of space through a new occupation of site in tension with what precedes it' (2004, p.374).

While each trope emphasizes different configurations of the relationship between performance and place, all three commonly represent site-specific performance as recalibrating that relationship on less hierarchical and more interrogative terms than are usually found in spatially conventional performance. As Fiona Wilkie suggests:

> Simply put, site-specific theatre privileges place. It suggests that the act of dividing the activity labelled 'theatre' from the building labelled 'theatre' holds possibilities for responding to and interrogating a range of current spatial concerns, and for investigating the spatial dimension of contemporary identities (personal, communal, national and international).
>
> (2008, p.89)

Site-specific performance, in this way of thinking, involves performance assuming a more responsive and dialectical relationship to the environments (broadly defined) in which it occurs.

But site-specific performance does not always privilege place. Sometimes it uses place to privilege performance itself. Accounting for such cases requires a different way of understanding the spatial relations of site-specific theatre than is available in extant research. Tropes of heterotopia, dialogue, and palimpsest struggle to account for site-specific performances that are monopolistic in their approach to place; that is, performances that seek to appropriate place wholly within the apparatus of the theatre event and produce value through doing so, such as *Ditch*. A production like *Ditch* in the Waterloo tunnels invites an alternative model that helps to account for site-specific performances whose appeal is not only artistic but also economic.

In this chapter I aim to use *Ditch* as a starting point for a cultural-economic analysis of monopolistic performance. In doing so, I draw on Allen J Scott's (2008) examination of the socio-cultural economics of cities and on David Harvey's (2001) use of rent theory to theorize the distinctive spatiality of cultural forms under post-Fordist capitalism. Monopolistic performances produce their value by appropriating and trading self-consciously on the non-replicable qualities of places according to a logic that is substantially economic. As I will elaborate, this involves translating the agglomerative qualities of performance industries into experiential benefits of the theatre event as well as capitalizing on the extent to which site-specific performances are, at least symbolically, what economists call 'rent-seeking' (they offer participants in the event the opportunity to purchase a unique parcel of time and space for a limited time). I will also argue that monopolistic performance models types of theatrical, economic, and spatial productivity that are highly attractive within contemporary performance and urban economies, not only in London but in any number of cities around the world: it appears to achieve greater spatial efficacy than is often the case with performance events; it seemingly cultivates ideal economic subjects; and it apparently creates newly productive spaces within the urban environment. These things are particularly important at a time when cities are competing aggressively with each other to attract transnational capital, and they illustrate distinctive, and rarely acknowledged, ways in which site-specific performance is tied up with contemporary urban development. The appeal of site-specific performance, then, may indeed lie in the extent to which it asks participants to imagine alternative configurations of performance, place, and society. But the spatial and theatrical politics of these alternatives are rather more complex and ambiguous than might first appear.

Ditch

Ditch is set in Britain, in the near, but unspecified, future. The country is in a state of civil war after an environmental catastrophe, with a fascist government trying to subdue a restive population through military repression and forced labour. Much of Britain is socially and environmentally devastated. As one character proclaims to another: 'You let it get to this! You let the sea rise and flooded cities, burst river banks and destroyed our houses. You used up oil, make cars stop, forced us inta towns. You made us share rooms, put us in factories, fed us rations, let us get sick' [*sic*] (Steel, 2010, pp.85–86). The play is located in an isolated military outpost in the Peak District, the beautiful but sometimes desolate range of hills and moors in central and northern England. On the lookout for insurgents and refugees, the characters' existence is lonely and savage: food is scarce, living conditions are poor, and moments of hope (as when two younger characters fall in love and one becomes pregnant) are extinguished by death (both die – the young man in battle, the young woman murdered). *Ditch* is a dystopian portrait of a bleak future, a warning about the need for environmental stewardship and the dangers of authoritarian politics.

The play was first performed in April 2010 as part of the High Tide Festival at The Cut, a community arts centre in Halesworth, Suffolk, in a small, end-on auditorium. The production transferred the following month to the tunnels under Waterloo railway station in South London, in co-production with the Old Vic. Waterloo Station is one of the city's oldest and largest railway stations, and, like many termini in South London, its trains arrive and depart above street level on viaducts (unlike most trains in North London, which more commonly travel in trenches below street level). The vaults underneath these viaducts are often enclosed to provide work space, and, indeed, one of the aims of Network Rail (the consortium of private companies that owns many rail termini in Britain, including Waterloo Station) is to make these spaces as profitable as possible by renting them out for commercial use. The Waterloo 'tunnels' (for that is what they look like inside once the vaults have been enclosed – a series of brick tunnels running parallel to each other but perpendicular to the tracks above) were once used for railway equipment storage. In recent years they have not been needed for this purpose and their awkward location – accessed principally via a side street – makes them less than ideal for commercial use. As a performance space, however, the tunnels provide an undeniably evocative environment.[5]

Locating the venue for the first time is not easy, though, even with a map. The entrance to the tunnels is located along the outside perimeter of Waterloo Station, and is only scarcely marked. After finding the correct door and exchanging box office pleasantries, however, I entered the tunnels for *Ditch*. The tunnels were gloomy, dirty, and most noticeably, smelly: the damp was palpable and the mustiness powerful. There appeared to be blood on the dirt-covered ground. Pools of light and patches of darkness framed installations composed under the old brick arches: stretched animal skins hung from the roof; an old wooden wheel, no longer in use, was engulfed by vegetation; a small deer (stuffed, it became apparent) stood, isolated, in an antechamber (having passed by the bloody skins to get to it I could only think of it as a target). All the while, the trains rumbled immediately overhead; it sounded like rolling thunder, or, more ominously, distant artillery fire. The scripted play had yet to begin, but the audience was already immersed in the fictional world of the play.

The rest of the event, though, was located in what was very much like a conventional, end-on theatre auditorium (supplemented by a very conventional theatre bar constructed under an adjacent arch). This auditorium spanned the width of one arch, and was immediately familiar to a theatregoer: there was a stage at one end, risers of theatre seating faced it, and stage lighting hung overhead. At the same time, however, the auditorium amplified the atmosphere of the play more than a conventional theatre auditorium could – the stage floor was mud, there were old panels of rusting corrugated steel on the underside of the arch above the audience, and the strong smell of damp persisted (this would become even more conspicuous when it rained onstage and the mud that covered the playing area thickened). The performance space reiterated the post-apocalyptic register of the play more than a conventional theatre space could, yet it also offered the customary features of a theatre auditorium. It was evocatively fictive but reassuringly familiar.

Towards a theory of monopolistic performance

Once it moved into the Waterloo tunnels, *Ditch* became a monopolistic performance by capitalizing upon distinctive spatial and theatrical relations that could not be realized in a conventional theatre space like The Cut (or anywhere else, for that matter). The production achieved effect (and affect) through an interplay between the particular architectonic qualities of the tunnels, the script's diegesis, and the spatial configuration of the playing and spectating areas. One might argue that these relations could be explicated without recourse to a new model of site-specific performance. Indeed, at first glance the temptation is to assume that the two main spatial elements of the event – the installation space and the auditorium space – were somewhat at odds with each other, and, therefore, in a dialectical relationship for which tropes of heterotopia, dialogue, and palimpsest might serve adequately. But there was something else going on here: *Ditch* remade the tunnels as theatre. It capitalized on their distinctive qualities but subsumed these within the representational and spatial apparatus of the theatre event; the successful installation of a familiar theatre auditorium (as the final destination of one's travel to the production) signalled emphatically that the tunnels had been taken within the dominion of theatre. Here, performance not so much privileged place as appropriated it for its own purposes.

How, then, might the operations of such a monopolistic performance be understood more fully? What is the cultural-economic logic of this form of site-specific theatre? By way of beginning to address these questions, I will argue that monopolistic performance is characterized by at least two key features. First, it is especially agglomerative, in that it attempts to translate some of the distinctive industrial characteristics of theatre (and the particular spatiality these predominantly involve) into experiential benefits of the performance event to an unusual degree.

Second, it is symbolically rent-seeking, in that it extends theatrical authority over a portion of the urban environment and then capitalizes upon spatial elements found there that cannot be replicated elsewhere (or at least that are difficult to do so).

In his analysis of what he calls 'cognitive-cultural capitalism', Scott observes that cultural industries, although comprised of 'a rather incoherent collection of sectors', nonetheless have a number of shared features that distinguish them from other industries (2008, p.84).[6] One is particularly important within the context of monopolistic performance: the fact that cultural production tends to be agglomerative, particularly in large urban centres like London. In the most basic sense, agglomeration economies occur when firms of similar types cluster in particular locales (and often in identifiable districts). As Michael Ball and David Sunderland point out, they do this to reduce costs by operating in close proximity to their workforce and the consumers of their products (2001, pp.14–37). Modern cultural industries generally, and performance industries especially, are notably agglomerative; not only have theatres historically tended to cluster in cities (as well as districts within those cities), theatrical performance is unusual in the extent to which production and consumption predominantly happen in the same time and place (something that happens in few other enterprises).[7] Indeed, theatrical performance is distinctive because of the extent to which agglomeration often characterizes the economic organization of its industries *and* is a key experiential feature of its events (through the co-presence that these events usually, if not universally, involve).

Part of the appeal of being a spectator in the Waterloo *Ditch*, however, is the promise that 'being here together' will pay off in ways not possible in most performance events. Monopolistic performance, then, seeks to translate agglomeration to the diegetic and phenomenological registers of the performance more fully than a spatially conventional event does. *Ditch* illustrates how this happens. The playing area installed in the tunnel became a less privileged diegetic space within the event than it otherwise would have been – instead, diegesis appeared to be produced by the total performance environment and all of the agents within in it (including spectators). This environmental diegesis was assisted by the sense-perceptual intensification that moving *Ditch* into the tunnels involved: the military outpost in the play is dirty, damp, and smelly – and so were the tunnels.[8] In the Waterloo *Ditch*, agglomeration was not only an industrial and social characteristic of theatre generally, but also a narrative and experiential benefit of spectatorship within the individual performance event.

The value of monopolistic performance is also contingent on the extent to which it offers spectators an encounter with a place, but one where performance itself is the key intermediary. In this way monopolistic performance is rent-seeking; its theatrical exploitation of a particular portion of the environment operates according to a logic that is as much economic as artistic. Put simply, economic rent is unearned income: it is the difference between the price paid for a resource to its owner and the cost (land, labour, capital) of keeping that resource in circulation. The problem of rent has concerned economists since its notable theorizations in the nineteenth century by David Ricardo (1971) and, subsequently, Karl Marx (1981).[9] As Harvey observes, rents tend to arise today in two situations: when social agents 'control some special quality resource, commodity or location which, in relation to a certain kind of activity, enables them to extract monopoly rents from those desiring to use it' (2001, p.395); and when there is what economists call an 'inelastic supply' of resources (either by design or historical con-sequence) which results in the value of those resources being greater than would be the case if they were more widely distributed through the economy or could be created easily by others. Monopolistic per-formance involves both of these senses of rent. Its value hinges on its spatial distinctiveness in relation to other, more spatially conven-tional, events, and its scarcity, in that the locations in which it occurs are largely idiosyncratic and rare, or, if neither of these things, are only used theatrically for a limited time.

Fantasies of productivity

Explaining the attraction of site-specific performance in contemporary London is not easy, and its appeal is not reducible to a single characteris-tic, or a fixed set of characteristics, spanning all types of such work. But I will argue in this section that monopolistic performance is appealing because it models forms of productivity that are tremendously attractive within theatre itself and within London's broader urban economy, but which are very difficult to realize in both. Monopolistic performance brings together and appears to resolve – again, however temporarily and symbolically – some quite difficult theatrical, economic, and urban problems: of theatrical efficacy, of private property, and of spatial dis-use, respectively. In doing so, monopolistic performance offers itself as a privileged site through which to enact exemplary cultural-economic relations, both in London and in urban centres elsewhere.

Monopolistic performance is preoccupied with the long-standing and complex problem of theatrical efficacy: the ability of performance to produce desired results, both within a performance event and within the society of which that event is a part. Monopolistic performance, however, elaborates two distinct variants of this concern with efficacy: in the first instance, theatre's anxiety about the extent of its own productivity; and, in the second, the extent to which its use of place might improve that productivity in the interest of realizing a more effective performance event.

Site-specific performance generally seeks to address a sense – whether acknowledged explicitly or not – that the optimal operation of the performance event is diminished when the spatial elements available to that event are not fully capitalized upon. It seeks, therefore, to maximize its theatrical 'output' by mobilizing the full range of spatial inputs available to it. Site-specific performance responds to the fact that most theatre events treat their places of performance as spatially unremarkable, bracketing these places as, for example, scenographic challenges to be addressed through successful stage design. Monopolistic performance, however, draws attention to the way that place is both a constitutive element of the entire performance event and a set of spatial resources to be deployed *vis-à-vis* other material within that event. It implies that, unless the theatre machine uses all of its spatial elements fully, it fails to fire on all cylinders. What would otherwise be waste must be turned into fuel.

Monopolistic performance also trades on the privileging of private property ownership as the ideal economic relation between social subject and space under modern capitalism. Private property ownership creates a monopolistic relationship between social subject and place: it elevates an owner's claim to a particular parcel of space over competing claims. In a monopolistic performance spectators are invited to 'purchase', through the performance, temporary 'ownership' over a distinct and non-replicable time, place, and experience. This plays out a fantasy of property ownership that is difficult to realize in the broader urban economy of a city like London, where access to property ownership is restricted by high entry costs (and it neatly effaces the fact that this ownership is actually a rental arrangement). Monopolistic performance allows spectators to imagine themselves as productive economic subjects of a particular kind – the property-owning bourgeoisie – which is especially seductive when this role is progressively less available outside the theatre.[10]

Finally, monopolistic performance takes disused (or not optimally used) urban spaces and puts them into production. This is attractive for several reasons. The idea that the arts can play an important role in urban renewal is one that has gained particular currency in the past decade among theatre practitioners, politicians, and public policymakers.[11] A performance like *Ditch* brings what would otherwise be an unproductive space back into (legitimate) use, and, if only for a short time, integrates that space within London's urban economy. It also helps cultivate the sense of 'place difference' (Molotch, 2002, p.666) that is key to distinguishing cities from each other under transnational capitalism and making them more attractive places for capital investment, as well as for individual capitalists themselves.[12] Monopolistic performance, then, models two related, and highly appealing, forms of urban productivity: it appears to improve London's productivity as a place in itself, and it ostensibly contributes to London's ability to compete successfully with other cities under transnational capitalism.

By way of concluding, I want to reflect briefly on some of the challenges that monopolistic performance poses for analyses of theatre and space and also of urban cultural economics. In the first instance, conceiving spatially reflexive performance as monopolistic performance invites an alternative account of the spatial politics of performance to those most commonly available in performance research. Performance studies scholars have periodically framed the political potential of performance spatially, where, in David Wiles's characterization, performance offers 'a counter-site that speaks about other sites' and resists their dominance (2003, p.8). Monopolistic performance, though, draws attention to the ways in which some performance events appropriate places for their own uses and on their own terms – they subsume them within the apparatus of the event as much as entering into a 'dialogue' with them. This suggests that the relationship of performance to place should not be presumed to be interrogative. In some cases it may be; the existence of monopolistic performance does not foreclose the interrogative potential of other forms of site-specific work. But monopolistic performance demonstrates that the relationship of performance to place is sometimes less interrogative, and more acquisitive, than is commonly acknowledged.

At the same time, monopolistic performance throws into relief a tension between efficacy and productivity embedded in the operations of site-specific performance: a performance event can appear to be highly productive without being effective, and it can also be effective without being optimally productive. Many performance events that are not site-specific are perfectly capable of achieving semiotic, affective, and phenomenological efficacy without recourse to spatial reflexiveness or monopoly. Indeed, such events are effective not because they pretend that place does not matter, but, rather, because they are not overly concerned about the extent to which performance might achieve optimal spatiality. In spite of the impressive spatial choreography that site-specific performances often involve, the spectatorial experience can be rather dissatisfying. The event can try too hard to do spectators' interpretive work for them – the place of performance assumes a reiterative function, just in case spectators fail to 'get it'. What appears as a novel form of theatrical engagement with a place, then, can also signal an anxiety over the terms on which spectators undertake their interpretive labour in that place. And sometimes site-specific performance possibly gets its own spatial interpretation wrong – staging *Ditch* in the subterranean Waterloo tunnels is very atmospherically evocative but it arguably misreads the script, which repeatedly draws attention to its location on the open spaces of the Peak District. The productivity of site-specific performance, then, can circumscribe other forms of efficacy within the theatrical enterprise.

Monopolistic performances also complicate dominant ways of thinking about the relationship between cultural production, cities, and economics that have emerged from the social sciences in recent years. Although critics like Scott and Harvey offer sophisticated accounts of this relationship, they, like many other contributors to the field of urban cultural economics, often focus their attention on arts practices that are most likely to involve the creation of commodities (such as screen and popular music production). Monopolistic performances invite critics to account for cultural forms that, while undoubtedly related to the production and consumption of commodities in the wider market economy, are neither commodities themselves nor created by profit-making enterprises. Indeed, the ability of such performance events to model ideal cultural-economic relations under post-Fordist capitalism hinges on their resistance to the duplicability that characterizes so many commodities and the profit-seeking that characterizes so many commercial enterprises.

Site-specific performance has much to tell about the relationship between contemporary performance, place, and society. It is also the case that this story is more complex than scholars have previously imagined – accounting for the distinctive cultural and economic work that different forms of site-specific performance do in cities today requires different modes of analysis than critics have employed thus far. My attempt here to challenge dominant conceptions of site-specific performance is not to imply that these are always incorrect (or, by extension, to imply that site-specific performance is somehow malign). Rather, it is to argue for a more expansive consideration of site-specific performance's forms, operations, and material effects. The ambiguous spatial politics of site-specific performance should, ideally, prove both critically and theatrically generative.

Notes

1. I use the term site-specific performance in a broad sense, to denote performances that are consciously reflexive about their places of performance and trade on the distinctive qualities of those places *vis-à-vis* other places to achieve theatrical effect and affect.

2. I am indebted to Louise Owen for sharing her expertise on such relationships with me. It should also be noted that the London Development Agency (LDA) closed in March 2012. In its first comprehensive spending review in October 2010, the recently elected Conservative–Liberal Democrat coalition government promised a 'bonfire of the quangos' and removed national funding for the LDA altogether. The Mayor of London, Boris Johnson, had already stated his intention to abolish the LDA and fold some of its functions into the Greater London Authority.

3. It should be noted that Tompkins draws on Kevin Hetherington's (1997) complex application of Foucault – among others – in his analysis of the 'social ordering' of eighteenth-century modernity.

4. For Foucault, of course, all theatre is heterotopic, regardless of whether it is site-specific or not, but spatially reflexive work arguably draws greater attention to the spatial negotiations that performance involves and contrives an event that seeks to make these negotiations an experiential benefit for the spectator to an unusual degree.

5. *Ditch* was not the first performance in the Waterloo tunnels; Punchdrunk staged a series of installations there the previous year. The London International Festival of Theatre staged *Aftermath* in the Waterloo tunnels in July 2010 and other events have taken place there since. The Waterloo tunnels are also not the only site of their kind: performance collective Shunt has produced events in its vaults under London Bridge Station (further east along the River Thames) for several years, and, before that, under a rail viaduct in Bethnal Green in the city's east.

6. In addition to their tendency to be agglomerative, Scott argues that cultural economies have at least three common features:

> First, they are all concerned in one way or another with the creation of sign-value or symbolic value. Second, they are generally subject to the effects of Engel's Law, meaning that as disposable income expands, consumption of these outputs rises at a disproportionately higher rate. Third, they exemplify with special force the dynamics of Chamberlinian or monopolistic competition.
>
> (Scott, 2008, pp.84–85)

For the founding economic analysis of monopolistic competition (which, although relevant to site-specificity, is beyond the scope of this article), see Chamberlin 1962.

7. One might argue that live music performance functions similarly, but theatrical performance only occasionally has a recorded artefact that circulates independently of the live event; when it does this it is usually seen as a poor relation to the live event and is often consumed for documentary or pedagogical purposes.

8. This is not confined to *Ditch*. One can find similar qualities in Shunt's *Money*, which ran for more than a year in a former tobacco warehouse in Bermondsey. *Money* involved the construction of a self-contained theatre space (of a self-consciously mechanical sort) within the main hall of the warehouse that almost completely internalized – and rigorously disciplined – the act of spectatorship. The warehouse resembled a container for a very carefully designed theatrical machine.

9. In the classic formulation, rents arise in relation to land but economists have more recently been concerned with economic rent as it arises in relation to phenomena such as intellectual property, capital gains, the buying and selling of patents, and some of the more complex features of the global financial system (like credit default swaps) that have featured in the recent economic crises affecting many capitalist countries.

10. Even with the relative decline in residential property prices in London and the UK as a result of the recent 'credit crunch', incomes remain low relative to prices and lenders are offering significantly lower loan-to-value ratios than they were a few years ago.

11. For a perceptive analysis of how this process plays out in material but politically ambiguous ways, see Levin and Solga (2009).

12. The role of the arts in securing London's superior position vis-à-vis other 'global cities' within transnational capitalism has been explicitly proclaimed in a series of public-policy documents, most recently in the Mayor of London's cultural strategy for 2012 and beyond (Mayor of London, 2010). For a discussion of the role of theatre and the arts in reproducing London's globality, see McKinnie (2009).

Part II

Site-Specificity and the Narratives of History

3
Rehearsing across Space and Place: Rethinking *A Masque Presented at Ludlow Castle*

Susan Bennett and Julie Sanders

Paradigms of site-specificity have been deployed almost exclusively to inform interpretations of contemporary performances, yet surely these precepts might also serve to unlock the meanings of past theatrical events. As a challenge to conventional temporal restrictions on the use of site-specific theory, this chapter releases the moment of performance in one early modern theatrical happening. *A Masque Presented at Ludlow Castle, 1634* – sometimes known as *Comus* and often accredited to John Milton alone as author, although it is, we argue, more accurately regarded as a co-production – was a 'multimedial' theatrical event involving music, dance, and spoken verse: a mixed aesthetic typical of the masque as a dramatic form in the early seventeenth century.[1] This masque was created for the purposes of a site-specific performance for the inauguration of John Egerton, the first Earl of Bridgewater, as King Charles I's Lord President of the Council of the Marches and Wales – the administrative centre of which was located in the Shropshire county town of Ludlow.[2]

The Lord President's role in this border region of England and Wales was primarily a judicial one; he presided over local courts which acted as regional complements to the royal prerogative courts of the Star Chamber and the Chancery based at Whitehall near London.[3] He acted as the King's representative in the region. Egerton was simultaneously appointed Lord Lieutenant of the several counties that made up this administrative domain (Shropshire, Worcestershire, Herefordshire, Monmouthshire, and North and South Wales), underscoring the relationship between position and place that we will come to see forms a central strand in the masque proper. In tying together position and place, however, the masque also consciously unsettles that relationship, and in this way finds kinship with several of the more contemporary site-specific performances discussed in this volume. Site, space, landscape, and location are characterized in this particular instance, as in the sub-genre of site-specific performance as a whole, by 'ambiguity, contingency, and unsettlement'.[4] The physical and political geography of the region in which the masque was performed is crucial to the themes and tensions of power and governance that it plays out. The masque itself is highly attentive to issues of place and space, no doubt because this area and in particular the nearby Forest of Dean, a contested border region, had been the site of several outbreaks of popular protest (sometimes of a violent nature) over the encroachment of local customary rights by landowners and crown agents (Map 3.1). It was into this specific cultural geography that the Earl was consciously inserting himself and negotiating his role in 1634, and the masque can be understood as a vital tool in ongoing jurisdictional negotiations with the region and its inhabitants.

A Masque Presented at Ludlow Castle was staged on the evening of Monday 29 September 1634 at the Castle for a mixed audience of local citizens and dignitaries, as well as direct associates and employees of Egerton. The key roles were performed by members of the Earl's household, including his own children – 15-year-old Lady Alice and his two sons, 11-year-old John and 9-year-old Thomas – along with their music tutor Henry Lawes, who was by this time also a member of the King's Musick at court.[5] The children had prior experience of masquing culture, having performed in court productions in the early 1630s, and the family was interested in theatre as a form – the Earl's wife Frances was an active collector of published plays.[6] Lawes, in turn, as we will come to recognize, was a crucial collaborator with Milton in the creation and delivery of this site-particular production.

The Earl had actually been appointed to his gubernatorial position in 1631, but it was not until the summer of 1634, due to a combination of business and health-related reasons, that he was able to travel with his family to Ludlow to formally accept the role. The journey took four days and the Earl and his retinue were given various civic welcomes at towns and villages *en route*, arriving at Ludlow on 5 July. Records show that the Earl then spent several weeks in Ludlow, but after that set out on a 'tour of the territories for which he was now responsible' (Brown 1977, pp.76–86; 1985; and 1987, pp.1–12).[7] Over a three-week period the Earl conducted the equivalent of a royal progress, staying, along with his family and significant household members (including Lawes), at the homes of prominent noble families in the region, and often receiving theatrical welcomes in the process. All of the households

Ludlow Castle in its regional setting

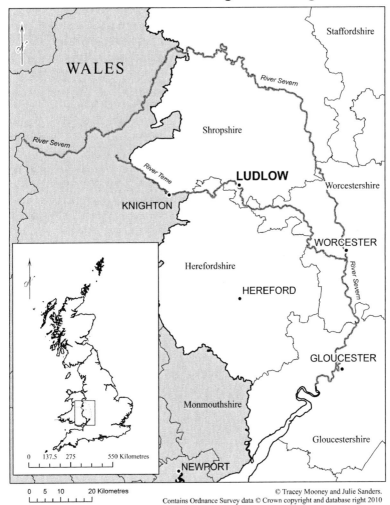

Map 3.1 Ludlow Castle in its regional setting.

he is known to have visited belonged to 'holders of posts related to his official duties [...] or powerful families to which he was related'. These included Eyton Hall in Shropshire, Chirk Castle in Wales – where we know a theatrical entertainment built around the occasion of a banquet was staged as part of the welcome for the Earl that August – Bretton

Hall in Flintshire, and Cholmendeley Castle in Cheshire (Campbell and Corns, 2008, p.77). Eventually, after what Cedric Brown describes as a 'substantial looping journey' (1985, p.31), the 'progress' reached Lyme Hall (better known today as Lyme Park) near Macclesfield, the home of Sir Peter Legh, a relative of the Earl through marriage.[8]

The party returned to Ludlow, after spending time at Lyme, on the evening of Wednesday 17 September. This was just 12 days before the masque was performed and there has been critical speculation as to how the Earl's children might have learned such demanding parts in such a short space of time; both Alice and John had more than 150 lines, while nine-year-old Thomas had a more modest 52.[9] But, as Brown has rightly suggested, the key to the story of the presidential progress that preceded the performance of the Ludlow masque is the time spent at Lyme. This cultured, relaxed place, known for its library of books and music, would have provided the perfect rehearsal space for Lawes and the children who were in his educational care. As Brown reflects, 'it seems likely that they [the children] would have had their parts with them at Lyme, [...] and that the rehearsal of this most literary, sophisticated entertainment was as it were their educational vacation project' (1985, p.35).

Milton, a writer who lived close to the city of London at this time and who is not known to have visited Ludlow at any stage in the proceedings, presumably furnished Lawes with a working script which he was able to alter and refine according to the pragmatic demands of performance through rehearsals at Lyme and then subsequently in Ludlow Castle itself. Lawes is, therefore, a collaborator not only in the respect that he provided the music for the production, but also in the way that he worked with the Egerton children to produce the final performance.[10] This mediatory and facilitating role is reflected in the part that he plays in the masque of Attendant Spirit Thyrsis, who acts as a veritable guardian angel and educative force, especially for the two boys, within the storyline of the drama. The Michaelmas Eve dating of the Ludlow masque also had resonance with these themes; in addition to harvest celebrations, Michaelmas Eve was traditionally associated with the Christian festival of St Michael and All Angels.

The plot of the masque, in brief, bears witness to the Earl's three children trying to make their way to Ludlow Castle for their father's inauguration. To do this they are forced to travel through a 'wild wood' (s.d. 0) – a site that has been read by critics as a complex blend of the literary forest, an obvious intertextual inheritance from Ovid, Spenser, and Shakespeare, and the material actuality of the Forest of Dean, one of the key areas over which the Earl would soon be asked to enact his jurisdictional powers.[11] While in the woods the boys become separated from their sister and she is in turn waylaid by Comus, a necromancer who heads up a 'rout' (s.d. 92) of half-humans/half-beasts, who abducts her, takes her to his 'stately palace' (658) and then attempts to assault her sexually by means of an intoxicating glass of 'liquor' (666). With the aid of the Attendant Spirit, disguised as a local shepherd, the Lady (Alice) is rescued and the family is able to reach the Castle in time for the state occasion.

By placing this plot summary alongside the earlier account of the regional progress that the Egerton household had recently undertaken, we can begin to unpack the way in which the plot trajectory of the masque re-performs and re-stages the experiential, collaborative, and educational journey of the children for public consumption. It is this kind of localized reference and allusion that encourages us to read this theatrical event as very much a co-production between the distanced figure of Milton and the active experience of the family, including Lawes, in the weeks leading up to the performance. The masque itself is enmeshed with the idea of experiential journeys (not least for the Ludlow Castle spectators on that September night in 1634), and the plot plays inventively with the potential of ideas of reflexivity and re-performance within the loaded site-specific locale of the Castle. Thus, a very particular theatrical event in 1634 finds purchase and rele-vance within wider discussions of site-specific practice and is in turn illuminated by some of the recent conscious destabilizations of assump-tions about how and in what ways site-specificity operates on creators, performers, and spectators.

Stage directions to the text indicate specific settings, moving in the course of the masque's 1023 lines from a 'wild wood' (s.d. 0) to a 'stately palace' (s.d. 658), through to the River Severn and, finally, 'Ludlow Town and the President's Castle' (s.d. 957). Conventionally it is thought that painted backdrops or shutters effected key scene changes and provided a wider allusive resonance, at its height in the final setting where the world of the audience would have been directly mirrored by the image onstage in a production generally presumed to have taken place in the Castle's Great Hall.[12] But, to extend the argument for *A Masque Presented at Ludlow Castle* as a co-production, we suggest that the entertainment may well have proceeded through the actual local material spaces and places invoked. If Lawes had successfully rehearsed his young pupils in their lines during the tour through the noble households of the region, and especially at Lyme, then the 12 days at Ludlow prior to the night of the performance could have been used profitably to rehearse the masque on site. As our reading elaborates, not only does this masque insist upon engaging multiple audiences across family, community, and region, but its physical demands presume a dramaturgy that the single location of Ludlow Castle's Great Hall could simply not fulfil (for a floor plan of the Castle, see Map 3.2).

The masque's opening direction reads: 'The first scene discovers a wild wood. The Attendant Spirit descends or enters' (s.d. 0). The marking of a choice here indicates a text that predates knowing what staging would be possible: 'enters' could indicate a simple movement into the Great Hall, but 'descends' suggests an actual forest setting where the arrival of the Attendant Spirit would be much more dramatic and provocative. In the same way that the dramatic journey of the masque plays off the actual presidential progress through the region recently undertaken by the performers, so here the imaginative space of the dramatic 'wood' is richly inflected by the material site of the Forest of Dean, located in the Earl's gubernatorial domains but also the site of regular daily practices for the local people present at this theatrical occasion.

Ludlow Castle as Site

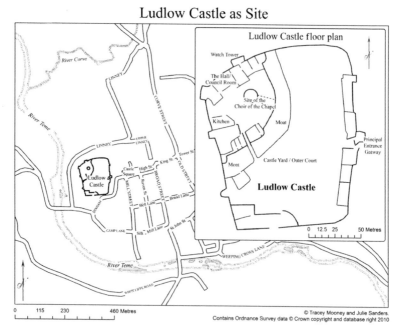

Map 3.2 Map of Ludlow Castle.

As several other chapters in this volume indicate, site-specific theory has a vested interest in exploring the spatial confusions presented by issues of insider/outsider status during performances within this recognized sub-genre. *A Masque Presented at Ludlow Castle,* although a historical document of a past performance, is recuperated for us as a moment of performance if we attend to its direct engagement with these same questions and confusions. In his opening speech of some 90-plus lines, the Attendant Spirit conjures the imaginative leap from the locality of the Castle grounds to the wider context of the Forest of Dean in all its social, political, and economic complexity. In other words, the site is cited so as to hail an 'insider' audience, well aware that the masque has as a purpose the examination of their own specific positionalities in and under the Earl's governance. As the Spirit establishes his relationship to the 'fair offspring nursed in princely lore' (34), he also instructs the wider audience on the perils of 'this drear wood,/The nodding horror of whose shady brows/Threats the forlorn and wandering passenger' (37–9). Against the natural backdrop, the Spirit then elaborates the threat of Comus, a necromancer whose 'orient liquor' can change human into 'brutish form' (66; 71). In order to protect his young charges, the Attendant Spirit explains that he must 'put off/These my skyrobes spun out of Iris' woof,/And take the weeds and likeness of a swain' (82–4) and, as he hears Comus's footsteps, become 'viewless' (92). In short, the Spirit assumes a habit common to the local people who would be a part of his audience in the Castle grounds, facilitating an easy disappearance in terms of the action, if keeping him very much in view among the spectators. At the same time, to see the music teacher dress up as a simple shepherd would doubtless be charming and entertaining for the audience, acting out a social mobility that the masque will continue to reference. From the outset, then, *A Masque Presented at Ludlow Castle* demands two distinct but interwoven architectures of response: one that affirms the Earl and his household in their royal duties and responsibilities, and another that powerfully reminds his subjects of their own and his place in the world.

The masque's next direction is elaborate:

> Comus enters with a charming-rod in one hand, his glass in the other, with him a rout of monsters, headed like sundry sorts of wild beasts, but otherwise like men and women, their apparel glistering, they come in making a riotous and unruly noise, with torches in their hands.
>
> (s.d. 92)

Here, place, costume, and sound (all things that the Attendant Spirit previously described through language) shift the ambience of the masque
from the eloquent and elegant poetry of its opening to chaotic and
unsettling action. The 'rout' – perhaps roles given to locals rather than
members of the household or actors – might well push their way
through the gathered audience. On the one hand, this carnivalesque
behaviour would provoke a comic, if surprised, response, even as the
monsters frightened or repulsed the audience; on the other hand, it may
well have recalled the specific acts of protest that had taken place in the
nearby Forest of Dean and Mortimer Forest in the early 1630s as part of
what is commonly known as the Great Western Rising, acts of protest
that consciously deployed carnivalesque costume, music, torchlight,
and physical performance.[13] Either way, the rout is clearly intended to
be an invasion of the audience's aural and corporeal space – a practice
that demands intimate connection for its effects and not the formal
separation of space typical of an interior setting.

Comus summons his rout to dance 'a light fantastic round' (144)
until he instructs, 'Break off, break off, I feel the different pace,/Of some
chaste footing near about this ground' (145–6), the cue for Lady Alice to
prepare to enter. If Comus and his followers have literally taken over the
performance space since their arrival, we are reminded that the Lady will
herald a more 'chaste footing', deftly gendering the action and empha-
sizing that women's movement must operate within a much smaller
spatial compass. The last lines in this sequence repeat the previous scene
with the Attendant Spirit, when Comus assumes a disguise as a villager
(again facilitating easy absorption into the audience) – a feat he accom-
plishes by 'magic dust' (165) – demonstrating to the very group into
which he now merges the dangerous tricks at his disposal. Thus, the
170 lines preceding Alice's entrance have affirmed the risks of her journey and produced the wood as a site of peril; her entrance can only be
received anxiously as Comus is among the audience, indeed passing as
one of them. Alice comes into the masque immediately recognizable as
her 15-year-old self, which is another vulnerable context since she is at
the very point of marriageability that is so crucial to the smooth conduct
and transfer of dynastic power.

The Lady provides an embodied performance of the Castle's power
stratum, but is distinctly out of place and explicitly at risk. Her first
words re-describe the 'sound/Of riot, and ill-managed merriment' that
the audience has just experienced first-hand and express her fears of
meeting such 'rudeness, and swilled insolence/Of such late wassailers'
(171–2) that, again, the audience knows is still among their crowd.

Further, Alice has no counter strategy to articulate; rather, she continues, 'yet O where else/Shall I inform my unacquainted feet/In the blind mazes of this tangled wood?' (179–81) and a few lines later worries about her brothers' whereabouts: 'But where they are, and why they came not back,/Is now the labour of my thoughts' (191–2). As the audience recognizes Comus's continued presence, it might, too, question why the Attendant Spirit, disguised now as a shepherd and also we assume among them, does not step forward to 'attend' her.

The audience is taken through several stages of dislocation, a ploy towards identification with Alice and, as such, key to the education embedded in the plot. How would spectators understand the separation of the Lady – in reality the daughter of their new governor – from the Attendant Spirit and from her brothers – the men whose task it was to keep her safe? Surely the audience cannot help but feel some culpability, that they are involved in this narrative of abandonment, complicit through their own failure to act, as Alice asks for 'a glistering guardian [...]/To keep my life and honour unassailed' (220–1). Moreover, how does this read as a welcome to Ludlow Castle on the part of the Earl of Bridgewater and, equally, on the part of the citizenry towards his arrival at Ludlow? In effect, there is a constant push to remind the audience of the larger geopolitical landscape that positions shepherds, villagers, and the ruling elite in highly specific ways. This resonates with strategies of spectatorial engagement more typically used to describe contemporary site-specific work.

Appropriate to her class and gender, Alice elects to sing, the effect of which is to bring Comus from his 'hidden residence' (248). Alice misreads her interlocutor as a 'gentle shepherd' (271) as she describes how her brothers left her 'weary on a grassy turf' (280). Comus, by contrast, revels in his local knowledge:

> I know each lane, and every alley green
> Dingle, or bushy dell of this wild wood,
> And every bosky burn from side to side
> My daily walks and ancient neighbourhood.

> (311–14)

Alice accepts his word (surely increasing concern among the spectators) and asks the 'Shepherd' to lead her to the cottage where he has promised her respite. Their exit marks the brothers' entrance, arriving with a series of questions about their sister to which the audience already knows the answers. Unlike the local knowledge and threat of magic that Comus has demonstrated, the brothers have only language at their disposal – a performance here that is languid, allusive, and full of excess. They can discuss chastity at elaborate length, but they can do nothing, in that place, to protect it.

Here the Attendant Spirit enters 'habited like a shepherd' (489) and is immediately recognized by the brothers as their father's employee – another emphasis on Lawes's work for the Earl in the care and tuition of his sons. What follows is more re-performance, where the brothers describe again the loss of their sister. The Spirit, like Comus to Alice immediately before, stresses his own strength of knowledge and practical experience of the woods – a stark contrast to the book-learned and untested accounts of that same space which the brothers provide. Lawes's character interrupts the poetic nimbleness of the Elder Brother and points to the inadequacy of his drawn sword to 'quell the might of hellish charms' (613). The Spirit describes his own comprehension of local plants and herbs that will more effectively provide the necessary means to defeat their sister's captor. What plays out here is a performance of recognition: for the Earl's governance to be exercised successfully in this border region, he will need local support. In this way the Attendant Spirit provides an education not only to the brothers, but also to the watching Earl, with reference to the role he has just assumed. In the culmination of the woodland setting, the brothers promise to follow the 'shepherd' to the necromancer's hall – a gesture towards the Castle that reminds all those present who has right of access and who does not.

The next direction heralds an entirely different scenography:

> The scene changes to a stately palace, set out with all manner of deliciousness: soft music, tables spread with all dainties. Comus appears with his rabble, and the lady set in an enchanted chair, to whom he offers his glass, which she puts by, and goes about to rise.
>
> (s.d. 968)

It is reasonable to imagine that the Egerton party and their guests returned to the Castle, after the scene in the woods, for a waiting banquet, while the citizenry found their entertainment at a (temporary) end. Feasting in the Great Hall would launch an on-site celebration of the Earl's new position and provide some time for the children to rest and prepare before their next scenes. But any happy mood among the guests is eventually broken by a resumption of the masque's action and the reappearance of Comus and his rout – a powerful reminder to the audience of their duty of care for Alice, a responsibility that might well have been forgotten amid the pleasures of food and drink. As Barbara Lewalski has noted, the audience would have expected 'the court scene to be the main masque after the antimasque in the dark wood with the antic dances of Comus's rout' (2000, p.77), but, thwarting expectations, the outsider Comus has penetrated the Castle environment and made it his own. Again, this performative act produces both place and its interpretation, actions that connote real-life thresholds, crossed and transgressed as they were at this time with remarkable frequency.

Comus addresses Alice on a life of elite leisure, showing the audience that he can perform this rhetoric just as ably as they can and prompts Alice's distressed response to her 'false traitor' (691) that this is far from the 'safe abode' (694) he promised her: 'What grim aspects are these,/These ugly-headed monsters? Mercy guard me!' (695–6) – a reference to Comus's rabble, of course, but also perhaps extended to the occupants of the banquet tables. Alice, in effect, performs chastity and sobriety in contrast to the behaviour of viewers internal and external to the masque proper, even as she is under a spell and unable to move from the chair in which Comus has seated her. But her words are a model of temperance and control, demonstrating a promise of the kind of governance that the Egerton family would bring to the region: both actions and words rehearse possible future (literal) performances of legislated power.

Alice's grace and eloquence is interrupted by Comus as he reminds her she is 'but young yet' (757). This keeps the 'real' Alice in focus and re-imposes the awful tension that characterized the previous scene in the woods: that the material site itself is no guarantee of outcome, rather contested knowledges will determine individual fates. Through a series of didactic engagements, repeated and compounded in the action of the masque, both the Egerton children and the audience are cast as experiential learners. As the three children work through the lesson prepared for them by Lawes in front of their new neighbours, that audience is made breathtakingly aware of the instruments of legislation that the Earl's appointment inscribes. This lesson reaches its climax in the scene where Comus puts the glass to Alice's lips, a crucial threshold that he cannot be allowed to cross literally or figuratively. The audience must grapple with the potential consequences for Alice, but also for the family and, beyond, the wider regional politic. Like Alice they have a choice: to be complicit with the action or to feel the force of it. Comus rages:

> Come, no more,
> This is mere moral babble, and direct
> Against the canon laws of our foundation;
> I must not suffer this, yet 'tis but the lees
> And settlings of a melancholy blood;
> But this will cure all straight, one sip of this
> Will bathe the drooping Spirits in delight
> Beyond the bliss of dreams.
>
> (808–13)

Even in this dramatic moment, Comus reminds Alice and the audience of legal jurisdiction ('canon laws'), and that a navigation of physical geography is inherent to this administrative centre of the council.

Predictably, Comus is unsuccessful in his claims on young Alice's body, as the brothers 'rush in with swords drawn, wrest his glass out of his hand, and break it against the ground; his rout make sign of resistance but are all driven in' (s.d. 813). This is a remarkably powerful dramaturgy: the audience is all too aware that it has failed to provide a safe context for the Earl's daughter, even in their designated space of the Castle, at the same time as the brothers' 'rescue' has been enabled by the Spirit's skills. And, as the Attendant Spirit's next lines make evident, their action has been neither effective nor conclusive: Alice is still under Comus's spell and cannot move from the chair. The Spirit says, 'What, have you let the false enchanter scape?/O ye mistook, ye should have snatched his wand/And bound him fast' (814–16). In short, the boys' education is not yet satisfactorily complete and, it is implied, neither is the audience's since they are equally culpable in their 'mistook', seeing the battle as a comic action leading to a happy ending. But the masque has more, yet, to teach its various audiences, a further lesson that requires the reabsorption of the Castle audience with the larger viewership.

Thus, the Attendant Spirit proposes a new setting to see 'a gentle nymph not far from hence,/That with moist curb sways the smooth Severn stream' (824–5). This introduces Sabrina, mythical goddess of the Severn river – the border between England and Wales and a key element in the geography of the region over which the Earl now governs – who must be relied upon to unlock the spell and free Alice. As he prepares the audience to return outdoors, the Spirit relates how Sabrina was 'Made Goddess of the River; still she retains/Her maiden gentleness' (843–4) and how he will summon her with 'warbled song' (854) and 'adjuring verse' (858). It is tempting to read the break in scene as time for the Castle audience to engage in some sober reflection on their flawed response to what took place in the Great Hall.

Once on the riverbank (Ludlow Castle stands in a raised position above the River Teme, a tributary of the Severn),[14] the spectatorship for the masque is again extended: the elite audience that has witnessed the previous scenes in the Castle is joined by the audience of citizenry who saw only the woodland scenes (and who must wonder what has happened, in the interim, to Alice and her brothers). The Attendant Spirit delivers the song and verse promised in the Great Hall, with a summons to Sabrina to appear: 'Rise, rise, and heave thy rosy head/From they coral-paven bed' (886–7); and to the audience to 'Listen and save' (889). The stage direction here reads, 'Sabrina rises, attended by water-nymphs, and sings' (s.d. 889). This description has often led critics of this masque to wonder how this might have been staged in the Castle setting, but understanding this event as a peripatetic performance allows for a more dramatic revelation of the lesson, explicitly contextualized by the border geographies that have been consistently, if ambivalently, referenced.

Sabrina touches Alice 'with chaste palms moist and cold' (918), once again illustrating the importance of incorporating local knowledge with able and appropriate governance and care. Then, 'Sabrina descends, and the lady rises out of her seat' (s.d. 921) – an extraordinary moment of symmetry that displays for both insider and local audiences the gender-inflected presence of power. With danger allayed, the Attendant Spirit signals yet another move:

> Come lady while Heaven lends us grace,
> Let us fly this cursed place,
> Lest the sorcerer us entice
> With some other new device.
> Not a waste, or needless sound
> Till we come to holier ground,
> I shall be your faithful guide
> Through this gloomy covert wide,
> And not many furlongs thence
> Is your father's residence.
>
> (938–47)

The address here extends to all members of the audience to join in the festivities 'Where this night are met in state/Many a friend to gratulate/His wished presence' (948–50) in the Great Hall of Ludlow Castle.

The final stage direction marks the re-entry and re-incorporation into the Castle space for festivities that this time include the full spectatorship, as an official welcome to their new management: 'The scene changes, presenting Ludlow Town and the President's Castle, then come in country-dancers, after them the Attendant Spirit, with the two brothers and the lady' (s.d. 957). Dances ensue, punctuated by two songs from the Attendant Spirit – the first marking the carnivalesque and, so, temporary nature of the masque (the shepherds must leave the Castle and return to work) and the second presenting the children to their parents. Here, Alice and her brothers, now properly prepared for their new environment, predict the Earl's success in his duties if he, too, has assimilated the educational message conveyed through the geographical turn. In effect, the masque has been a rehearsal for the Earl's duties that lie ahead – to see his daughter married, to govern the region, to represent the King among them. If the festive re-entry to the Castle displays success, this is nonetheless tempered by the Attendant Spirit's epilogue, the last lines of which indicate a marked provisionality:

> Mortals that would follow me,
> Love Virtue, she alone is free,
> She can teach ye how to climb
> Higher than the sphery chime;
> Or if Virtue feeble were,
> Heaven itself would stoop to her.
>
> (1018–23)

If the performance is at an end, this is, in effect, only the beginning of real labour at Ludlow Castle. The lesson, for all this masque's varied audiences (the family, the nobility, the citizenry) lies in the working through of competing knowledges and the realization that the successful management of space (whether this registers as Alice's body or the geographic boundaries of the Earl's responsibilities) depends on active and reflective engagement.

It remains true that most of the critical discussion of *A Masque Presented at Ludlow Castle* concerns itself with the text's place in the *oeuvre* of Milton's poetry. But, as we hope to have shown here, the masque required significant elaboration and realization on-site to achieve its dramatic effects. Yet those few critics who have paid attention to possible performance conditions have limited discussion by narrowing the debate to the either/or of indoor/outdoor staging. Our turn to site-specificity imagines a hybrid and peripatetic form that affords different engagements for the different audiences that this masque addresses. This credits a much more active role in the production of meaning for Lawes, as well as for the Egerton children and the various spectator groups. In effect, we propose a reading that explores not just the generic designation of 'masque', but the very conditions that enabled it to be 'presented at Ludlow Castle'. To understand performance on-site, then, is not – or at least not only – an argument for attention to physical details (a built environment with measurable dimensions and practical effects), but one that insists on the wider conceptual and jurisdictional site in which any performance takes place.

Acknowledgements

The authors thank the Social Sciences & Humanities Research Council of Canada for its financial support of this research collaboration.

Notes

1. On the masque form in the early modern period, see Butler (2008) and Bevington and Holbrook (1998).
2. See Westfall on the 'multimedia; displays' constituted by household theatre in the early modern period (1997, p.46).
3. There was a comparable position in northern England, which was held in the early 1630s by Sir Thomas Wentworth, future Earl of Strafford and one of the King's chief councillors.
4. The phrase is that of our editors, Joanne Tompkins and Anna Birch (see the introduction, 'The 'place' and practice of site-specific theatre and performance', p. 1).
5. Entries in the Bailiffs and Chamberlains' Accounts for 1633–4 note payments to 'some officers when we were invited to the maske', Shropshire Record Office LB 8/1/155. f[11v]*; reproduced in Somerset (1994, p.113). This and related entries are discussed by John Creaser (1984).
6. The boys had appeared as pages in Thomas Carew's *Coelum Britannicum* in 1632. Among the dramatic texts recently purchased by their mother was work by Ben Jonson (*The New Inn*); see Brown (1985, p.33).
7. These details were uncovered and published by Cedric Brown in a series of groundbreaking articles based on readings of documents in the British Library and the Huntington Library's Ellesmere papers (Ludlow to Lyme fragmentary accounts, Huntington MS EL 6678–6683). The details are deftly

summarized in the recent biography of Milton by Campbell and Corns (2008), especially Chapter 5.

8. We know that Lawes was a member of the party that sojourned at Lyme since some months later he wrote a letter of thanks to Legh for his hospitality; see Brown (1985, p.31) citing a letter dated 5 February 1635 from the Legh of Lyme Papers in the John Rylands Library, Manchester.

9. It had taken Queen Henrietta Maria and her court women some four months of rehearsal to prepare Walter Montagu's *The Shepherds' Paradise* for performance in 1632/3; see, for example, Ravelhofer (1999).

10. The textual history of *A Masque Presented at Ludlow Castle* is notoriously complicated and can only be gestured at here. The masque is extant in at least three variants, including the so-called Trinity Manuscript in Milton's own hand, which is presumed to represent early versions of the text; the presentation copy that was made for the Egerton family, which is often held to represent the text as performed; and the 1637 published version which was issued under Lawes's name. In this chapter, line references refer to Cummings's collated text edition of Milton (2000): the anthologizing of *Comus* [sic] as poetry has further contributed to a limited understanding of the collaborative site-specific context of its first performance which we seek to address here. For a full discussion of the implication of the variant textual states of the masque, see Brown (1985). Milton had authored another site-specific entertainment just two years earlier for another branch of the family based at Harefield House in Middlesex. *Arcades* (1632), written in honour of the Dowager Countess of Derby, with its interest in ideas of place and 'neighbouring' communities is an intriguing companion text to the Ludlow masque and is discussed in greater detail in this context by Brown (1985; and 1995, Chapter 3). Critics have suggested that it was Lawes, who had strong London links with the musical circles that Milton is known to have abutted at this time, who introduced the writer to the families (see, for example, Brown, 1985, p.12).

11. This particular context for understanding the Ludlow masque is examined in detail in Sanders (2011).

12. This reading is frequently produced by the deployment of the term 'scene' at this point in the text (see, for example, Brown, 1985, p.51 which suggests that the masque was effectively a journey across a room with each 'scene' at one end). The *Oxford English Dictionary* online indicates that in the seventeenth century, with particular relation to court masques, the term did refer specifically to '[t]he material apparatus, consisting chiefly of printed hangings, slides [...] set at the back or sides of the stage and intended to give the illusion of a real view of the locale' (*Oxford English Dictionary*, 2011, 6a). But the Ludlow masque, as we are arguing, is a departure from court masquing traditions in a number of ways and bears more relation to contemporary provincial entertainment at noble households, such as Ben Jonson's *Love's Welcome at Bolsover* staged in Derbyshire in July 1634, which involved a degree of peripatetic experience, moving between indoor and outdoor spaces. To this end, the phrase 'change of scene', which can suggest relocation, not least through movement and travel, becomes a double motif in the Ludlow masque. Earlier critical work that has offered valuable speculation about the possibilities of outdoor performance in relation to the

masque include Hunter (1983), which provides a speculative promptbook as an appendix, and Demaray (1968), especially Chapter 5 on the 'Staging of *Comus*', though both have tended to opt for either a wholly indoor or outdoor performance rather than the suggestive hybrid that we argue for here.

13. The details of the Western Rising can be found in Sharp (1980, pp.174–5); the carnivalesque aspects of a number of the protests are discussed in Sanders (2001).

14. Demaray (1968, p.97) discusses the symbolic potential of the views of both the River Teme and the Corve valley from Ludlow Castle for this section of the masque.

4

Embodied Presence and Dislocated Spaces: Playing the Audience in *Ten Thousand Several Doors* in a Promenade, Site-Specific Performance of John Webster's *The Duchess of Malfi*

Jane Collins

Theatre, according to Herbert Blau, 'posits itself in distance' (1990, p.86). This distance is a psychic and a physical necessity rooted in what Blau calls the 'scopic drive', the erotic pleasure generated by gazing at that which we cannot touch but that might touch us. Thus, for Blau, the delineation of the stage edge, the boundary between actor and audience, is fundamental to the act of viewing (for a discussion of Blau, see Collins and Nisbet, 2010, pp.5–10). Site-specific performance, in which the embodied presence of the audience is a component of the scenography, collapses distance and physical boundaries. There is no fixed stage edge; the line between the fictional space and the real is fluid and unstable. The audience becomes 'dislocated' in the sense of not knowing their proper place, position, or relationship to the events depicted. When this spatial dislocation is compounded by a mode of 'playing' that blurs the psychic boundaries as well – 'who are the actors here? What is my role?' – the audience is further displaced from the security of their position as viewing subject.

I discuss here a site-specific adaptation of John Webster's Jacobean revenge tragedy *The Duchess of Malfi*, directed by myself, designed by Peter Farley[1] and developed in conjunction with Prodigal Theatre Company;[2] the potential for psycho/spatial play between the actors and audience produced new readings of a canonical text. Through the analysis of three key moments in this production, I suggest how these meanings emerged and examine the ways in which performers, audience, space, and site colluded: I argue that the spatial properties of the site afforded the actors opportunities for 'play' which embroiled the audience in the moral ambiguities of Webster's text in ways that a more formal staging would not have permitted.[3] Through their embodied engagement in the narrative, the audience was forced to confront their own conflicting responses to the reprehensible actions of the protagonists and examine their own complicity in the Duchess's suffering and eventual death.

The production took its title from the Duchess's lines:

> I know death hath ten thousand several doors
> For men to take their *Exits*: and 'tis found
> They go on such strange geometrical hinges,
> You may open them both ways: any way, for Heaven sake,
> So I were out of your whispering.

(Act IV, Scene 2, 215–19; original emphasis)

Doors opened 'both ways' throughout this production, sometimes with farce-like speed and precision, at others ineffably slowly. They contained the audience in small intimate spaces and opened outwards onto expansive public worlds: an integral component of the scenography was their physical materiality, their capacity to slam and creak, reveal and conceal, and to let in light and to enclose in darkness.

Ten Thousand Several Doors was presented at the Brighton International Festival in various rooms of the Grand Central in Brighton, UK, in May 2006 and again in 2009. The Grand Central overlooks Brighton railway station and is a popular drinking house for Brighton's commuters; it also houses a theatre on the first floor.[4] The production exploited the building's natural light, ambient background noise, and the claustrophobic atmosphere of its smaller rooms. The action also extended to the bar and the station concourse.

With the seats removed, the theatre becomes a black playing space of approximately 6 by 11 metres. The shuttered windows on two sides can be opened to reveal the main concourse of Brighton station and also the road that runs alongside the building (Image 4.1). The theatre is directly above the bar, and, in spite of expensive insulation, sounds drift upwards. This continuous, low-level background noise, sometimes punctuated with laughter, intruded into the most intimate or tragic moments of the performance: a commentary of indifference from the

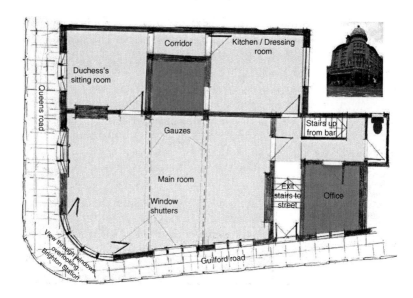

Image 4.1   Plan of the first floor of the Grand Central including Nightingale Theatre and adjoining rooms. Courtesy of Andrew Nesbit.

'real' public world of the bar to the suffering of the characters in the fic-tive world of the play. There are four other rooms on this floor: a small sitting room with a large bay window which also affords a view over the station; a kitchen that doubles as a dressing room; a toilet with a washbasin; and a tiny office. These rooms have an air of shabby gen-tility. Posters of past productions and photographs of the conversion of the space to a working theatre vie with period fireplaces and numbered doors which attest to the building's use as a hotel more than 50 years ago. The space also has a 'behind the scenes' theatricality about it, highlighting what is revealed and what is kept hidden in performance. Utilizing all the rooms enabled us to play with the accepted taxonomies of theatrical space by offering the opportunity to be at once 'onstage' and 'backstage'.

Playing the audience

The movement of the audience through these rooms was carefully managed by the performers. This tight control of the audience as an 'embodied presence' problematized the relationship between the spectator and performer, as reviewer Dorothy Max Prior was able to discern:

> It is a production in which the role of the audience is thrown into question. We are – what? Priests in the confessional box, therapists, hospital psychiatrists? All and none of the above. We are not invisible: we are played to and acknowledged as we move from room to room. But we are powerless voyeurs, and in the unfolding scenes of double-dealing, betrayal and violence somehow complicit in our non-intervention.
>
> (2006, p.24)

The dislocation of a conventional viewing position challenges contemporary audiences, but ironically, this engages with the play's early modern roots. In her analysis of Elizabethan staging, Bridget Escolme speculates that the objectives of Shakespearean stage figures in the early modern period 'are bound up with the fact that they know you're there' (2005, p.16). She continues: 'the shifting distance between performer and audience might be constitutive of the ways in which [these] plays produce meaning' (Escolme, 2005, p.18). Escolme's study looks at Shakespeare, but the potential for play on the distance between the performer and audience is equally applicable to the production of meaning in Jacobean drama. The explicit theatricality of Jacobean stage convention with its sensationalist effects, tricks, and fakery appears to demand an exuberant performance style which shifts rapidly between representational 'acting', which does not acknowledge the presence of the audience, to presentational 'performing', which does.

Whereas conventional venues usually reinforce representational performance, the size and variety of playing spaces in the Grand Central accommodated the shifts in style that presentational performing affords. There was also actual physical contact between performers and the audience given the intimacy of some of the smaller rooms. This apparent collapsing of distance blurred the boundaries between the fictive and the real. According to Philip Auslander, actors' presence is tied up with their 'psychophysical attractiveness to the audience, a concept related to that of *charisma*' (1997, p.62; original emphasis); this presence does not precede the performance but is created by it. In *Ten Thousand Several Doors*, the performers manipulated 'presence' as they charmed or coerced the audience around the site. Sometimes acting in character, at other times, to paraphrase Auslander, apparently 'just being themselves'[5] (1997, p.28), they directed the audience's attention or persuaded them of the validity of a particular character's point of view, playing the conversational intimacy of the smaller rooms against the formality demanded by the larger spaces. The form and function of these rooms contributed to the performance's aims in a way that a traditional theatre venue could not.

The blurring of the fictive and the real also underpinned the scenography. There were no fixed or grounded elements to the design other than those properties inherent, or apparently inherent, in the site itself. This fluid visual/spatial dynamic was produced by the embodied presence of the audience as they moved around the space, oscillating between observers and participants. Max Prior's review makes this point:

> Voyeurism – getting an eyeful, peeping through the keyhole to gain forbidden knowledge – is played upon throughout. The scenography of the show is one of the main dramaturgical tools in creating this play of revelation and concealment: light, shadows and a wonderful moment of complete darkness; mirrors that give sudden shocking reflections of performers or audience; sudden glimpses into an inner sanctum; veils, curtains and shutters opening and closing.
>
> (2006, p.24)

Manoeuvred by the actors into complicity in a fabricated culture of duplicity and violence, the audience did not know where they stood (sometimes literally) as viewing subjects in relation to the events depicted: the duplicity the characters practise on each other in the text was turned outwards and practised on the audience. This strategy intensified engagement in the action while simultaneously raising self-consciousness through a process of what Escolme (2000) describes, in a discussion of Webster's characters, as 'seduction and deconstruction'. The audience is forced to confront the ways in which these charismatic but morally reprehensible characters manipulate meaning and exercise power over the body of the Duchess and their own embodied presence in the space. As the performance developed, this spatial and moral disorientation and reorientation became even more acute as the realities of space and place, truth and illusion were progressively conflated by exploiting the opportunities offered up by the site. The particular ways in which this site-specific venue was mobilized, in other words, conditioned the audience's response to events.

Staging the real

The history of the site informed the costumes. Farley's designs suggested the 1950s, the actual heyday of the Grand Central as a hotel. Given the eclectic mix of modern and retro styles that coexists in contemporary Brighton, though, these blended easily with the clothes of the regular customers downstairs in the bar where the performance started. It was only when the actors appeared together as a group upstairs with the Duchess in her 1950s 'Living Doll'[6] gown that their stylistic unity became evident.[7] Farley's subtle enhancements of the material qualities of the rooms themselves also highlighted the period and created the illusion of an actual lived-in domestic place that simultaneously retained its identity as a performance space. He was not striving for historical accuracy and no attempt was made to disguise the kitchen/dressing room, for instance, as other than what it was: a place where the Duchess's men (that is, the actors) hang out when they are off duty/offstage.

The only overtly theatrical modification that Farley made to the site was the addition of two black gauze curtains that traversed the main playing area on the first floor at separate intervals. This enabled the creation of a number of different scenographic frames within the one space and also allowed us to contain the performers and the audience within these frames in the course of the action. Thus the Duchess's secret marriage to her steward, Antonio, takes place in a corridor of light between the gauzes with the audience looking in from either side unacknowledged by the performers. Later, this situation is reversed when the audience is literally trapped in between the gauzes in the dark and the action played out across them. Antonio addresses them directly; they are cast as members of the Duchess's household, confined to their 'chambers' while a robbery is investigated – a plot cooked up by Antonio to divert attention from the untimely birth of his and the Duchess's first child.

Despite the addition of more overtly theatrical components (such as the curtains), the close quarters of the venue served to highlight the site and reinforce the additional meanings that each room communicated. This duality of function was reinforced by the engagement of all the senses in the scenography. Owing to the size of the rooms and the close proximity of the actors as the audience moved around the site, the heady fragrance of the Duchess's perfume – Chanel, of course – merged with the smell of cheap aftershave worn by the male chorus and the more subtle aromas of the expensive cologne worn by the Cardinal and

Ferdinand. Was this a carefully constructed differentiation of power and authority or simply an indicator of the actors' personal tastes? These olfactory sensations underlined and attenuated the meanings being produced by the other senses. Were the damp tea towels slung across the kitchen/dressing room and the steaming tea urn a behind-the-scenes glimpse of 1950s domestic life or indices of the offstage world of a group of actors in the process of making tea for the interval?

Presence and dislocation

The typical relationship between actor and audience is elaborated by Maaike Bleeker to include the recognition of self by the viewer as one who views:

> 'Presence' results from a relationship between a body seeing and the image of a body seen, and both sides of this relationship as well as what connects them, are embedded in culture. Within this relationship, 'presence' is an experience of confirmation of the body seeing rather than a quality observed or present in a body seen.
>
> (2008, pp.127–8)

In this re-staging of Webster's play, confirmation includes not only the acknowledgement by the viewer of their pleasure in the performer's charisma and the power of the performer to seduce, but also to a questioning of their own subject positions in relation to what they 'see' and participate in. The modern audience becomes embroiled in a culture which is alien and yet recognizably their own. The distance between the canonical text and the embodied present is collapsed by the 'play' of the actors in combination with the architectonic features of the site. Not knowing where one stands in relation to events can lead to questioning and reflection. The following three scenes isolate moments of spatial and psychic 'dislocation' generated by the site that, in combination with Webster's sophisticated stagecraft, draw the audience into the rich and moral complexity of his dramatic world.

Moment 1: The 'pilgrimage to Our Lady of Loretto'

As the action progresses, the Duchess's brothers discover that she has married again against their will but they do not know to whom. She publicly dismisses Antonio as a 'false steward' but secretly plans to rendezvous with him and flee with the children. Then, in a pivotal scene that changes the play's axis, she takes Bosola into her confidence.

Bosola, who works for her brothers, persuades her to change her plans, saying:

> Let me think;
> I would wish your Grace to feign a pilgrimage
> To Our Lady of Loretto, scarce seven leagues
> From fair Ancona.

(Act III, Scene 2, 305–8)

Ferdinand orders the shutters in the main theatre space to be opened and the audience is directed to look out of the windows onto the street below. The Duchess, her servant, and three children are seen making their way down Guildford Road towards Brighton station; as Max Prior (2006, p.24) recounts, '[W]e peer out of the window to see the Duchess and her children scurrying towards Brighton Station in an attempt to escape her guards, passers-by unsure whether to intervene' (Image 4.2). They wait at the lights and then cross the road onto the station concourse where they are greeted by Antonio. The Duchess and Antonio embrace and move towards the platforms when they are intercepted by one of Ferdinand's men, who hands them a letter. As the

Image 4.2 The Duchess of Malfi, Miranda Henderson, with her children and servant Cariola, Ignacio Jarquin, viewed from the windows of the Grand Central on their way towards Brighton station. Courtesy of Matthew Andrews.

Duchess realizes that she has been set up and her plans for escape have been foiled, she looks up towards the windows and the audience. Antonio reluctantly makes a break for it with their eldest son while she is marched back across the road with her servant and the two other children towards the Grand Central and the theatre.

Positioned at the windows, the audience are simultaneously actors in and witnesses to the dramatic events played out below as the fictive world of the play encounters the realities of Brighton. The presence of mimetic action set in one temporal zone collides with the presence of Brighton commuters in another, and these parallel realities are further complicated for the audience by the running commentary from Ferdinand and the Cardinal, who are also watching from the windows. This narration by the two brothers was improvised in response to the random events which intervened in the action. Sometimes, heavy traffic meant that the Duchess had to wait a long time to cross the road with the children, or a bus would stop between the window and the station, blocking the audience's view. Meanwhile the actors extemporized about road safety, the Green Cross Code and the problems of heavy traffic in Brighton, often eliciting comments from the audience. The spontaneity of these moments of simultaneous showing and telling collapsed the established frames of the performance while at the same time reinforcing the dramatic convention of the triangulation of knowledge. The audience are both spectators and participants; their presence is acknowledged by Ferdinand and the Cardinal but not by the Duchess. They share knowledge with the brothers that the Duchess is not party to, until she looks up at the window, at which point they become implicated in the set-up. Moreover, the effect of the brothers' witty banter, which the audience realizes cannot have been planned in advance, makes them laugh and draws them further into their orbit, aligning them closer to the staging of the cruel events that follow.

Having established that the Duchess has been intercepted, Ferdinand orders the shutters to be closed and the audience to sit on the floor at one end of the theatre space, thereby reasserting the delineation of the stage edge. He produces a 'fake' hand that he plays with, showing off his tricks. However, when he takes this 'play' into the audience, moving among them, shaking 'hands', stroking their hair, and eventually sitting down with them on the floor, the fictive and real boundaries become blurred again. When the Duchess and her children are brought into this space and placed in front of them, the audience are momentarily caught between these vulnerable stage figures and her increasingly unstable brother. The children are pushed into the small adjoining room and Ferdinand orders the lights to be switched off; then, in the dark (actual rather than the stage dark of Jacobean performance), he and his man Bosola continue to torment the Duchess. Opening the shutters extended the space to incorporate the 'real' world beyond the play, but this expansion of site was only temporary and served to intensify the claustrophobic atmosphere in the theatre when they were closed. The locked shutters and the darkness heightened the audience's awareness of the isolation of the Duchess and the imminent danger to her children in the next room, familiar to the audience as a domestic space in previous scenes and not, as it were, 'offstage'.

Moment 2: Wax dummies

Ferdinand:
I come to seal my peace with you: here's a hand,
                    Gives her a dead man's hand
[...] (Act 1V, Scene 1, 43–4)

Duchess:
What witchcraft doth he practise, that he hath left
A dead man's hand here? –

Here is discover'd, behind a traverse, the artificial figures of ANTONIO and his child; appearing as if they were dead.

Bosola:
Look you: here's the piece from which 'twas tane;
                              (Act 1V, Scene 1, 54–6)

David M. Bergeron (1978) speculates that the Jacobean audience would have recognized the figures with which the Duchess is tormented as wax funereal effigies popular with high-ranking people at that time. In this sense, the stage illusion or special effect would have had a symbolic as well as a dramatic impact. The lifelike quality of the figures, the result of advances in wax moulding techniques, convinces the Duchess that they are 'true substantial bodies' (Act 1V, Scene 1, 114) and Bergeron points out the way that Webster exploits their theatrical potential to raise the stakes of horror and the grotesque:

> Though the theatre audience is initially caught in the stage illusion of these wax figures, Webster finally widens the ironic gap of perspective by informing us and letting the Duchess persist in the belief that the figures truly are Antonio and the children dead.
>
> (Bergeron, 1978, p.335)

For this production we used photographic slides that had a forensic quality and attested to the believability of photography in the pre-digital age (though, of course, constructed digitally). Our intention was that the audience should also be convinced of the veracity of the images of dead Antonio and the young boy whom they had moments before seen running away on the station concourse. It was a raw and cruel moment, difficult to watch as the grief-stricken Duchess was forced to contemplate the dead bodies of her husband and son before being removed from the space by Bosola. Ferdinand immediately tells the audience that this was a trick, like the joke fake hand; he says: 'Excellent; as I would wish: she's plagued in art' (Act 1V, Scene 1, 110). This comment makes the audience aware that they have also been 'taken in', compounding the sense of phenomenological uncertainty which had been built up in the previous scenes. Now, not only what I see but also what I feel is being blatantly manipulated. The men find the whole episode hilarious, and despite Bosola's protestations, Ferdinand makes it clear that he has more tortures in store for the Duchess: 'To bring her to despair' (Act 1V, Scene 1, 114).

The men exit and the venue once again shifts the audience's perceptions about its role and place. The door to the next room is opened by one of the children, who beckons the audience to follow her. They file past her grieving mother (who is lying on the daybed) into the adjacent kitchen/dressing room, one of the smallest rooms of the venue, where the men, indifferent to the Duchess's suffering, are drinking tea and playing darts. Bosola is working out on a punchbag as Ferdinand slicks back his hair in the mirror. Is this a dressing room, or a kitchen, or both? The men joke with the audience as they pass through the space. Are they 'acting' or just being themselves? When they address the women, these jokes have a hint of sexual innuendo. In the tiny kitchen/dressing room the audience is caught between the inappropriateness of this intimacy and enjoyment of the actors' banter. The collapse of distance and physical boundaries that the venue presents reinforces the effect and affect of the audience's enforced complicity in the action. As the audience leave, one of the men waits outside the door and courteously directs them to the bar downstairs for the interval. The interval will in fact be incorporated into the performance, and the public space of the bar will be the next site for dramatic action.

Moment 3: The dance of the madmen

Ferdinand:
And, 'cause she'll needs be mad, I am resolv'd

To remove forth the common hospital
All the mad folk, and place them near her lodging:
There let them practise together, sing, and dance,
And act their gambols to the full o'th' moon:

(Act IV, Scene 1, 124–8)

Visits to London's Bedlam Hospital were popular as an early modern spectacle: unfortunate inmates were often called upon to sing and dance for the entertainment of these audiences. Although a discussion of the ways in which madness was performed is outside my remit here, there has been a tendency in recent productions of Jacobean plays to interpret the mad scenes through the empathic lenses of pity and fear. These representations often take their sensibilities and visual cues from Victorian imagery. Escolme (2008) gives an example of a production of *The Duchess of Malfi*:

> The RSC's [Royal Shakespeare Company's] 2000/1 production offered Victorian rocking and muttering madmen, incarcerated within the production's central glass box. On show behind the glass, these are exploited objects of pity from an era of dirty white asylum clothes and straightjackets. They speak the lines of the mad doctor, lawyer and priest, but not so we can hear them. They certainly don't sing and dance.

A close study of Webster's text offers up other possible readings of 'the mad folk' in *The Duchess of Malfi* which concur more closely with the notion of madness as spectacle and point to their strategic positioning within the narrative as a dramatic device, geared to have a specific effect on the audience. In a reading of *Ten Thousand Several Doors* in this context, Escolme (2008) explains that our production:

> pushes the mixture of delight and embarrassment and delight in embarrassment to a contemporary extreme when the actors lead us down into the pub itself for the madhouse scene. Here both the Duchess and the audience are placed before a seedy little stage and made to watch a misogynistic stand up show, complete with a grim routine with a ventriloquist's dummy dressed exactly like the Duchess. We are cast as punters and laugh nervously at the jokes – they're ghastly but very well timed – feeling, perhaps both, complicit in the Duchess' humiliation and mildly disconcerted that the real punters in the pub might think that this is genuinely what we have come to see.

In the text, much of what the madmen say is satirical. What is more, their exchanges are peppered with misogynistic and scatological references, Jacobean jokes that reinforce many of the implicit fears around the loss of male agency and power which are the main drivers of the Play. To develop Escolme's point about the stage figures in this period always being aware of the audience, one might equally speculate about Webster's awareness as a dramatist of the potential affect on his audience of these disturbing and yet comic stage figures.

The madmen could be there to make the audience laugh, and the context in which this happens, a comedy show for a grieving wife and mother, represents the torture of the Duchess by her brothers. She believes that her husband and her son are dead. The audience know otherwise. From our place in history, we can only speculate as to the moral and ethical complexity for the Jacobean audience created by the effect of a grieving widow positioned onstage between them and a group of deranged jesters who sing, dance, tell bad jokes, and, however reluctantly, make them laugh.

These effects are realized through the use of the Grand Central bar as both theatre venue and site-specific location. The type of 'theatre' venue here becomes intertwined with another, related site-specific location, that of the 'end of the pier show' for which Brighton is known. The Duchess's brothers presented this tacky 'end of the pier show' when the audience was directed downstairs to the bar for the interval. They were given just enough time to order drinks before the Cardinal's stand-up routine commenced, followed by Ferdinand's ventriloquist act. The Duchess, who was clearly distressed, was placed between the stage and the audience. Although spatially the 'seedy little stage' was situated to one side, a microphone meant the show was clearly audible, if not always visible, to the other customers in the bar. Escolme (2008) describes the high degree of 'skill' in the delivery of the material, certainly from the Cardinal, who managed to get the audience laughing through a series of well-timed but fairly innocuous gags before directing his misogynistic jokes at the Duchess. Not knowing the context, the 'real punters' in the pub often continued laughing, especially at Ferdinand's crude ventriloquist act. The audience were momentarily caught between their knowledge of this fictive world, the role they had been cast in, and the 'real' reactions of those around them, produced by another 'layer' of audience: those participants who were not attending the theatre but just happened to be in the pub. When Ferdinand's act collapsed into bathos, the paying audience was told to drink up by the actors and ushered upstairs to the 'theatre' where the spatial and psychic boundaries of the performance were once more redrawn.

Playing this scene in the Grand Central bar not only merged form and content, but also placed the action outside the disciplinary certainty of dramatic convention, further unsettling the relationship between audience and performer. In this public space, the responses of the 'real punters' could not be distinguished from those of the audience, nor could they be predicted or controlled. In dealing with these site-specific contingencies, the actors increased what Auslander calls their 'psychophysical attractiveness' (1997, p.62) while simultaneously colluding in the humiliation of the Duchess. What is the place, position and relationship of the audience to these exchanges when there is no stage edge, no apparent physical or physic boundaries to the action? Do they react as punters, as audience, or as themselves?

'What is "present" to us,' according to Hans Ulrich Gumbrecht, 'is in front of us, in reach of and tangible for our bodies' and that this effect is also 'subjected, in space, to movements of greater or lesser proximity, and of greater or lesser intensity' (2004, p.17). In her account of early modern audience relationships, Escolme notes the '[a]wkward, unpredictable as well as easy, conventionalised encounters' (2005, p.18) that the audience would have had with the performers. The possibility of such unpredictability, in conjunction with the fluidity and instability of both the objects in space and space itself, was intended in this staging to literally displace the viewer from their position as subject. Blau uses the word 'touch' in 'the double sense of physical touch and the emotionally touching' (1990, p.84). In *Ten Thousand Several Doors*, the play on distance afforded by the spatial properties of the site heightened the erotic charge between performer and audience and increased emotional engagement in the action. Continually dislocated and relocated as an embodied presence in the space, the audience became physically and psychically caught up in the visceral energy and desires of the protagonists; the audience's emotional responses were never allowed to settle. To re-stage this text as a site-based work offers the opportunity to explore the moral ambiguities it suggests by blurring the boundaries between the fictive and the real in performance. This production also reminds us of the manipulative potential of site-specific performance to destabilize the certainties between what we see, feel, and think.

Notes

1. Peter Farley is a designer and senior lecturer in Theatre Design at Wimbledon College of Art in London.
2. Prodigal Theatre was established in 1999 and is based in Brighton. In 2004, Prodigal reopened the Nightingale Theatre after years of closure, with Steven Berkoff as the venue's patron. In 2006, Prodigal were the resident company

and actor-managers of the space. The collaborative partnership with Prodigal built on and developed ideas explored by Collins and Farley in *Webster's Women*, a practice-based research project that examined the female characters in *The White Devil and The Duchess of Malfi*. The work was greatly enhanced by Prodigal's rigorous approaches to training and performance which produced a highly attuned level of ensemble playing that became an integral part of the stylistic language of the final production. Miranda Henderson and Alister O'Loughlin, the founders of the company, played the Duchess of Malfi and Bosola. Ignacio Jarquin, the musical director, played Cariola, the Duchess's waiting woman. For more information on the philosophy and work of Prodigal Theatre see www.prodigaltheatre.co.uk.

3. Webster's text was pared down to its narrative bones, but the basic dramatic framework and teleological structure of the play remained intact.

4. The Nightingale Theatre's current artistic policy is to offer the space for artist-led developments and residencies. The incumbent director/managers have also opened up the rooms on the second floor as potential playing spaces and readopted the signage – kitchen, bathroom, bedroom – associated with the Grand Central's history as a hotel (Nightingale, 2011).

5. This is paraphrased from Auslander's chapter entitled ' "Just be your self": *logocentrism* and *différance* in performance theory' (1997, p.28).

6. 'Living Doll' is a song written by Lionel Bart and recorded by Cliff Richard and the Shadows (then called the Drifters) in 1959.

7. Language was similarly employed to create the impression of familiarity and to act as a distancing device as the performers shifted between speech in the modern idiom and Jacobean verse.

5
Haunted House: Staging *The Persians* with the British Army

Mike Pearson

In an originary moment of Western drama, in Aeschylus' *The Persians*, a ghost appears...

> Come, friends, let us speak the old words, sing the songs of good omen.
> Let us raise the dead.
> Conjure up the soul of Darius as I honour the earth and let it drink.
> (Queen, *The Persians*; adaptation: Kaite O'Reilly)

> Lord of the dead, earth itself,
> let him ascend from forgetfulness.
> Let our Persian god, born in Susa,
> rise from the dark slumber, below.
> Release the divine Darius...
> (Chorus, *The Persians*; adaptation: Kaite O'Reilly)

In August 2010, I directed a site-specific staging of Aeschylus's play for the newly launched National Theatre Wales (NTW)[1], whose first season in 2010/11 – 12 works in 12 months at different locations – focused upon 'a "theatrical mapping" of the country' (McGrath, 2009, p.10). John McGrath, NTW's artistic director, explains: 'We will explore the land through theatre, and theatre through the land. Each piece will be developed out of, and in response to, its Location [...]. Location isn't just about site, it's about how our memories live in geography and space' (2009, p.10).

The 'development' of site-specific theatre invariably involves an admixture of desire and necessity, the implementation of sets of both programmatic and pragmatic addresses to the possibilities and problems of a location. Outside the controlled environment of the auditorium,

69

it offers new creative opportunities as well as requiring extended techniques of production management – of providing for, and attending to, audiences and performers alike. This production of *The Persians* illustrates this admixture, while also engaging with place and performance in Wales.

While the 'response' of site-specific performance might refer directly in its subject matter to the history and past or present usage of a place, in an enacted reciprocity or symmetrical occupation, the relationship of site and performance might equally – after architect Bernard Tschumi (1994, pp. XXI–XXIII) – be one of *conflict* or studied *indifference*. Performance might resemble a transitory tenure that resists explicitly 'pointing at' or 'pointing out' the location: ambivalence can be equally and mutually revealing. Whether explicitly referenced or not, site will always constitute a stratum of meaning within the stratigraphy of the dramaturgy (Pearson, 2010, pp.166–70).

In the early 1990s, and much influenced by Tschumi's theoretical perceptions, Cliff McLucas, designer and co-artistic director of Welsh theatre company Brith Gof, began to characterize site-specific performance as the coexistence and overlay of two basic sets of architectures: those of the extant building or what he called the *host*, that which is *at* site – and those of the constructed scenography and performance, or the *ghost*, that which is temporarily brought *to* site. The site itself became an active component in the creation of performative meaning, rather than a neutral space of exposition or scenic backdrop for dramatic action: 'It's the "host" which does have personality, history, character, narrative written into it' (McLucas cited in Morgan, 1995, p.47). However, *host* and *ghost* might be functionally independent. Significantly, they might have quite different origins and ignore the other's presence; they are coexistent but not necessarily congruent. Their alignment – both conceptual and spatial – might be asymmetrical, but the performance remains transparent. Cathy Turner espouses the creative potency of an uneasy fit: 'Each occupation, or traversal, or transgression of space offers a reinterpretation of it, even a rewriting' (2004, p.373). In addition, 'the "ghost" is transgressive, defamiliarizing, and incoherent' (Turner, 2004, p.374), creating a fruitful disjuncture. So, a drama with a ghost is spectrally present; it is not 'of' the place but finds temporary affordances there.

On 10 August 2010 as for the first time the Chorus open their shirts to expose white body armour, beating their chests and raising their arms in invocation, 'rise from the dark slumber' Darius does, the dead 'Eternal Leader': his large back-projected video image appearing in a room-sized aperture on the upper storey of the 'Skills House', his highly amplified voice echoing across the hilly landscape. Haunting the house...

The singular Skills House stands on the edge of Cilienni – or in its army designation Fighting In Built Up Areas (FIBUA) – a specially constructed replica village built around 1990 on the Sennybridge Training Area (SENTA), close to Brecon Beacons National Park in mid-South Wales (Pearson, 2010, pp.135–9). SENTA is the British Army's third-largest live-firing estate, covering 24,000 hectares of upland terrain; public access is strictly prohibited. It was compulsorily requisitioned in 1940, and a population of 219 individuals from 54 homes were moved out; they never returned. Heaps of stones that were once the scattered farms typical of the region still mark the land; with the footings of the ruined chapel, they are reminders of a community and economy largely invisible to those authorities that regarded the area as unpopulated (Hughes, 1998; Carruthers, 2007). Eviction was swift. There was a degree of political opposition: Welsh pacifist and playwright Saunders Lewis and the young Gwynfor Evans, subsequently Plaid Cymru's first Member of Parliament, addressed public meetings. But it is largely with hindsight that the seizure is regarded as one of those moments in recent Welsh history in which places – Welsh-speaking places – were 'disappeared', most notably with the construction of the reservoir at Tryweryn to provide water for Liverpool in the early 1960s. It advances an appreciation of *cynefin* – a conceptualization of environment that includes human dwelling and agency – and the repercussions of its compromise or loss in such events: 'Land and language are two strands that tie the Welsh-speaker to his *cynefin* or locale. [...] There are other links such as remembrance of things past' (Lewis Jones, 1985, p.122). Welsh commentator Ned Thomas also discusses remembrance in the context of landscapes:

> Wherever you look in the modern Welsh culture you find the word 'remember'. [...] Even the landscape takes on a different quality if you are one of those who remember. The scenery is then never separate from the history of the place, from the feeling for the lives that have been lived there.
>
> (1973, p.72)

And it continues to rankle. While the present landscape seems scenically attractive and benign – munitions are surprisingly quickly absorbed by the soft sub-soil, leaving little surface scarring – it resonates with political undertones. When performance occasions visitation, for some – 'those who remember' – the events of 1940 will be an inescapable facet of interpretation; the site is already freighted. It is the first level of haunting: of both the cleared land and of a certain national imagination.

FIBUA is a place of simulation, where urban warfare is rehearsed, scenarios tested and choreographies of corporeal engagement inculcated. It is a cluster of simple houses with steel-shuttered windows outwardly German or Balkan in appearance[2] – where darkened rooms have trapdoors and hidden tunnels; where there is no plumbing; where the barn bears no trace of agricultural labour; and where gravestones have neither names nor dedicatory verses. Here one might find the odd pile of spent blank cartridges hinting at some past incident or an emplacement of ammunition boxes and scrawled graffiti in ad-hoc constructions of homeliness, but not a single bullet hole (the risk of ricochet being too great). And there are no signs of domestic habitation, of paint, wallpaper, furniture: architecture as the barest of outlines.

The Skills House is a three-storey, concrete-block building with a pitched roof. All the windows and doorways are simply empty openings. It has no façade. The troops who gather in the small grandstand opposite can see into rooms two deep, into exposed staircases and the basement as they watch colleagues attacking and defending the structure, all sallies and repulses exposed for their inspection and instruction: a precisely controlled context for action, and viewpoint for its apprehension – linked *orchestra* and *theatron*. The impression is of an open-fronted, life-sized doll's house. Incongruously, there is also a projecting forestage.

FIBUA is a place *of* performance or at least of rehearsal for performance, occupied sporadically by different casts whose temporary presence and passing to theatres of war elsewhere linger: another, poignant, haunting. Here, NTW's production of *The Persians* was conceived and sited.

The Persians was first presented at the City Dionysia in Athens in 472 BC. It survives as the earliest drama in the Western canon recorded in anything close to completeness and the only Greek tragedy based upon a historical event. Its subject is the destruction of Xerxes' navy at Salamis only eight years previously – which Aeschylus himself doubtless witnessed – and the aftermath. Uniquely, it relates the battle and its repercussions from the perspective of the defeated invaders. No Greeks are named: there is no mention, for example, of Themistocles who inspired the building of an Athenian fleet to match the terrestrial *phalanx*. For the Greek audience, the names of Persian generals and places evoked an exotic world – alien and fascinating, yet a real and present danger; as immediate yet enigmatic and difficult to recall as those commanders and towns in Helmand province or north of Basra in reports of today's encounters. It stands on a cusp in societal development: at Salamis, human fallibility and responsibility are beginning to equal divine intervention as causal effects; in *The Persians*, the failure of military strategy is no longer simply a matter of fate. Within 50 years, Herodotus will include a detailed description of events in *The Histories*:

> The purpose is to prevent the traces of human events from being erased by time, and to preserve the fame of the important and remarkable achievements produced by both Greeks and non-Greeks; among the matters covered is, in particular, the cause of the hostilities between Greeks and non-Greeks.
>
> (Herodotus, 1998, p.3)

Aeschylus' drama is rudimentary in form, with four principal characters – Queen, Messenger, Darius, Xerxes – and a Chorus. At the outset, Queen and the Chorus await intelligence of the conflict with gathering apprehension. A Messenger appears with news of disaster. In the ensuing confusion, Darius is summoned from beyond the grave and consulted. Finally, Xerxes arrives, alone, having lost and abandoned his retinue. Structurally, there are four distinct phases or movements, each presaged by an arrival, entrance or exit; throughout the conceptual and creative process for the NTW production, these were referred to as Premonition, Revelation, Recrimination, and Chaos, providing the schedule for sectional rehearsal.

The Persians is a drama of anticipation and consequence, of reportage and repercussion: a warning against reckless adventurism. Its principal concerns are *hubris* and its ensuing nemesis. As revelation follows revelation, the only possible outcome is grief and chaos. There can be no cathartic resolution, for this concerns foreigners. But it is cautionary – of the threat to establishment – rather than chauvinistic. In Kaite O'Reilly's adaptation, there is no attempt to modernize the text; it is full of anachronistic talk of spears and chariots and quivers. And there is no simple equation of antique and contemporary figures or circumstances: no attempt to figure Saddam Hussein as a latter-day Xerxes, for instance. O'Reilly's tone is plain but robust rather than poetic; the words issue easily – despite the archaic names of people and places – from modern mouths.

Tom Holland suggests that in the original performance, the sacked temples – still in ruins and left as a reminder of the city's ordeal – provided the backdrop; that the bleachers on which the audience were seated came from the timbers of wrecked Persian ships and the stage awning from the captured Persian royal tent (Holland, 2005, pp.359–60). At the Skills House, the contemporary audience also sit on a simple wooden rake, but *The Persians* is now highly mediatized: the experience of war is re-imagined in the era of 24-hour news – of images of far-off populations and countries whose names barely register, and a constant attention and intrusion into both public and private affairs. It is, however, too easy to read the juxtaposition of text and site as some direct allusion to, or allegory for, current world events. Instead, this is an attempt to lay bare the eternal nature of vaunting human ambition through the collision of ancient and modern, in the coexistence of, or frictions *between*, performance and location: drawing out themes of the cult of personality, the collapse of the old order, the threat of regime change, and the incipient danger of a reversion to barbarism and ritual.

At 7pm the audience assembles at the central army base in the nearby town of Sennybridge, where the range's small, permanent staff is housed and where the NTW company lived in barracks and ate in the canteen during rehearsals. Each member of the audience is issued with a waterproof, windproof poncho and given stern warnings not to touch anything on the ground. They are then transported by coach on a 20-minute journey to the village, across an unfamiliar and dis-orienting landscape, accompanied by a recorded musical soundtrack: an intimation of things to come. As they disembark at the boundary chicane of FIBUA, a martial anthem plays in the distance. They walk through the empty village, passing burned-out military vehicles and closed, unpainted houses. Few will have been to this restricted place before; it is eerie, disconcerting.

What is this place, they might wonder? A community without men, the women and children closeted safely out of sight of visitors? A thread-bare country stripped and bankrupted by war effort? A dismal 'victory museum' displaying the captured detritus of past wars, as in North Korea? An abandoned community in a military 'no-go' zone? A deserted film set? War-ravaged Athens? Disconcertingly, the deserted streets have Welsh names. And who are we, this audience, assigned a kind of col-lective identity in our matching khaki garb? Are we a procession; a demonstration; tourists; weapons inspectors; the straggling survivors of conflict? Persians? Greeks? With so little to go on, anything might happen here.

The audience arrives at the central square where, in front of the mock church, there is a dais with flags, three chairs, three megaphones, a large portrait photograph (that will eventually be disclosed as Darius), and a single male figure. There is also a small 1950s Peugeot van with mounted loudspeakers from which the anthem repeatedly and remorselessly issues.[3] Suddenly, there is the sound of a blaring car horn and a heavy, black Rover 100 sedan of similar vintage to the van approaches, driving straight into the midst of the crowd and coming to rest. The Chorus – three men in cheap suits – emerges, kissing the ground, waving, shaking hands, embracing spectators, like the arrival of Radovan Karadzic at some secret meeting in Pale, Kosovo: a modern *parodos*. The awaiting figure – who ran to meet them, jogging beside the car – is identified as one of their number, though he will remain silent throughout the performance. They are Darius's men – 'understudies to power, rulers by proxy for the warring Xerxes' – as much nightclub bouncers or secret-service agents as junta: intimidating and menacing, their forceful entry and proximate energy already too large to imagine confined to an auditorium. They are media men too: they know how to create an impression, as preening and pompous as Mussolini, for the outside broadcast (OB) camera that immediately focuses on them. In motion, they aim for the barely restrained power and taut masculinity of Toshiro Mifune in Akira Kurosawa's film *Throne of Blood* (1957) and, at rest, for the compositional precision and rigour of Bill Viola's slow-moving video groupings (Viola, 2010).

They mount the dais – clapping, saluting the crowd – and begin their oration, using the crude amplification. They are affirmative, bullish, and bombastic, describing the departure for Greece of Xerxes and his armies: a roll call of passing military might that 'we' witnessed 'on this spot'. They predict the assured victory of formidable force – of overwhelming size and strength – with extravagant mimetic hand gestures and poses that might, as with their Athenian forebears, be understood by visiting foreigners. This is a triumphalist rally, the audience cast unwittingly as Persians even if they cannot escape the reality of the Welsh FIBUA site; such is the fervour generated that many applaud. But the mood is tense. Anything might happen here.

The speeches reach a climax. A procession of loudspeaker van, the Chorus carrying Darius' portrait, and audience forms; it proceeds to the Skills House and grandstand, where the seating rake has been extended to accommodate 140 spectators on uncovered wooden benches.

The Skills House itself has been modified: all safety rails – a pre-scribed feature of health and safety protocols, even in army training – have been removed. In the main interior spaces, mobile walls are installed, galvanized metal on one side, wood on the other. Suspended on overhead, front-to-back tracks, they can be shifted forwards and backwards, angled, and rotated. Their movement during performance creates varying spatial configurations – temporary rooms, short-lived passageways – facilitating new articulations of 'on' and 'off,' between public and private; exposing different surfaces; and offering kinetic counterpoint to weighty passages of text – some equivalent to the Greek *periaktos*. The house is illuminated by discretely placed weatherproof neon strips and halogen lamps, operated primarily by passing perform-ers as they enter or leave rooms. At eight strategic points there are wall-mounted video monitors. And the soundtrack is already running.

But what is this place and why is the audience assembled here? A continuation of the rally perhaps, a celebration for the dedication of the 'Darius Memorial Home for War Veterans'? An annual gathering at his shrine or tomb? Or an assembly to witness the recommence-ment of work on a half-finished, speculative construction, familiar from present-day Greece?

As they are seated, the audience see themselves and the Chorus hold-ing the portrait aloft on the upper screen, from the OB camera clearly now radio-linked to the projector. Whatever this is, it is apparently some kind of public media event; and the audience are here as bussed-in par-ticipants. On some evenings, their view includes distant mountains, rainbows, vivid crimson sunsets, a large moon. On others, they will hud-dle in driving rain, the house topped by black clouds or shrouded in swirling mist.

The Chorus hangs Darius' portrait on an interior wall. There is an *impasse*. As they wait, they begin to express doubts concerning the state of affairs, but *sotto voce*. Yet they are heard clearly, for all performers wear radio-microphones: all text in the production is to be amplified. The audience is party to intimate thoughts, whispered asides, private misgiv-ings, privileged conversations from individuals and groups of performers at different locations in the house, without the need for unnatural vocal projection – here, outdoors and in unstable weather conditions. The array of audio speakers is located in, around, and beneath the grand-stand: the audience sits within a sonic envelope in which voices and the continuous, pre-recorded musical soundtrack are mixed. Only Darius ever speaks directly from the house. The effect is to keep the text close and intimate and the quality constant, though performers may be distant or even unseen, as the production turns increasingly away from the audience into the interior of the house.

And the Chorus appears in strange, distorted close-ups on the video monitors; only gradually is it apparent that their non-speaking member is wearing a small camera on his wrist, providing shots from the very midst of their group. The mediatized dimensions of this performance prompt new questions about 'site' and 'location' that are beyond the scope of this chapter.

The Queen finally arrives in a matching white Rover, picked up by the OB camera for the audience, even before the Chorus sees her. Two Chorus members rush out across the grass to meet her and escort her, while the others police the audience closely. She might bring purpose to this gathering, but she is too distracted to address the crowd; whatever should have happened here is upset and compromised. She has been disturbed by a dream. As she relates her terrible premonition, the animated reactions of the Chorus, hidden behind a wall, are seen on the monitors. The Queen herself appears throughout on the large screen, her red costume and blond hair striking at scale in the fading light, her slightest facial responses apparent; the OB camera pursues her relentlessly, paparazzi-like.

In the house she touches nothing. As she begins to question the Chorus about the nature of Athens, they move walls to create 'corridors of power' – half-glimpsed in their roving conversation by the two cameras, becoming visible and then disappearing on the various screens, though their voices remain constant.

The situation is disturbed by the mediated arrival of the Messenger, breaking through on all the video monitors as if by satellite-link from a war zone. These monitors attract and focus the attention of both performers and audience alike as an unexpected phenomenon, both within the narrative and the production matrices. As the Chorus repositions walls to reveal the multiple screen images better, the Queen is sequestered in a closed room; the audience witnesses her private conversation and increasingly distraught responses to the news of Xerxes' defeat only as a projected image from the ever-attentive OB camera, which occasionally also provides shots of the Messenger, caught incidentally on one of the monitors (Figure 5.1).

The Chorus is dispersed, watching and addressing the Messenger from several positions simultaneously; engaging in silent solo and group actions that respond to and then increasingly echo and enact the

Image 5.1 The Messenger reports. National Theatre Wales, *The Persians*, directed by Mike Pearson. Courtesy of Farrows Creative.

account of the battle and subsequent disastrous retreat. Their activities are compartmentalized and framed in the open-fronted rooms. The *kabuki* theatre style provides an inspiration for the physical composition of the Chorus; at various times, their actions resemble *kata* – techniques such as *danmari* (a mass tableau or the slow-motion pantomimic struggle for an object) and *ma* (pauses marking emotional highpoints and visual climaxes) (Brandon, Malm, and Shively, 1978, pp.66–8; 84–6).[4]

The audience watches a complex combination of live and mediated action and pre-recorded video that includes extreme close-ups of considerable scale: activities of different orders and intensities, with perfect attendant sound. The OB camera provides candid footage as well as staged oration and 'direct to camera' interjections; the audience is always made aware of the presence of the crew going about its business. *The Persians* begins to resemble a live film, which the specific architectural configuration of the Skills House suggests, accommodates, and makes possible, forcing a further redefinition of 'site'.

The footage of the Messenger was pre-recorded against a number of cubic concrete Second World War anti-tank defences on a pebble beach in South Wales and then played, as if simulcast, at the Skills House. He spoke directly to camera with increasing urgency for almost 20 minutes while leaving pauses of appropriate estimated length for the live verbal responses of the Queen and the Chorus. Filling these gaps successfully in performance – to create the illusion of a dialogue in the present – would prove to be one of the most challenging aspects of rehearsal. But the video assured a similar dynamic drive night after night, particularly when presented simultaneously on the eight monitors; and the combination of heightened, highly charged acting by the Queen with the televisual style of the Messenger proved to be a revelation of the production, as the conjunction of live and pre-recorded material successfully maintained dramatic intercourse and tension.

After an admonition to do their duty and prepare for Xerxes' return, the Queen exits. The Chorus is now racked with unease, their rule under threat, the empire in danger. (In reality, as Aeschylus has introduced a second actor, their very dramatic function is also in question.) And as they become increasingly disturbed – pushing, grabbing each other, cannoning around a small room – the endemic violence of this society is made evident.

The Queen re-enters in black robe, hair in disarray, lamenting but defiant. As she descends, so the Chorus retreats to the basement where with incantatory voices and flagellant actions they summon their dead master Darius: suits discarded, they resort to ritual. The Queen never looks at the looming, oversized projected image of Darius (Figure 5.2). Isolated on the forestage, she always faces to the front, in a conversation that is initially accusatory and then conciliatory, and that sustains the illusion of being pursued in real time. As the Chorus creates a moving frieze of extreme positions against a lower concrete wall, a stratified picture is created: Chorus, Queen, Darius. The Queen finally retires and there is a hope of resolution, of welcome for the returning Xerxes. But the Chorus remains agitated, taking stock, counting what has been lost.

Image 5.2 Darius appears. National Theatre Wales, *The Persians*, directed by Mike Pearson. Courtesy of David Hurn.

The OB camera picks up Xerxes first, running from a distance, his amplified, panting voice heard in the sound matrix. He enters the basement through a side entrance and calls up through the house, which is now fully illuminated and glowing in the gathering dusk. The Chorus meets him like rabid, snarling dogs, their reversion to barbarism almost complete. He wears anachronistic dress: distressed body armour and a kilt. He is shepherded out onto the forestage; it is a rough and accusatory homecoming, the consequences of over-weaning militarism now fully internalized within this royal edifice, this 'House of Darius'. He is remorseful but resilient, eventually relating his own state of trauma at having witnessed the massacre of his friends. As the soundtrack swells, he becomes more assertive: the grief is to be shared in a scene of increasing mayhem. The Chorus engages in extreme actions, spinning dervish-like in closed spaces, seen only on the monitors; smoke pours through cracks, as their acoustic, chanting voices become wordless. Xerxes reaches a climax of exulted grief, and finally collapses. The Chorus – now resembling the penitents in Francisco Goya's painting *A Procession of Flagellants* (c. 1812–14) – descends to carry him up the staircases, extinguishing lights as it travels. As it enters the Queen's room, there is sudden silence and a blackout, as if the power plug of the production has fallen out of the socket.

The performance ends. But as the audience walks back to the coaches through the shadowy village, there is a disturbing coda: keening female voices seem to issue from distant houses.

The impetus to create at site is frequently cast in the realm of the Latin prepositional accusative – *in, inter, trans* – of motion towards and into; of mobility; of entry and encounter; of *ad*-venture. I'm thinking here of Jeffrey Kastner and Brain Wallis's (1998) typology of land art – integration, interruption, involvement. But what might be the nature of performance prefixed with *clam*, unknown to; *ob*, in front of; *juxta*, close to; *penes*, in the power of? Or in the prepositional *ablative* indicating rest: performance 'in the presence of', 'together with', 'adjacent to' the site.

What then is the relationship between FIBUA and *The Persians*? What do they bring to or disclose in each other? As a restricted military site, FIBUA is beyond the remit of those regulatory bodies that license public events. Anything might indeed happen here: the use of vehicles, the mass movement of audiences. Its ground plan certainly informed processional routes, entrances and exits, and the placement of scenes. But it is already in a theatrical mode, providing the daily setting for war games; the amplified sounds of air attacks, repeatedly broadcast from the church tower, accompany exercises in the village. Any inclination to theatricalize FIBUA further – decorating it or using its domestic buildings domestically or explicitly indicating this or that feature – would be the equivalent of a double negative. Though mute, it speaks for itself, and in complex and shifting ways. What is this place, it demands, for you?

The Skills House is a place of extreme scrutiny where, under normal circumstances, a detailed appreciation and understanding of action and response may eventually be a matter of life or death. With its attendant grandstand, it is made for performance. *The Persians* identifies and aligns itself with this function, providing views of movements and encounters while at the same time acknowledging and countering it with the installation of masking walls. The scenography is plumbed into the architecture in a congruent manner; it is on the same orientation – the mobile walls fit apertures and lighting is hung on convenient architectural projections. But there is here an uncharacteristic proliferation of screens – complex technology in the sparest of locations and in an exposed landscape setting – though even this finds parallel in the surveillance cameras throughout the village linked to central equipment in the church.

The production involved no major works of construction. The seating rake was extended but left unroofed to preserve the stark and inherently dramatic coexistence of two distinct architectural entities:

grandstand and house. While the ponchos gave a collective identity to audiences – the more so in adverse conditions – they ensured individual security against wind and rain. With an option to withdraw exposed elements of the performance back into the house, weather became a potentially active component of spectatorship: most strikingly in views riven by diagonals of heavy rain, or partly obscured by intervening moorland mist.

FIBUA is almost diagrammatic in aspect. It is a series of simple shapes and unadorned spaces that can stand in for any 'elsewhere': Northern Ireland, Kosovo, Iraq, Afghanistan. Serious business usually happens here. Its emptiness is profound: in its latency, its emptiness, potential resides. It awaits – anticipates – action, imaginaries, all that is brought to it. Anything might be said or done here. But it lacks the vernacular detail of everyday life, the traces and patinas of human occupancy; it remains unmarked. The living would be tough indeed here. In *The Persians* at FIBUA, then, rather than *host* and *ghost*, there is perhaps *ghost* and *ghost*, two spectral presences: impermanent, provisional site and transitory performance – that was removed within one day, leaving only the filled holes of attaching bolts and screws... and the vague recollections of audiences. It is a mutual haunting in which one momentarily summoned the other into existence, each revealing and relying upon the other conditionally. This flickering of site and performance was achieved by respecting the independence and integrity of the two without forcing the performance to be an allegory for recent events in the Middle East, or the site a symbol of military endeavours.

Access to FIBUA was limited in duration. *The Persians* was rehearsed initially in a studio in Cardiff. Brought to the Skills House in a state of prefabrication, it expanded to fit the building, responding directly to its specificities: architectural, environmental, spatial, and acoustic. Its dramaturgy was conceived as a series of horizontal strata – text, action, music, technology, and scenography – developed discretely and then combined at site. The task was to find an effective accommodation through the overlay, deletion, and preferential highlighting of detail: relocating choreographic sequences, pushing phases of soundtrack. The overall effect was of site-specific theatre as *mix*, an apposite term with so much reliant upon the efficacy of live audio and video mixing. One danger was that the pre-recorded sequences of video would set an inflexible dynamic. The rapid, rolling delivery of the Messenger and the more measured tones of Darius countered this, as did the concentrated and compensatory engagement of the live performers with recorded imagery that remained, by definition, unresponsive. And the music – by a composer acknowledged for his film and television scores – supported, illuminated, and prodded the action, without ever becoming emotionally dominant.

At FIBUA – at a place where there are seemingly no preconditions for theatrical exposition – a *hybrid* emerged: of dramatic stage traditions as exemplified by the work of the Queen, Darius, and Xerxes; of practices of physical theatre and devised performance apparent in the work of the Chorus; of mediatized and mediated installation.

But the ranges at SENTA are no *tabula rasa*, a place rendered a-historical through its removal from the quotidian purview. What then might 'legitimately' be said and done? *The Persians* made no direct thematic reference to either the troubled history of the landscape, or its contentious current usage: little could be gained from agitation that would never lead to repossession by Welsh communities, or criticism of a professional army under substantial stress in its international responsibilities. Yet its co-presence served to render both palpable.

The Persians achieved popular and critical success.[5] And in the elision of place and performance, a small instance of cultural transformation is achieved; not as a permanent reclamation of place, but as an ephemeral act of national theatre that acknowledges and restores a tradition of experimental practice in Wales and that augurs further initiatives in site-specific theatre. This is a theatre distinct in its concerns and practical approaches, differentiated from the conventions of its English neighbour.

An originary moment ... at this site ... specifically ...

Notes

1. *The Persians* was presented on 11–14 and 16–21 August 2010. Direction – Mike Pearson; Text adaptation – Kaite O'Reilly; Conceptual design – Mike Brookes; Scenic design – Simon Banham; Music – John Hardy; Video – Pete Telfer. Queen – Sian Thomas; Darius – Paul Rhys; Xerxes – Rhys Rusbatch; Messenger – Richard Harrington; Chorus – Richard Lynch, Richard Huw Morgan, John Rowley, Gerald Tyler; Lady in Waiting – Rosa Casado.
2. The plans – used in several similar installations in the UK – are from a time when the Third World War, if non-nuclear, was imagined to be a major tank battle in Germany.
3. As Magnum agency photographer David Hurn, who documented the project, commented: 'When I visit a country with flags, large portraits and music like that, I know I'm in trouble.'
4. Of course the multimedia components of this production contribute yet another dimension that is yet to be fully explored in site-specific performance.
5. See National Theatre Wales (2010).

6
Toiling, Tolling, and Telling: Performing Dissensus

Kathleen Irwin

In 2007, Father Keith Heiberg, the parish priest of Ponteix (Saskatchewan, Canada) invited Knowhere Productions to devise a site-specific performance to mark the community's centennial planned for July of the following year. Knowhere Productions Inc.[1] is an artists' collective that defines its approach, in the words of Grant Kester, as 'the facilitation of dialogue among diverse communities' (2004a, p.1). We are, like others who have moved outside the institutions and systems of conventional stage practice, '"context providers" [...] whose work involves the creative orchestration of collaborative encounters and conversations' (Kester, 2004a, p.1). The project was proposed as a vehicle to catalyse consensus around the specific conditions of this rural and economically marginalized community, challenge stereotypes, valorize its historic culture, encourage its inhabitants to repurpose its accumulated knowledge, and apply it to a strategy for a sustainable future. Over the 12 months leading up to the event, the conversations and processes of consensus-building employed to help the community to 'imagine beyond the limits of fixed identities, official discourse, and the perceived inevitability of partisan political conflict' (Kester, 2004a, p.8) brought the project, in many ways, to a successful, positive, and sought-after conclusion. However, the notion of consensus – at the very centre of community-oriented practice – is, in part, what this chapter seeks to problematize. As the producer of the event, I understand it, somewhat cynically, as a panacea applied simplistically to address the complexity of performing with and for a community. I want here to reconsider the term consensus and its antithesis, dissensus. In examining the capacity of these terms, what I hope to add to the ongoing discussion is my own perspective – that of an artist whose work, over a number of community-engaged projects produced in rural Saskatchewan,[2] has made me somewhat wary of seeking consensus and creative collaboration.

In considering collaborative art practice, Kester (2004a, p.15) characterizes consensus and its absence as the difference between the positive sense of collective identification required to break down our defensive isolation and to honour a consciousness shaped by common experience, and the negative sense of collective identity that does much to repress specific difference. On the other hand, the philosopher, Jacques Rancière (2009a), argues that dissensus is the productive supplement to the consensual game of domination and rebellion, of ruling and being ruled, that characterizes all social and political activity of which art-making is profoundly a part. By examining the specificity of Knowhere Productions's performance, I attempt to parse the binary of consensus/dissensus alongside the notions of identity and locationality that are critical to site-specific and community-oriented practice. Through its very groundedness, perhaps more than other forms of creative activity, site-specific work manifests the nuances and relations of place to social and cultural selfhoods, passages and migrations, claims and counterclaims, ownership and its loss. This is critical in that it suggests ways and means for alternative voices to speak from positions of knowledge through local experience.

Consensus and its absence

Steven Corcoran (2010) introduces the idea of a consensual turn in society in his introduction to Rancière's *Dissensus: On Politics and Aesthetics*. Corcoran writes, '[t]he present day circumscription of political activity, we know, is everywhere permeated and suffocated by the notion of consensus' (2010, p.4). A consensual vision involves an attempt to define the preconditions that determine choice as objective and univocal, the logic of which is a feature of the contemporary managerial state where it usually involves collaboration rather than compromise. Instead of one opinion being adopted by a plurality, stakeholders are brought together until a convergent decision is reached. However, according to Corcoran's (2010, p.5) interpretation of Rancière, some of the ways that consensual vision is activated reduce the multivariate components of a population into a single voice and by arrogating the right to individual expressivity to the powerful, the expert, and the professional: those who are seen to be qualified to lead or speak rather than those who are not generally taken into account.

The abstract notion of consensus is made concrete, for example, in labour negotiations, where its end – a legally binding arrangement – is facilitated by the rhetoric of consensus, assuring a form of general agreement to expedite action for a limited amount of time and a limited segment of the population. In community-oriented performance, gathering consensus is the initial activity in creative place-making, in order to define, mediate, express, and eventually ameliorate local issues. It marks the moment in which consent is granted to artists to negotiate the representation of, or to speak for, a group of individuals. In reality, consensus in such circumstances is, at best, a utopian enterprise existing always just beyond the collective reach. This shortfall is the nexus of debate for artists, participants, and critics for whom the collaborative process raises issues in equal measure, of dissensus, contestation, of who speaks for whom, and, indeed, who is heard.

So, the impossibility of consensus, and the potency of dissensus are the lens through which I frame the following investigation of Knowhere Productions's *Windblown/Rafales* (2008), a site-specific performance in a rural, French-Canadian Catholic town that defined itself historically in opposition to the federalist, hegemonic strategy to colonize the Canadian West with English Protestants or others who, from necessity, might adapt quickly to this uniform norm. While their connection to the fur trade (and later farming) made the French settlers vital in opening up Saskatchewan, they were only one of a number of waves of immigrants.[3] Political dissent, strong ties to the Church, the French language, and the land continue to mark the character of the inhabitants of Ponteix and their collective enunciation as an outsider/survivor community. This identificatory unity is constructed and maintained through the hierarchical structure of the Catholic Diocese that regulates its parishioners by strategically including/excluding individuals and certain historical moments from its narrative. Typically, this formation of community effectively excludes those who are outside the predetermined unification, social, and religious conventions. For this reason, the parish priest's invitation to perform in this closed community presented an intriguing opportunity to enter into, observe and possibly rupture, in a creative way, its logic and rituals. Not surprisingly, during our eventual engagement, the delineations of insider and outsider positioned the Knowhere Productions's collective sometimes within the consensus-building apparatus, and sometimes outside it – although always attempting to make the matrix visible through our enacting of it.

This fundamental ambivalence that characterizes community-oriented practice makes it difficult, if not impossible, to do the essential socially oriented work that underpins it – that of drawing together into one voice those who are not seen to have one, those who Rancière characterizes as society's unaccounted for. For Rancière (2009a), consensual community is unrealizable as it is first and foremost the voices of those qualified to speak that will be heard.

I ask two questions: does the mechanism of consensus-building – that which aims to univocally express a will, an identity or a desire – rather conceal the apparatuses of power, making inaudible the multiple voices that nuance the shared creative act? And is it not dissensus rather than consensus that must be enacted by the artist who locates herself, both literally and figuratively, at the crossroads of collaboration?

Landscape: the specificities of this place

As geographer Randy Widdis writes, 'location is essential in understanding a wide variety of processes. In just about every facet of life, location matters and this is certainly the case for western Canada' (2006, p.131). Too frequently, outsiders see the physical uniformity of this region as synonymous with a lack of complexity or differentiated cultural background. Ponteix is a case in point: its rich and distinct heritage, so strongly linked with the Auvergne district in France, sets it apart from other small communities in the region. Historically, the town and its French Catholic identity are defined by the ambit of the bells of Notre Dame d'Auvergne, the Church at its centre. The circumference within which the church chimes are audible delineates the border between home and away/location and dislocation. So bounded, the town appears inward-looking in relation to the openness of the vast Canadian prairies. The French community has primarily defined itself against the federal policy that encouraged the flattening of ethnic difference, and the manner in which the spire of the church disturbs the prairie horizon asserts the town's discrete cultural enterprise.

At this juncture, in the first decade of the twenty-first century, Ponteix still defies the hinterland notion of an amorphous Western region and asserts itself as a place willing to reconsider itself in relation to the changing world around it; it thus problematizes the notion of local identity within a larger national project. Forged by homesteading, hardship, and cultural oppression, the people of Ponteix exemplify what Rob Shields describes as a 'tremendous complicity between the body and environment [... as] the two interpenetrate each other' (1991, p.14). The mythic scope of struggle of the early settlers to subdue the land is reified in the arid landscape and the extremities of the climate; *Windblown/Rafales*, the title of the performance, essentialized the multifaceted struggle of their forebears in this place.

The intent of the performance, scheduled at the centre of a week-long celebration of a francophone way of life sustained against the grain of the dominant culture, was not merely to enact a memory play but to look critically at the town's current situation, reflected in its diminishing population and loss of traditional cultural practices, and to consider its options: in other words, to define what it means to be a rural community at the turn of the twenty-first century. The invitation by Father Keith necessitated an investigation, defined by certain limitations, of the town and particularly the history of its founder, Father Albert Royer, who at the turn of the twentieth century dreamt of settling a francophone community devout in its worship of Mary. Royer's aspiration was fanned by the federal government, who promised affordable land and a paradise in the Western prairies – a veritable Garden of Eden. In reality, the land was not readily arable and the weather unforgiving. This initial deception and the ensuing disillusionment shaped the blueprint for Saskatchewan's agrarian experience and forged an outsider identity that portrayed Royer's faith community as self-contained, self-sufficient, and a dissenting voice within the Canadian settlement project. A hundred years later, our sponsor urged us to affirm this vision by considering certain historical moments and ignoring any records that challenged the image of the righteous, toiling and independent community bound by the regular and regulating tolling of the church bells.[4] Ponteix's desire to perform itself with the help of Knowhere Productions represented a desire to look Janus-like backwards for confirmation of this identity and forwards to re-vision the town as a vital part of a new and diversified Western Canadian economic model.[5]

Knowhere Productions: context providers

For the members of the Knowhere Productions collective, the offer to collaborate with the town of Ponteix was an opportunity to practise our mandate to explore, through multi-performative means, the relationship of a local population to a particular place and time.[6] Our productions, typically site-specific and devised, emphasize themes, myths, and legends that reveal the complex relationship between our physical environment and ourselves. In this instance, the possibility to consider place-making through the lens of colonizing practices and the urban/rural dichotomy was appealing and germane to the terms of the company's practice. The issues that have marginalized this population resonate strongly within Canada, where the drift towards globalized networks has decimated local economies and dispersed rural populations to urban centres. Those remaining on the land struggle to reconstruct an identity from memory fragments and fading photographs. Shields underscores this, suggesting that the images and stories retained are merely partial, piecemeal, and able to be prised open. He writes, '[p]lace-images, and our views of them, are produced historically, and are actively contested. There is no whole picture that can be "filled in" since the perception and filling of a gap leads to the awareness of other gaps' (Shields, 1991, p.18). Figuratively speaking, Knowhere Productions inserts its performances into these intervals.

Father Keith had proposed a mutually beneficial relationship whereby the town would gain insights into its own situation through the filter of our performance and we would gain access to a unique, historic locale at a crucial and transitional moment. Seduced by the possibilities this afforded, we agreed. In July 2007, an information session was organized by and for stakeholders at which options were weighed, input gathered, the pros and cons assessed. At the end of the meeting the general agreement was to move tentatively forward, working on the understanding that members of the community would be collaborators and partners, that the town's history would be respected and that our process of observing and devising a performance over time, something quite foreign to the residents, would be accommodated.

A few words on this process are in order here. Knowhere Productions attempts a respectful interaction with community members through an assiduous, open negotiation that is mindful of the complex insider/outsider dichotomy. We are aware of the potential for our own creative agenda to gloss local considerations and we avoid this by a thorough investigation of archival records and by interacting with and interviewing, where possible, everyone in the community. Boarding in people's homes or bunking down in empty buildings, we are ethnographers observing daily rituals and rhythms. However, we remain outsiders and are clear that our function is to bring a fresh perspective. We want to unpack stereotypes about a site, its inhabitants, and its past; to do this we listen for the ever-present dissenting voices that contribute to a more complex representation of the community in the performance.[7]

As a place of memory and a charged discursive field, Ponteix provided valuable opportunities for our consideration. Contrary to the normative reading of events provided by the scions of the community, we discovered a rich polyphony of voices. The historical texture was visible in its heritage buildings, particularly the well-proportioned Catholic Church, built to accommodate a congregation triple the town's current population. Twice reconstructed after being razed by fire (1923)[8] and by cyclone (1929), Notre Dame d'Auvergne is a metaphor for the town's struggle. Adjacent to the church, the parish hall, built to function while the church was under repair, suggests a communal will to survive. To the west of the church is the Convent of the Sisters of Notre Dame funded by the Michelin Tire Company, which had its headquarters in the Auvergne district of France where the Mother House was and still is located. Nearby stands the oldest of the buildings, the Gabriel Hospital, built in 1918 in time to administer to homecoming First World War veterans and victims of the Spanish flu pandemic. These buildings were our stages.

Over a few weeks, the performance took shape first on paper and then on foot. We determined that the projected audience, an ageing demographic that reflected the outward migration of young people, would initially congregate for a musical prologue at the church steps before moving into the nave for the first of a series of performed events (Figure 6.1). Next they would visit the hospital for a perambulating performance along its central corridor and through the adjoining rooms. Following this, the actors would lead the spectators to the convent orchard for a dance performance or, for those who could manage it, a longer walk down the main street reminiscent of the church's annual Marian procession,[9] before ending the event in a performance at the parish hall. Mapping this trajectory on foot through the town site represented our second interaction with the community. After this, we began to rough in the other details: the integration of puppets (standing in for both ancestors and children/the past and the future), an epic poem written for the occasion, an original musical score, choreography, sound, video, and sculpture installations.

Simultaneously, we researched the archival sources available to us to flesh out the content of the performance. Understanding how Ponteix defined itself was not difficult. The library and museum were replete with diaries and records of immigration and arduous homesteading. A local poet, novelist and playwright,[10] a fiddle band, the sisters of the convent and the parish priest all provided us with the flavour of a rapidly disappearing way of life, an idea of the cycle of the church calendar and how its progression once marked time as surely as the

Image 6.1   Windblown/Rafales (2008). Stanza One – 'I am a part of all that I have met.' Actors (back to front): Derek Lindman, Eugenie Ducatel, Regena Marler. Courtesy of Glenn Gordon.

church bells delineated space. The tourist centre distributed brochures illustrating Ponteix's new marketing strategy as a retirement community. The publicity identified its attributes as a friendly, well-serviced, heritage community with strong values. Much of what we gleaned – the music, the bells, and the traditions – was written into the script. On top of the historical threads that were forming the armature of the performance, we superimposed a poetic line borrowed from Tennyson's *Ulysses*. The historic figure of the founder, Father Royer, referenced the ageing adventurer in whose memories smoulder discontent and defiance in the face of his inevitable decline. The layering of modalities, historical detail, and poetic subtext is a Brechtian strategy that we frequently use to distance and objectify the reading of the performance.

As newcomers into the community, our daily activity had been closely monitored. However, within a week, the townspeople were accustomed to seeing the costumes, puppets, and props as we introduced them into rehearsals. We were encouraged to roam and ask questions and, through this means, a rapport developed. The parish priest provided meals at his home and neighbours hosted barbeques where we gathered gossip and shared stories. A key element of the process was the incorporation of these anecdotes into the script. Details gathered from sidewalk conversations frequently contradicted the overarching narrative of hardworking, devout settlers, and the pious, charitable sisters. They supplied alternative stories of outsiders set more against the deteriorating buildings on the main street than the church and its associated buildings.[11] These sites were never reproduced on the ubiquitous postcards and calendars that showed the town's iconic structures – the church and its religious statues, the parish hall, hospital, and grain elevators. We observed that the town's built environment delineated and differentiated the social strata of the community and this fuelled the development of the working script in interesting ways. For example, the procession through the town was expanded as new monologues written for street corners and alleys were inserted – these were the stories of drunkards and drifters that ran against the dominant narrative. When these were finally performed, the audience literally saw themselves in the store windows and heard themselves in the actors' inflections of their own stories. The reflected images were ambiguous; they contained the notion of consensus, of collective identity, and the possibility of dissenting voices – the voices of those typically unaccounted for in the grander narratives of settlement and survival (Figure 6.2).

Image 6.2   Windblown/Rafales (2008). Stanza Three – 'To strive, to seek, to find, and not to yield.' Actor: Regena Marler. Courtesy of Glenn Gordon.

The cut: between a rock and a hard place

At the conclusion of the performance and the week of centennial cele-bration, through comments heard and letters received, we understood that, for the spectators and those commissioning the work, the produc-tion was deemed provocative, stimulating, entertaining, and reaffirm-ing. From a population of 329 individuals, 250 people, old and young, attended the public performance (Statistics Canada, 2006). We had, it appeared, captured the essence of the town – how it 'really was'. However, the consideration of the relationship between an audience, a landscape, and its history has lead to more questions than answers. The event's critical assessment, shaped by multiple disciplines and diverse agendas, is challenging. The absence of adequate markers to measure aesthetic or social value trouble this practice for the artists who disturb the underlying imperatives of a consensual and collaborative process.

Both Kester (1995) and Claire Bishop (cited in Roche, 2006) have engaged critically with this subject from differing perspectives and their work has polarized the dialogue between those who contextualize the work in this genre as art and those who position it within a range of socially ameliorative activities. Kester defends this practice on the level of social interaction or intervention, defining it 'as a specific form of art practice with its own characteristics and effects, related to, but also different from, other forms of art and other forms of activism' (2004a, p.11). Bishop, however, writes that while the creativity behind socially engaged art may 'rehumanize' a 'numb and fragmented' society, its cri-tique focuses mainly on the artist's process and intentions, or its social outcomes, to the neglect of the work's aesthetic impact (cited in Roche, 2006).

From a philosophical point of view, Rancière (2010) characterizes this as a dilemma in aesthetic practice, between representational media-tion and ethical immediacy. By leaving the spaces reserved for it and becoming a social practice, Rancière suggests that the addressing of art in 'real life' induces, as Corcoran expresses it in his introduction, 'a *cut* between the intention of the artist and the outcome on the spectator's behaviour, between cause and effect' (2010, p.19; original emphasis). The cut implies a productive distance, a form of dissensus or conflict 'between a sensory presentation and a way of making sense of it' (Rancière, 2010, p.139). The cut also underscores the ambiguous relationship between the autonomy of the artist and the heteronomy of the act. He suggests that those who insist that such art is isolated from politics are 'somewhat beside the point' and 'those who want it to fulfill its political promise are condemned to a certain melancholy' (Rancière, 2010, p.133). It is never satisfyingly one thing or another and this tension is troubling.

At this point I need to affirm my primacy as scenographer rather than social activist (although I may fulfil that role at times). In relation to conventional stage design, the role that I perform recognizes found space as a text among other texts, such as the script or musical score. While not abandoning conventional elements of design and composition, a scenographer working in this way is always conscious of the patina of life. Where a stage designer may employ colour, texture, rhythm, balance, light, and shadow to develop a visual language within the proscenium, a scenographer maps a site through myth, memory, personal narrative, and material detail, thereby framing a specific place within a local and global context. This process results in a kind of performance in which narratives form and fragment, proliferate and disperse, revealing the interpenetration of people, place, culture, and history. It is a way of working that privileges 'looking', operating within the space of the glance between artist and spectator as the co-creator. Kester (2004b) suggests that this moment of exchange is creative and generative: 'marked by both risk and possibility. The risk of doubt and uncertainty, and the possibility of an opening out to the other; a movement from self-assurance to the vulnerability of intersubjective exchange.'

Simulacra and authenticity: puppets and people

Performance theorist Maaike Bleeker (2008) also addresses the dynamic of 'looking' in the theatre context. She writes that the illusion of objectivity, the notion of vision as true and objective, and the im/possibility of seeing someone or something 'as it is', is the central paradox of representational strategies in theatre – there is a failure in representation if what we see is recognized as being other than authentic (therefore theatrical) (Bleeker, 2008, pp.2–3). In the example that I provide here, the artists' brief was to see the town 'as it is', to look beyond the stereotypes and the facades of the buildings and perform 'what we saw'. What we observed was a community reconsidering its collective identity as francophone, rooted in faith and unified by a sense of itself as outsider. The tension between old and new generational ways of thinking was apparent, the re-visioning merely partial. Janus-like, some looked forward while others looked back. The very notion of Ponteix formed and reformed as we tried to grasp it. Practically speaking, the impossibility of comprehending the situation fully was our rationale for using half-human-scale puppets to stand in for what we ourselves could never fully understand or perform, the sense of the unrepresentable other: the community 'as it was'. The puppets were a form of simulacra, a void onto which subjective memories, fears, hopes, and desires might be projected. Their use exemplified recognition of multiple subjectivities, the absence of a collective voice, and a refusal to seek consensus. Indeed, this heterogeneity suggested the efficacy or potential of dissensus. It was a strategy that moved our working brief from the necessity of seeing the community 'as it is' and merely theatricalizing its exteriority, to providing an opportunity for those unaccounted for to be active, generative and reciprocating – to be, according to Rancière, 'an emancipated community of narrators and translators' (2009b, p.23). This, he suggests, requires spectators, who play the role of active interpreters, to develop their own translation in order to appropriate the 'story' and make it their own.

In the broadest sense, *Windblown/Rafales* was about reconstituting pasts, acknowledging milestones, looking critically at Ponteix's current contingencies and expressing hopes and concerns for the future. It marked a moment introduced into the public record as collective re-identification, a significant act of place-making and dissent. As an aesthetic and a political gesture, it demonstrates the possibility for individuals to become a jurisdiction of equal voices – a rupturing of the classifications and hierarchy of the local Catholic Diocese and the municipal governance structure in relation to those who do not, nor have ever, counted within the community.

Negotiating the terms of art and social practice without losing an understanding of who and what is being represented and the relative value of the activity on any numbers of levels is the crux of the creative dilemma. The inherent tension lies in the ability of the artist to operate under the Kantian terms of autonomy or heteronomy – either in accordance with reason and moral duty or in accordance with one's desires – either independent of daily life or connecting to the hope of changing life.

Read in conjunction with Kester's (1995) critical assessment, these issues respond to the ethical turn in much of today's art practice. He sees the dilemma of community-engaged artists who assert their position as a 'vehicle for an unmediated expressivity on the part of a given community', as a 'potentially abusive appropriation of the community for the consolidation and advancement of the artist's personal agenda' or as a means to align with the ideology that defines arts policy and funding (cited in Kwon, 2002, p.139). He adds that the community artist is, in many cases, being positioned as a kind of social-service provider, placed in the position of providing alternatives to existing forms of social policy (Kester, 1995). This, Kester argues, produces a response to the work, which is to 'provisionally accept its identity as art but to limit critical engagement to a straightforward calculation of political efficacy' (2004a, p.11). Bishop (cited in Roche, 2006) suggests that discussion of this genre of work should be undertaken, not provisionally as a social project that may or may not produce quantifiable results, but within art criticism. Reading such work merely as social programme, she writes, is problematic as this makes for a situation in which 'there can be no failed, unsuccessful, unresolved, or boring works of collaborative art because all are equally essential to the task of strengthening the social bond' (Bishop cited in Roche, 2006). While sympathetic to addressing social agendas, she argues that it is also crucial to discuss, analyse, and compare such work critically as art. The collaborative or interactive fact-of-the-matter does not, in itself, guarantee its significance. What is important is how it addresses and intervenes in the representational conventions of the time – how it innovates and critiques.

These matters are elemental and represent a considerable tension for artists who work in this manner and sometimes struggle to find a creative and critical context for their work beyond the local community, the funding institutions, and the infrastructure of professional theatres and galleries, which have so defined the terms of representation and value. Following Rancière (2010), this is the dilemma of working between the regime of representation, the praxis that defines institutionalized art, and the regime of aestheticized practice, which declassifies all prior formulas, finds its 'poeticity [sic]' in the world, and operates against the praxis of differentiation of high and low art found within modernism.[12]

Does the notion of dissensus abrogate the perennial and vexing question at the heart of socially engaged practice: is it art or is it social activism? Resisting this opposition, Rancière argues for an understanding of a relationship that binds autonomy and heteronomy in the realm of the experiential – a common sensorium of experience. Thus, art from the aesthetic regime provides an opportunity for equality that allows for dissensus, a supplementation that permits redistribution of the differentiating categories of power and reconfigures art as a political issue. Dissensus represents the cut between the intentionality and outcome –

the unknowable quotient of that which is produced, that which cannot be anticipated or measured but which points towards the demonstrative power of the multiplicity of local instances of political and artistic innovation. It is a form of efficacy, an enunciation that invents novel relationships between things and meanings that were previously unrelated, 'between reality and appearance, the individual and the collective' (Rancière, 2010, p.141).

Performing dissensus

This chapter has taken up the term 'dissensus' to attempt to understand the tension and the potential in Knowhere Productions's creative practice, exemplified in this particular production of *Windblown/Rafales*, and to address the oppositions and binaries inherent in the doing and in the critique of the kind of work in general. To actualize the terms of dissensus, according to Rancière, this way of working makes a new sense of things by helping to break down what is perceived as natural, as an unquestionable order that destines 'specific individuals and groups to occupy positions of rule or of being ruled, assigning them to private or public lives, pinning them down to a certain time and space, to specific "bodies," that is to specific ways of being, seeing and saying' (Rancière, 2010, p.139). Its efficacy to overturn stereotypes is exemplified in the ability of the practice to take on the task of making a collective 'conscious of its own secrets, [...] by delving to the depths of the social, to disclose the enigmas and fantasies hidden in the intimate realities of everyday life' (Rancière, 2010, p.127). For artists invited into communities, this is never an easy position to facilitate, maintain, or justify. It feels problematic because it reveals a failure of representation in that it conflates daily activity and performance and opposes the art of the representation with that which is unrepresentable and, to invoke Bleeker (2008), unknowable. Challenging and perplexing, it requires, as Bishop writes, 'intelligence and imagination and risk and pleasure and generosity, both from the artists and the participants' (cited in Roche, 2006). Although evoking a better world, it does not plot the course nor calculate how long it takes to get there. It reveals the unsteady relationship between people, objects, and places – the supplement that is tantalizing and potently affective and effective. This argument, of course, does not signal the end of the discussion about site-specific performance practice, but I hope that it liberates artists who work in this way from the burden of consensus.

Notes

1. The company's founding members (2002) include Kathleen Irwin, Associate Professor in the Theatre Department, University of Regina, Saskatchewan, Canada; Andrew Houston, Associate Professor in the Department of Speech and Communication, University of Waterloo, Ontario; and Richard Diener, Third Eye Media (Regina, Saskatchewan).
2. Knowhere Productions has produced several large-scale community based, site-specific productions: *The Weyburn Project* (Weyburn Project, 2002); *We the City* (2005); *Crossfiring/Mama Wetotan* (Crossfiring, 2006); and *Windblown/Rafales* (Windblown, 2008).
3. As land was colonized in Western Canada in the late nineteenth and early twentieth centuries, federal policy favoured the model of immigration that had settled Upper Canada with English speakers, while the Canadian Colonization Association (largely responsible for assisting immigrant families in the provinces of Manitoba, Saskatchewan and Alberta) distributed land to German Mennonites, Russian Jews, Ukrainians, French and French Canadians, Icelanders, and others. Nonetheless, all were expected to function and do business in English (Hedges, 2008, p.374).
4. As Father Keith's request was made in good faith, the details that he wanted omitted cannot be revealed. In a general sense, the stories involved members of the clergy whose contact with parishioners was not appropriate, stories of feuding families and apocrypha surrounding certain historical events. An example that I will give, as it illuminates a widely accepted but unsubstantiated claim, is that members of the Ku Klux Klan burned the church to the ground in 1923.
5. According to a Canadian federal government website, the underlying objective of the Western Diversification Plan is to create 'a stronger West and a stronger Canada'. Several guiding principles are used to help assess these initiatives:

   • Increased economic activity that improves the viability, prosperity, and standard of living for individuals and communities across Western Canada.
   • Increased economic research in the areas of community economic development, leading-edge technologies and entrepreneurship to provide a sound base for economic development in areas of importance to Western Canada.
   (Western Economic Diversification Canada, 2007).

6. In 2002, Knowhere Productions produced *The Weyburn Project*, a large-scale, site-specific event in an abandoned mental hospital in Weyburn, Saskatchewan. The event was captured in a video documentary entitled *Weyburn, Archaeology of Madness*, produced by 3rd Eye Media Productions in association with Wolf Sun Productions Ltd. and broadcast frequently on Saskatchewan Community Network.
7. Our process of interviewing individuals in their homes and on the street (often for hours at a time) brings many stories and multiple perspectives to the surface.

8. Although unsubstantiated, many claim that a local unit of the Ku Klux Klan set the fire (see footnote 4).

9. The procession, a ritual of thanksgiving initiated in the troubling years of the Great Depression, is staged annually on 16 July throughout the town of Ponteix. Led by the parish priest, it involves the entire population. Throughout the event, the sisters of the convent sing and the bells of the church are rung. Church dignitaries carry a wooden sculpture of the Pieta (early eighteenth-century France), seated with a recumbent Christ. The sculpture, brought to Canada in 1907, has several apocryphal stories connected to it, including the claim that when the Church was razed in 1923, the fire stopped at the foot of the Virgin.

10. Yvette Carignan, an 85-year-old daughter of an original settler, was a storehouse of information and historical detail. She generously provided hours of interviews, some from a hospital bed.

11. These stories were typical of the indigent and picaresque who populate any town, small or large.

12. Rancière distinguishes between three regimes of art-making. The first is the ethical regime, following Plato, in which works have no autonomy and are to be questioned for their truth and their effect on the ethos of the community. The second, the representative regime, depicts the truth of action through which its moral, political, and social significance is borne out. In the third form, the aesthetic regime, these regulated relationships are undone, but the shift brings with it,

> a promise of a new form of individual and community life [...that] now addresses itself, at least in principle, to the gaze of anyone at all [...]. Art in the aesthetic regime finds its only content precisely in this process of undoing, in opening up a gap [...] between a way of doing and a horizon of affect.'
>
> (Rancière, 2010, p.16)

Its power resides in its expression of the poeticity of the world and its egalitarian relationship to its subject matter, the equality of all subjects. The irresolvable contradiction in this, Rancière believes, is that 'everyone and anyone is now entitled to intervene in any form of discourse, use or be addressed by any language and be the subject of representation' (2010, p.17). In a regime of unlimited representability, the orders of logic and differentiation that determined aesthetic principals formerly and were understood, more or less, universally in the Western world are unfixed from the political and the social, art and non-art, words and things.

Part III

Site-Specificity and the Slippage of Place

7
Beyond Site-Specificity: Environmental Heterocosms on the Street

Susan Haedicke

Contemporary artists performing on the streets of European towns and cities do not seek to hide the everyday world that surrounds their performances. Rather they create an inextricable link between the fiction of theatrical performance and the reality of the public space in which it intervenes. Fantasy and actuality are simultaneously visible and tangible to both casual passer-by and intentional spectator. Here fiction does not work in opposition to reality; rather, the imaginary reinterprets, confuses, subverts, or challenges the real. The onlookers, who see familiar sites through a lens of artistic imagination, experience a re-vision of what seemed established or permanent, and that unexpected shift in the experience of what was, moments before, a familiar world, causes an experiential shock.[1] As boundaries between the fictional and the actual (between art and non-art) become permeable, perhaps indistinguishable, the audience-participants wander in sites with multiple levels of reality. This blurring of the imaginary and the quotidian has the potential to change how the public sees, understands, and experiences daily life in today's world.

Given this potential for efficacy, it is not surprising that many street artists insert their artistic responses to controversial socio-political issues into actual public spaces and engage passers-by who do not expect an aesthetic experience. As far back as 1994, Una Chaudhuri called on artists to imagine new ways of thinking and acting in relation to the environment, and many other authors writing on the relationship between art and environmental issues – notably Robert Macfarlane (2005b) and Bill McKibben (2005, 2009) – insist that artists must play a role in raising public awareness about the seriousness of the problem. Street performances are particularly well-placed to bring this issue to the public's attention.[2] To perform climate change, many street artists intervene in busy public spaces where they play with and challenge concepts of site-specificity that tie the artwork to a geographic location.[3] Sometimes the performance responds to a particular place, but more often it alters the meaning and function of a type of public space that has become so familiar that it is no longer seen. These street performances focus less on exposing socio-historical contexts of the sites than on using the actual public spaces to add a 'real world' dimension to what I call the imagined environmental heterocosms created in their interventions. These performed, alternative climate-changed worlds are responses, in part, to sites that do not exist geographically, but certainly have a presence in environmental debate. As the meaning of site-specificity for these performances breaks loose from particular places, yet never loses sight of them, 'site' refers to locational circumstances augmented by spatio-politico-cultural discourse.

Three contemporary street performances – Metis Arts's *Third Ring Out: Rehearsing the Future*; Opéra Pagaï's *Entreprise de Détournement: Chantier #5: L'Ile de Carhaix-Bretagne*;[4] and Motionhouse's *Cascade* – play with extended concepts of site-specificity as they use recognizable public locations associated with everyday activities to comment on the proximity of the environmental crisis, both spatially and temporally. Thus, the site is simultaneously a geographic location and a more abstract space of environmental discourse. The performance strategies and uses of the actual sites of these three interventions vary significantly,[5] but the visible presence of the recognizable public space seen through a performed environmental dystopia vividly emphasizes that climate change does not just happen elsewhere, but *here*. As the familiar space morphs into a strange place, the public space recedes as a specific geographic location and instead acts as a tool to highlight the immediate urgency of climate change. Physical site expands into the discursive realm. And, in fact, the more integral the actual public space is to the performance event, the more the discursive site wedges itself into the body of the spectator, as the experiential shock of being in a transformed familiar place reveals previously unimagined possibilities.

Site-specific art originated as part of the shift from modernist notions of autonomous, self-referential art forms to socially engaged ideas of contextual art where meaning is constructed by the artwork's relationship to surrounding conditions. Art historian Rosalyn Deutsche identifies site-specificity as an aesthetic strategy in which context was incorporated into the work itself[... A]rtists extended the notion of context to encompass the individual site's symbolic, social, and political meanings as well as the discursive and historical circumstances within which artwork, spectator, and site are situated.

(1996, p.61)

The original impulse of this strategy, she argues, sought to expose the fact that public spaces are not politically or socially neutral; the artwork intervenes in the site 'by making the social organization and ideological operations of that space visible' (Deutsche, 1996, p.68).[6] For performance scholar Nick Kaye, site-specific practices 'articulate exchanges between the work of art and the places in which its meanings are defined' (2000, p.1); site-specific performance also 'frequently works to *trouble* the oppositions between the site and the work' (2000, p.11; original emphasis). Expanding on these ideas, art historian Miwon Kwon has traced the genealogy of site-specific art from a physical link between artwork and spatial location to 'the cultural mediation of broader social, economic and political processes that organize urban life and urban space' (2002, p.3) – what she calls a 'discursive paradigm'. She argues that 'the operative definition of the site has been transformed from a physical location – grounded, fixed, actual – to a discursive vector – ungrounded, fluid, virtual' (Kwon, 2002, pp.29–30). Here the artwork's connection to the physical place is

subordinate to a *discursively* determined site that is delineated as a field of knowledge, intellectual exchange, or cultural debate. Furthermore, [...] this site is not defined as a *pre*condition. Rather it is generated by the work (often as 'content'), and then verified by its convergence with an existing discursive formation.

(2004, p.26; original emphasis)

Like the artworks Kwon analyses that use multiple sites to create meaning, these productions rely on concepts of site as a physical location, a participatory practice, and a scientific and imaginative discourse concerning climate change. These street performances create three very different palimpsests of an embodied environmental debate superimposed on an actual place. Just as Kwon describes Mark Dion's multilayered site-specific work *On Tropical Nature*, these street performances insert the discursive 'site of effect/reception' into the physical 'site of action/intervention' (2002, p.29). In *Third Ring Out*, the discursive site is in dialogue with the actual geographic site (the city in which the show is performed), but that location is presented in simulated images. In *Entreprise de Détournement*, the actual place as defined by the people and practices forms the jumping-off point for the discursive site. In *Cascade*, the discursive site in the form of intertextual images dominates the geographic location. As an understanding of site-specificity becomes 'unhinged', to use Kwon's term (2002, pp.33–55), from physical places and even from their rich socio-cultural context, site becomes an amalgamation of geographic location and spatio-political discourse. 'Unhinged' site-specific performance opens the possibility for new ways of seeing, understanding, and experiencing the links between larger, often controversial, social discourses and lived spaces.

Third Ring Out, Entreprise de Détournement, and *Cascade* offer street performances in familiar public spaces that create palimpsests of actual, imagined, and discursive sites (real geographic locations, imagined dystopias, and environmental discourses). Their use of frequented locations not usually associated with artworks or art-making highlights the spatial proximity of climate change, and the ephemerality of their interventions emphasizes its urgency. Site-specific street performance is naturally transitory, leaving a public memory of the temporarily changed site in the communal imagination. Yet it is that brief 'Ah-ha!' moment when a familiar place becomes unfamiliar that activates the experiential shock. For the productions by Metis Arts, Opéra Pagaï, and Motionhouse, the interacting multivalent sites become sites of socio-political struggle where spectators can begin, in the words of Robert Macfarlane, 'to entertain hypothetical situations – alternative lives, or futures, or landscapes – as though they were real [... and to] connect present action with future consequence' (2005b).

In 2010, Cambridge, UK-based Metis Arts (a performing arts company that seeks to engage audiences interactively with pressing social issues) brought to life what James Graham Ballard (cited in Macfarlane, 2005b) called the 'invisible literature' of climate change[7] by placing it into an interactive performance frame:

I walk quickly and arrive, a bit breathless, at the top of Greenwich Park Hill on a glorious sunny June day. One's eye travels through time from the Royal Naval College and the Queen's House, remnants of the past in the foreground, to the tall office buildings of Canary Wharf, the Saint Mary Axe Building (the 'Gherkin') and the Millennium Dome, all testaments to the twenty-first century on the other side of the river. I reluctantly pull myself away from the panorama and join a small group waiting for the start *of Metis Arts's production, '**Third Ring Out: Rehearsing the Future**,' an interactive performance, programmed in the Greenwich and Docklands International Festival. Soon we are summoned to the Observation Point that I had just abandoned, and a 'tour guide' conjures up an image of environmental harmony and a sense of well-being as she points out the blue water of the Thames, the green expanses of the park, and the important historic buildings we can see in Greenwich and the London skyline.*

That comfortable sense of security is soon overturned as we are suddenly and hurriedly herded into a large shipping container, and the door closed. We have become a 'local emergency response cell' responsible for our sector of the city. The date is June 2033, and the consequences of climate change in terms of soaring temperatures and severe storms are causing chaos in the city. The Thames flood barriers have failed, food shortages are causing civil unrest, the Millennium Dome is a centre for flood refugees, and a more intense storm is on its way. The table around which the 12 participants sit displays a large interactive map of our sector of East London and Greenwich. We are instructed about our resources to cope with the worsening situation (small plastic figures representing police, rescue workers, food distribution sites, and so on that we can place on the map), and we are given our voting consoles with which to decide on key issues that affect our survival: should we 'green' the city or develop a large beach on the river bank to deal with the rising temperatures? Should we improve sea defences for all of the UK or just London? Should we allow flood refugees in? Should we save the Tower of London or historical records and data? We learn information about what is happening outside the container from live performers and simulated news clips of our city displayed on the large screen. The scenario develops in response to our votes on policy decisions that have significant consequences on budgets and events. Our initial good will and generosity wanes as we watch the Tower of London collapse and as funds become scarce and our survival seems less certain. Events happen at a break-neck speed. After about an hour, the two officials who have guided us through the process are called away on an emergency mission, and we are left alone in the container. We hear what has happened to our climate-changed city, and finally the doors of the container open. Our officials greet us as we emerge into the daylight, and, in different roles, explain how to access the website to continue the interactivity and give us each our own password.

Site-specificity, climate-change issues, and an imagined environmental heterocosm converge in this 'interactive simulation of a climate changed world set in the future' (Metis Arts, 2011).[8] *Third Ring Out: Rehearsing the Future*[9] is specific to each city in which it is performed: the large interactive table map and the video clips display the events on the streets of that particular city. We watch 'news footage' displaying images of familiar sites, now damaged or destroyed by environmental disasters, and listen to 'broadcasters' describing devastation, social unrest, and police repression in locations we know well. In a literal sense, *Third Ring Out* declares that this can happen here, what it will be like, and that our choices and actions will determine the outcome.

The show's site-specificity is, however, more complicated than its interlocked connection between the performance's simulated environmental heterocosm and the actual geographic site depicted on the large map and in the videos. In *Third Ring Out*, the concept of site is multi-layered, including: first, the 'locational' site of the specific city in which the performance takes place; second, the 'imagined' site of that city in the future as an environmental dystopia; third, the 'virtual' site on the Metis Arts website that spectators can visit weeks after the performance to assess their decisions against those of other 'local emergency response cells' or scroll over the 'Scenario' to learn through embedded lectures, scientific reports, and charts what happens to the earth as the temperature rises; and last, the 'discursive' site as the production and its larger frame encourage the audience to enter the socio-political debate on climate change. Although *Third Ring Out* does not add new information to environmental discourse from a scientific perspective, it does contribute to an eco-literacy for the public. This eco-literacy acts both as an inquiry into the symbiotic relationship between humans and nature and as a critique of how we live in and care for our world. The interactive show offers an experiential learning tool as audience members make policy decisions and then must respond to the consequences of these decisions. Within the frame of the performance, we are held responsible for the future. The narrative that we construct through our votes (which varies within certain parameters for each production) develops a multilayered and ambiguous site, and it thus corresponds to Kwon's explanation of the discursive site that 'textualizes spaces and spatializes discourses' (2002, p.29). In *Third Ring Out*, the imagined dystopia, with its uncannily familiar reality, spatializes the debates around climate change by placing its consequences in actual recognizable locations, and it textualizes the places we know well by overlaying them with narratives of a frightening future. The performance depicts a world not yet experienced, but one that has enough in common with our own daily life to allow us to place ourselves easily within its new frame.

Conceptually, *Third Ring Out* is provocative and innovative, and its use of multiple paradigms of site increases our awareness of and knowledge about climate change. It is not at all obvious, however, that participation in this production (either on-site in one of the urban locations or later online) will actually lead to eco-activism. Although our votes affect the direction of the narrative, we only have three options and never have time to discuss or even reflect upon our decisions. This lack of agency, even within the performance frame, diminishes the conviction that activism can result in social change and allows us to remain comfortably on the level of playing a video game. In addition, although *Third Ring Out* plays with multiple layers of site, these layers simply accrue rather than interact, and thus they do not deepen in meaning from a spatio-discursive dialogue. Once we enter the container after our initial moments looking at the London skyline, we see the 'crisis' engulfing our city only through simulated images. This offers a provocative version of Guy Debord's 'society of spectacle', where 'spectacle is not a collection of images; rather it is a social relationship between people that is mediated by images' (1994, thesis 4:12, p.12). He argues that passive observation and contemplation of images of life have replaced direct, lived experience; images have become the new reality, and reality is reduced to images. People have become alienated from actual life, from each other, and even from themselves. The representation of the city in altered video footage and an interactive map, as opposed to 'lived experience', and the limited voting choices make the outcome seem preordained and result, I believe, in the passivity Debord predicted.

Like *Third Ring Out*, *Entreprise de Détournement: Chantier #5: L'Île de Carhaix-Bretagne*[10] plays with an intentional dialogue of multiple sites – locational, imagined, and discursive – to address environmental issues. While the discursive (or functional) site in *Third Ring Out* is choreographed through limited spectator choices, mediated images, and an informative website, *Entreprise de Détournement* uses unexpected and surprising improvisations to insert the discursive site into both a public space in the city and the bodies of the city inhabitants who become unintentional audience members. The actual urban site and the specific socio-historical context of that particular city always remain visible in spite of, or perhaps because of, the superimposition of an alternative fictional reality. Like Metis Arts, Opéra Pagaï (a French street-theatre company based in Bordeaux) relies on audience participation, but instead of offering limited choices and an informational website as forms of interactivity, *L'Île de Carhaix-Bretagne*[11] creates a temporary installation that resembles a corporate product demonstration. This faux-exhibition, set up in a busy public space, offers 'facts' and proposes 'solutions' to living in a climate-changed world, but ones that verge on the ridiculous, encouraging spectators to dispute their veracity and viability. Director Cyril Jaubert insists that the goal must be to push spectators to ask themselves questions.

Opéra Pagaï developed *Entreprise de Détournement* as a series of site-specific performative interventions.[12] Each one is tailored to a specific city and takes place only once over several days. Company members begin the research process for each unique intervention by permeating the city for about a week as curious tourists or faux-journalists asking the local inhabitants questions about life there. After leaving the city, the actors use their research to determine a recurring irritation or concern of the inhabitants and, over the next few months, they develop a narrative – a balance between truth and fiction – that intervenes as a seemingly actual event into the daily life of the city (for example, the pseudo-scientific exhibition in *L'Ile de Carhaix-Bretagne*) during the performance intervention. In this final stage of the project, the actors 'perform the city' through composite characters inspired by the anecdotes and opinions of the inhabitants themselves, collected months before on the research foray, and recontextualized into peculiar and, at the same time, credible situations. The actual urban residents themselves also perform the city in their responses to the intervention. As curious and sceptical residents engage with the actors – not as performers but as the individuals whom they say they are (scientists in *L'Ile de Carhaix-Bretagne*) – the audience participants enter a story space, both physically and symbolically. They thus transform the actual place into an alternative world: a heterocosm with new rules that they ostensibly accept; a spatial palimpsest where a new reality overlays the old. The inhabitants on ordinary errands become actors in the reframed and self-reflexive performance of their city – sometimes oblivious that they have stepped into a fictional world; sometimes suspecting that they are being teased, but since they lack confirmation, they often play along.

L'Ile de Carhaix-Bretagne of *Entreprise de Détournement* took place for ten days in November 2007 in the ancient capital of Brittany, Carhaix-Pougher, a small rural city in the middle of the Brittany peninsula. On the initial research trip, the actors found that a key anxiety was the diminishing population as many of the residents and their family members felt compelled to leave the city for work, education, or excitement. Some of the inhabitants even mused that global warming might make their city more appealing. The actors decided to play with the unlikely event that in 100 years, climate change would cause the sea to separate

Brittany from mainland France, thus creating l'Ile de Carhaix-Bretagne (Carhaix-Brittany Island) with the inland city transformed into a beach resort. During the durational performance installation, the actors, now as a group of independent research scientists, set up an exhibition to explain this 'inevitable' geographic upheaval so that city inhabitants could prepare themselves and make the best of the future. The exhibition playfully juxtaposes pastoral with apocalyptic imagery of the city of the future to insert a 'hijacked reality' intervention into the environmental debate. Passers-by walk around an experimental aquatic vegetable garden where chickens roost and rabbits nibble lettuce leaves in floating upturned umbrella-pens and where plants grow in pools of sea water that are also home to fish; this is, we are told, a much more efficient way of gardening and fishing at the same time (Image 7.1). The 'scientists' explain that cows take up too much space as more and more of the land becomes submerged under the rising oceans, and so they need to graze on small barges floating on the sea. Grass grows on these barges, but it is hydrated by sea water and so it makes the cows' milk very salty. A prototype of a bicycle-boat to allow farmers to go

Image 7.1 Opéra Pagaï, *Entreprise de Détournement: Chantier #5: L'Ile de Carhaix-Bretagne* (Carhaix, France, November 2007). Courtesy of Opera Pagaï.

to the tiny islands to milk the cows is available for spectators to 'try'. Official-looking posters provide supporting evidence for their claims. Other posters draw the new map of the area showing the rise in property values as inland homes become prime coastal properties, and one alters a photograph of the city's cathedral to include a lighthouse installed on its roof. Some posters offer details on climate change refugees and explain how Carhaix will become the port of entry for migrants. The members of the research group speculate that many Chinese will migrate to the island, so a couple sit in front of their small *cabane* (beach cottage) dangling their feet in the water as they practise Chinese. While the scientific basis of the predictions is purposefully shaky, their whimsical nature encourages an imaginative and emotional engagement with their possibility. Passers-by participate in the discursive site of the performance installation as they wander around the aquatic garden, read the posters, debate with the faux-scientists on the likelihood of their climate-change forecast, and offer suggestions for other inventions for the new way of life: they actively engage with the issues. Put differently, the pseudo-scientific exhibition offers both fact and fiction (actual and imaginative information). And, the audience's literal presence in the performative installation in an urban public square, as well as their imagined presence in their climate-changed city of the future, enable them to enter the discursive site and thus engage in the environmental debate. One woman, seriously studying the proposed map of the Brittany Island, explains – or jokes – 'My house will be on the beach. Maybe I should wait to sell it.'

This strategy underscores that the disastrous effects of climate change can happen *here* through the spectator's embodied experience of the site. On the one hand, the physical location of the event is diminished by the discursive site of environmental debate; on the other, this actual site is paradoxically re-experienced, re-interpreted, and received in a kind of heightened relief. These politically charged interconnected experiential sites have the potential to change how the public sees, understands, and lives daily life in today's world and, in so doing, propose a provocative social critique. These performances thus respond to the plea made by US environmentalist and author Bill McKibben (2005) for artists to implant climate-change scenarios into the communal imagination through stories, not just facts, because 'though we know about it, we don't *know* about it. It hasn't registered in our gut; it isn't part of our culture' (2005; original emphasis). Without that visceral understanding, he argues, people may just stand by and observe the environmental shifts around them, but are unlikely to agitate for change.

Motionhouse (a British dance company based in Leamington Spa) complicates the discursive site even further by overlaying the palimpsest of fictional event in an actual public space with a complex intertextuality of visual images and actual events. The performance of *Cascade*[13] starts with music and dance, yet the larger frame of the show begins earlier as passers-by, curious about the tilting red roof of a family home in Jubilee Plaza (in front of the entrance to the Canary Wharf underground station), begin to dawdle close by.[14] Some ask a group of people clustered around the large sound system about the show, and many choose to join the crowd beginning to form the semi-circle around the performance space, demarcated by sandbags. One by one, the four dancers start to warm up on and around the roof, sometimes interacting with each other, sometimes doing crowd-pleasing acrobatic movements, but also sometimes stopping to talk to someone in the audience: they are both one of us and separate from us. These casual conversations between audience members and performers, not 'in character' and not really as themselves either but rather in a liminal space between actual and fictional, start a human connection that has a significant impact on the reception of the piece. Spectator and dancer exchange pleasantries about the weather, the clatter of the overland train on the bridge behind the stage space, or the tiny house roof in contrast to the surrounding tall buildings. Thus, when the actual performance (physical urban dance) begins and we watch the family members struggling to get home in the wind and rain, grabbing the sandbags that divided our spaces and tossing them frantically to each other in an attempt to secure their home, gasping for air in the ever-shrinking attic space, climbing onto the roof, slipping off and eventually drowning, we are moved and shaken not just by the aesthetic images, but by a sense of personal loss. Talking to the dancers and losing the sandbag barrier between us places us within the larger frame of the event and casts us in the role of witness, participating in the catastrophic events, but unable to change them. We must accept some responsibility for the events – not as they occurred, but as they are understood, documented, interpreted, and contextualized. Here as witnesses, we enter into the discursive site.

Although *Cascade* eschews the participatory engagement of *Third Ring Out* and *Entreprise de Détournement* in favour of a stationary spectatorship, it complicates the act of spectating. Here an audience member is not a passive spectator watching an unfolding narrative in a self-contained world, but rather what Jacques Rancière calls an 'emancipated spectator' (2009b, p.22). Audiences witness the dancers embody reconstructed and recognizable media images of devastating floods, and as the performance 'link[s] what one knows with what one does not know', the spectators become 'active interpreters who develop their own translation in order to appropriate the "story" and make it their own story' (Rancière, 2009b, p.22). *Cascade* does not offer answers, but instead creates multiple narratives simultaneously that compel audiences into 'performing' acts of discovery, understanding and meaning-making, and thus 'participating'. As the concept of site is separated from a physical location, so too is the notion of participation separated from walking around a place. Rancière explains: 'Being a spectator is not some passive condition that we transform into activity. It is our normal situation. We also learn and teach, act and know, as spectators who all the time link what we see to what we have seen and said, done and dreamed' (2009b, p.17).

This form of participatory engagement is set in motion by the performance's intertextuality of visual images. This intertextuality is achieved through the dancers' embodied re-presentation of familiar media images of flood victims, and it widens the frame of reference from the tragic events that happen to one family to larger questions of why this happened and when or where it will happen again. Motionhouse's Artistic Director Kevin Finnan admits that the initial inspiration was drawn from the images of Katrina's devastation of New Orleans in 2005. However, the number of floods worldwide since then – in the UK, Sri Lanka, Malaysia, Pakistan, Australia, and Brazil, to mention just a few – makes the site to which the piece is specific both a collage of all these geographic locations and the controversial discourse around climate change. As Kwon claims, in discursive sites 'the site is now structured (inter) textually rather than spatially' (2002, p.29). The site in *Cascade* is not just a recreation of something that happened in the past, although after-images of the flood pictures linger in our imagination. It is not an exaggerated fantasy created to scare us into action. Instead, it represents a possible dystopian reality superimposed on an actual familiar reality to create a form of site-intertextuality. The physical location is one text, but it is augmented by and re-imagined through other texts that narrate multiple facets of daily life.

Baz Kershaw suggests that we 'be on the lookout for the reflexivities of paradox' as we develop models of performance that 'might dissolve the boundaries between performer and spectator to produce participants in ecologically responsive action which recognizes and embraces the agency of environments' (2007, p.317). *Cascade* offers that paradox in terms of participatory engagement. Although we do not physically participate in the action, we do enter the discursive site quite viscerally as the complicated site-intertextuality of remembered, reconstructed, and embodied images, superimposed on an actual outdoor location, gives *Cascade* its power as a political site-specific choreography. *Cascade* transforms statistics and charts of 'invisible literature' into a recognizable and personal tragedy as the jagged and twisted movements of the dancers' bodies and their contorted faces resonate with well-remembered media images documenting real lives destroyed by environmental disasters. While it is easy to both see and not see the surrounding city, it is impossible to forget the familiar images.

Marianne Moore gives both serious and whimsical advice to would-be poets in 'Poetry' as she insists that poems must offer genuine experiences and observation, not sheer flights of fancy. If they do not:

> the result is not poetry,
> nor till the poets among us can be
>   'literalists of
> the imagination'–above
>   insolence and triviality and can present
> for inspection, imaginary gardens with real toads in them,
>   shall we have it. (2003)

Contemporary street artists seem to have listened. Adapting Moore's dictum, one can argue that site-specificity in street performance fills real public places with imaginary (or fictional) actions and situations and, simultaneously, places real objects, situations, and experiences in imaginary spaces. Rather than an artistic response to a physical place, site-specific performances like *Third Ring Out, Entreprise de Détournement #5*, and *Cascade* create intertextual spatio-conceptual constructions that intervene in larger socio-political discourses. In other words, the spectator-participant-witness enters the intertextual performance site both viscerally and intellectually, joining the dialogue between the actual public space (with its socio-political context that prevents it from ever being a neutral or 'empty' space) and the discursive site of political and cultural debate on climate change. This embodied entrance into an inherent contradiction of an actual and imagined place causes an experiential shock. And, as a resident of Carhaix-Pougher testifies: 'If it is true, it's a catastrophe. But...it makes me reflect...(long pause); it inspires me.' Perhaps one more person has entered the discursive site.

Notes

1. I adapt Jacques Rancière's idea of 'perceptual shocks' and James M Jasper's notion of 'moral shocks' here. Rancière describes a 'perceptual shock' in

political art as a disruption in 'the relationship between the visible, the sayable, and the thinkable', a rupture that overturns expectations and 'resists signification' (2004, p.63). Jasper explains that a 'moral shock' occurs 'when an unexpected event or piece of information raises such a sense of outrage in a person that she becomes inclined toward political action' (1998, p.409). In both cases, the result is a change in understanding, attitudes, and behaviour.

2. In addition to the performances discussed in this chapter, several street artists explore the performance possibilities around the issue of the environment, including WildWorks, *A Beautiful Journey*; Spirale, *Le Cercle*; Ilotopie, *Les Oxymores d'Eau* (a spectacle performed on the water with the lighting and sound completely powered by renewable energy gathered during the day); Compagnie KMK, *Roman Fleuve* and *Les Jardins Migrants*; Strange Fruit and Graeae, *Against the Tide* and *The Garden*; and Wired Aerial Theatre, *As the World Tipped*, to mention just a few.

3. In her survey of British site-specific (performance, Fiona Wilkie places connections between artwork and place on a spectrum: site-specific ('performance specifically generated from/for one selected site'), site-generic ('performance generated for a series of like sites'), site-sympathetic ('existing performance text physicalized in a selected site'), outside theatre, and in a theatre building (2002b, p.150).

4. A word-for-word translation of *Entreprise de Détournement: Chantier #5* does not make sense in English. The looser translations, *Ventures that Hijack Reality: Site #5* or *The Hijacking Reality Crew: Site #5*, give a better sense of the French. Thanks to Anne Gonon of HorsLesMurs for help with the translation.

5. Using Wilkie's categories, *Entreprise de Détournement* is site-specific whereas *Cascade* is site-sympathetic. *Third Ring Out* falls between site-specific and site-generic as it is '*re-located*, that is, re-worked to fit each new site' (2002b, p.150).

6. See Deutsche's 'Boys' Town' and '*Tilted Arc* and the Uses of Democracy' in *Evictions* (1996). While analyses of the meaning of 'space' are outside the scope of this chapter, many cultural geographers interrogate the intersections of space and politics. For example, Doreen Massey focuses on the social idea of place as that which 'can be imagined as articulated moments in networks of social relations and understandings' (1994, p.154), and Gillian Rose suggests a provocative way of thinking about space as 'the articulation of collisions between discourse, fantasy and corporeality' (1999, p.247). These concepts of space can complicate ideas about site-specificity.

7. Robert Macfarlane explains Ballard's notion of invisible literature as 'the data buried in "company reports, specialist journals, technical manuals, newsletters, market research reports, internal memoranda." It exists as paper trail, as data stream. It also exists, of course, as journalism, as conversation, and as behaviour' (2005b).

8. This piece was created by Zoe Svendon and Simon Daw of Metis Arts. It won the Tipping Point Award (for a creative response to climate change) in 2010.

9. A video clip of the performance is available on the Metis Arts (2011) website: http://www.3rdringout.com/about/project/.

10. A video clip of the performance is available on the Opéra Pagaï (2011) website: http://www.dailymotion.com/opera-pagai#video=xqq7s3.
11. Details on this event were gathered in interviews with Cyril Jaubert, artistic director of Opéra Pagaï (2010), and Michèle Bosseur (2011), co-director of Le Fourneau, Centre Nationale des Arts de la Rue: Bretagne in Brest, which helped to produce the event.
12. Six have been created at the time of this writing. I discuss *Chantier #3: Mobil Home 'Container'* in my book on street arts, *Contemporary European Street Arts: Aesthetics and Politics*.
13. For a video clip of the performance (not the one that I saw in London), see Motionhouse (2010): http://www.youtube.com/watch?v=RJhkvjQxvNE or Motionhouse (2011).
14. I saw the performance at the 2010 Greenwich and Docklands International Festival.

8
Repetition and Performativity: Site-Specific Performance and Film as Living Monument

Anna Birch

How can repeated visits to one urban and historically inflected 'site' create meaning for local and global stakeholders? I was presented with a provocative canvas in and from which to explore this question when I discovered that Mary Wollstonecraft (1759–97) had lived and worked on Newington Green and had met her mentor, Richard Price (1723–91), on 'the Green' in north-east London, around the corner from where I live. Site-specific performance and film have provided my tools to produce a gender-inflected response to both the Wollstonecraft legacy and the practice of theatre production itself. Wollstonecraft herself offers a positive female role model for the twenty-first century, but the mode of production in this performance and film project encourages and extends the identification and ownership of that legacy in a number of key ways. In the absence of a physical monument to Wollstonecraft and her accomplishments,[1] I have generated a living monument that resists a single narrative, offering a discursive view of the identity of Mary Wollstonecraft herself and more widely of identity and its construction. This iterative monument interrogates traditional forms of monument construction and the process of commemoration while nevertheless being integrally connected to site.

This chapter examines how site shifts its 'specifics' through the use of iteration and multimedia, and how such a shift facilitates a performative reconstruction of identity and place. Each phase of the *Wollstonecraft Live!* project returns to the same site, inviting audiences to conjure up both the literal and performed ghosts of the past. Site-specific performance allows for new ways of viewing, unhampered by what Baz Kershaw calls the *'disciplinary system'* (1999, p.31; original emphasis) found in building-based theatres. Spectators are invited to experience – and re-experience – the performance as an embodied event outside a conventional theatre venue; iteration provides a very different reception process than that found in a theatre building.

First, some background on Wollstonecraft[2]: my neighbourhood has a 300-year history of political and religious dissent, with 2009 marking the 250th anniversary of Mary Wollstonecraft's birth. When I discovered that she had been a 'neighbour' of mine, I investigated her contribution to human rights and feminism and became fascinated with what her legacy could continue to offer. Britain's first feminist, author of *A Vindication of the Rights of Woman* (1792), wife of the radical philosopher William Godwin (1756–1836), mother of author Mary Shelley (1797–1851), and a radical dissenter, Wollstonecraft was the founder of Western feminism in the eighteenth century, one of the first human-rights campaigners and abolitionists, a pioneer travel writer as well as a single parent (to her first daughter Fanny Imlay, prior to her marriage to Godwin). Wollstonecraft visited France during the French Revolution, where she became even more convinced that improving women's rights would improve all human rights.

Newington Green itself is a small park with benches and playground equipment, surrounded in part by bushes, and it is open to the public; today it is a regenerated 'greenspace'.[3] It also acts as a traffic roundabout in a busy part of north-east London. In the distant past, its location beyond the city boundaries made it an appropriate site for clandestine meetings and dissenting behaviour. Today, a transport hub of sorts, the Green witnesses a series of arrivals and departures, and the site-specific performance of *Wollstonecraft Live!* engages with that movement: this neighbourhood has, since at least the seventeenth century, had a history of migrant populations moving in and settling. Current demographics for Newington Green indicate a lower-middle-class population with English as a second language (Islington Council, 2001). Linking the radical writing of Mary Wollstonecraft, who argued that the liberation of women would be the liberation of all humankind, and the history of dissent from the eighteenth century with the migrant populations now living at Newington Green provides a means to examine the multiple histories represented by the people living and working in and passing through the Green. Global and local links are thus a part of the dramaturgy found on Newington Green. This compression of time and space in twenty-first-century communications encourages the linking of both history and space.

A brief description of two of the interventions – 2005 and 2007 – sets the scene. *Wollstonecraft Live!*, written by Kaethe Fine,[4] celebrates the life of Mary Wollstonecraft through a multimedia history in which Fragments & Monuments, my film and performance company, conjures up the life and times of Wollstonecraft through performance and film on-site in Newington Green. The past is brought into the present through the script, costume, location, and audience participation. The *Wollstonecraft Live!* script includes Fragments & Monuments's narrative film biography, *VINDICATION* (2005), exploring the moment when Wollstonecraft first met Godwin. The project started with the intention of capturing a performance of Fine's script on video that would be used as an ongoing document and artefact. This film of *Wollstonecraft Live!* was made and later projected back onto the site of the initial performance and streamed online in the 2007 *The Wollstonecraft Live Experience!* This is a practice that keeps to Fragments & Monuments's aesthetic of filming each site-specific performance and returning to the site of performance to project the film back onto its original site (for the company's full chronology see the Appendix); the site thereby accruing a layering of previous iterations of performance in addition to its layering of history.

For the 2005 event, Fragments & Monuments arranged access to two spaces at Newington Green for the four evenings it was performed: *Wollstonecraft Live!* began in the Unitarian Chapel on the north side of the Green (where Wollstonecraft is known to have prayed in pew 19), and then continued as a walk outside through the Green where she ran a school for girls. Audiences discovered throughout the procession how Wollstonecraft articulated the case for women's suffrage in her famous 1792 treatise. In the process, Newington Green became a film set for a fictional biopic of her life, crewed by three actors who each played the title role. Extras were chosen from the audience as the story of her life was told through rehearsals for the film, her letters and prose, political writing of the time and Godwin's grief-filled narration, creating a multimedia, site-specific performance of her life in her church and her Green. The audience gathered outside the chapel and the film crew captured their arrival as if to a gala opening.[5] Filming from the outset of the evening invited the audience to see themselves as performers at the event. Inside the chapel, the atmosphere was celebratory as people discovered a space that in the main they had not seen before. The chapel is small and refurbished in a now-shabby 1970s style. The audience sat shoulder to shoulder as congregations have sat for more than 300 years. An Assistant Director welcomed the audience and assigned roles to random audience members as 'extras' for the filming of Wollstonecraft's life. Following the screening of *VINDICATION*, a sermon from Mary

Wollstonecraft (played by Sadiqua Akhtar) introduced her writing to the audience; she was then joined by two more Wollstonecrafts.[6]

The three performers cast to play Wollstonecraft all wore white 'box' dresses (Images 8.1 and 8.2). The box skirts produced a critical engagement for the spectator about the restrictions historically placed on women: the box dresses affected the movement of the performers playing Wollstonecraft in such a way that their choreographic choices needed careful management. The Wollstonecrafts negotiated the narrowness of the chapel aisles by lifting their dresses and adjusting their movement. They performed a chorus (its movement choreographed by Sarah Rubidge) of Wollstonecraft's own writing before settling into pew 19, their box dresses spilling out over the sides. The Wollstonecraft actors performed more of her writing, narrating it in a stop-start sequence, as a video recorder might stop and playback. This technological interruption and repetition sets up the technological and multimedia vocabulary that is integral to the scenography of the performance as a whole.[7]

Eventually the three Wollstonecrafts escaped pew 19 and, lifting their box dresses, rushed out of the chapel. The women in these dresses connected the dramatic action from their introduction inside the chapel

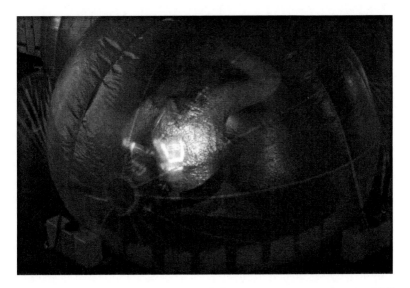

Image 8.1 Mary Wollstonecraft (Ros Phillips) as cinematographer in *Wollstonecraft Live!* (2005) projected onto the Portavillion Bubble (2010). Courtesy of Jana Riedel.

Image 8.2   The Wollstonecraft Live Experience! (2007) still image captured at *The Wollstonecraft Live Experience!* outdoor screening. Courtesy of Neil Wissink.

to outside on the Green, as the audience were instructed to follow them onto Newington Green itself. The audience negotiated a busy road between the chapel and the Green, halting traffic as they crossed, inhabiting the neighbourhood itself as the queue became visible to anyone passing through Newington Green. In the dark, the car lights picked out the audience, wrapping them into the dramaturgy and making the procession of audience, performer and camera crew another layer of history in the life of the Green. The production designer, Tina Lonergan, created a film set on Newington Green, as if Wollstonecraft were shooting a film of her life. Once in the Green, the audience became a part of the film location, which was set up with large film equipment cases, costume rails (as in the cover photo to this volume), lighting rigs and a technical desk, completed by a camera and track. The three Wollstonecrafts swapped their period jackets for tool-belts as they took up their new role as film crew. The audience sat on bundles of past issues of *The Guardian*, while large blocks made out of recycled books punctuated the set. As the audience made themselves comfortable, they could hear the traffic circulating around the Green as the action of the film shoot unfolded, while a minute's 'silence' was ordered by the Assistant Director as a sound check which reinforced the many functions of the Green; the effect for the audience was to increase their sense of being on this particular site of Newington Green in the night air surrounded by a purposeful film set. Later, a casting director interviewed the three Wollstonecrafts to select who might be the best one to play Mary herself. Each read further from her writing, a process that was projected onto large screens. The three performers were seen rehearsing, as actresses auditioning for the part of Wollstonecraft in the film-within-the performance, and as performers playing Wollstonecraft, suspending the power and ostensible certainty of a single narrative. In the production's multiple narrative, the audience were invited to complete the fragmented story for themselves. As the audience sat or stood on the Green, they came to understand more of the scale of her legacy. The performance was designed to offer a 360-degree experience of the Newington Green site as a historic site of dissent, layered with the practicalities of the early twenty-first-century urban experience and the historical presence of Wollstonecraft. After much negotiation, which included scenes between Wollstonecraft and Godwin, the film crew themselves argued about what to do next and the extras took over the film set in a comic sketch asking 'Who is Mary Wollstonecraft?', and the marriage scene between Godwin and Wollstonecraft was shot using the camera and track. Finally this scene was shared with the audience on the large screen:

SCENE 15: NEWINGTON GREEN SHOOT-PLAYBACK

ASSISTANT DIRECTOR

We can all move over here and watch the shot. Let's see how many more takes we'll have to do. Gather round if you want to. Right over here.

[*As the recorded tracking shot begins, we see it on the camera monitor. It is a slow view of nothing but the bushes and the trees of the Green. Mary, Godwin, park scene, extras, are not there, mysteriously, as if they have been erased from the film. But as the tracking shot progresses . . .*]

MARY THREE

(*she addresses the audience, Godwin watches*) Thinking of death makes us tenderly cling to our affections – with more than usual tenderness, I therefore assure you that I am yours, wishing that the temporary death of my absence may not endure longer than is absolutely necessary.

(Fine, 2005, p.38)

The effect of this final projection is to suggest that the Green itself as a site of historical dissent has been further strengthened by the specific intervention of *Wollstonecraft Live!* and the rehearsal, performance, and repetition of her own words, heard as the *'Videographers weave through the crowd capturing peoples' responses'* (Fine, 2005, p.38) to further enmesh the audience with the site and the history of the site.[8]

'Site' shifts were made to incorporate additional layers of time in Fragments & Monuments's 2007 iteration of the project. To make further connections across the facets of the project and across our audience(s), both 2005 films (*VINDICATION* and *Wollstonecraft Live!*) were projected onto Newington Green for *The Wollstonecraft Live Experience!* (2007) – an outdoor screening, picnic, and live music event streamed using the Internet from the park ranger's hut on the Green. The screening of the film *Wollstonecraft Live!* gave equal value to the site, performers, and audience, many of whom live and work around Newington Green and who were now captured on screen. A further set of visuals was generated and projected using Isadora software: our digital archive and the video capture of the picnic audience were underscored by live music from The Deidre Cartwright Trio, international jazz performers from the same neighbourhood. Finally, after dark, the *Wollstonecraft Live!* and *VINDICATION* films, featuring the three actors playing Wollstonecraft, were back-projected onto a 3.5 by 3.5 metre screen. The films thus became embedded onto Newington Green (Image 8.2).

The practicalities of the site called on other types of spatial considerations and implications: a safe and lit space was provided for our audience, in particular women who may not have felt comfortable being out at night. Picnic mats were designed and installed for the audience to sit on. Wollstonecraft's father's occupation as a handkerchief weaver in Spitalfields, East London, provided the starting point for the picnic mats, which displayed fragments of her writing. The specially designed mats created a context for the event on Newington Green, inviting the possibility of an embodied relationship between the audience and the legacy of Wollstonecraft's writing and its effects.

Fragments & Monuments's series of site-specific iterations deploy multimedia technologies in concert with live performance to extend the interpretational field of this specific site, without losing sight of the original location. The scenography of the legacy of Mary Wollstonecraft as a Hackney resident from the past creates a dialogue with that of the current population, who draw on new social networking media and technology to communicate with families that are often dispersed around the world. The multimedia in the *Wollstonecraft Live!* project brings with it a different inflection to both time and space, as Image 8.2 illustrates: the box dress worn by Mary Wollstonecraft in *Wollstonecraft Live!* is captured in a video clip projected onto Newington Green. As the audience discovered in the chapel, the box dress suggested both containment and an obstacle that needs to be managed and controlled. The projection screen is set against a backdrop of Newington Green itself where shopfronts glow as the evening sun sets, producing a fiery and dramatic scenography.

This cinematic ghosting of Wollstonecraft was captured as a still image at *The Wollstonecraft Live Experience!* picnic and brings Wollstonecraft back to the site when she is laminated onto the Green (through the use of digital photography).[9] The distribution of Wollstonecraft's image connects to the important distribution of her writing, made possible by the advances in printing at the time of the publication of her famous book.[10] Such layering and recycling reduces the likelihood of the erasure of history taking place, as well as providing an opportunity for participation between audience, performer, and site (see also the cover image).

The ghosting associated with *The Wollstonecraft Live Experience!* is relatively easy to read, since audiences are encouraged to witness how the same site is used and reused through successive iterations. This mesh of interconnections produced through both live and mediated iterations draws attention to the production of identity as a process. This processual aesthetic intends to share a series of fragments with the audience, inviting them to participate in finding their own story. Similar to the way that we find ourselves and our identity through experience and a process of cultural and social interactions, here the audience are invited to make space for the Wollstonecraft legacy by experiencing it first-hand on Newington Green and by being a part of a series of mediatized iterations in the form of still photography, film, and so on. During an interview about *The Wollstonecraft Live Experience!*, Lesley Ferris (2007) likened this layering and ghosting to fine art practices:

In the fine arts old masters would paint over their canvases perhaps for practical reasons and historians exclaim at this. In this postmodern moment photographers eg. Idris Khan [11] photographs old masters and layers his photographs one on top of the other to give a ghostly quality.

Repeated visits to the same site of performance based on the original performance of *Wollstonecraft Live!* (2005) achieve this ghostly quality, with the help of performance and film. Through my practice it has emerged that by moving outside the theatre space and beyond the proscenium arch, film, photography, and the Internet can be employed in site-specific theatre to provide a series of iterations both on and off the original site.

Yet it is not the ghosting of audience and actors so much as what is done with their images that extends and rethinks site as well as incorporating the vocabulary and potential of multimedia. The process of 'working on-site' is understood here as 'working on location' (as in film and television) to blur the boundaries between documentation and fiction, finished story and fragmented story. Film and photography enable the disparate aspects of site-specific performance to be brought together, which makes it possible to draw the site of Newington Green together with the performers and audience into a series of new artefacts that includes both short films and photographs. This fragmented dramaturgy of multimedia site-specific performance offers the audience/spectator the opportunity to discover, make, and re-make stories about Wollstonecraft and the site of Newington Green. The way in which Fragments & Monuments deploys multimedia is also embedded onto the site as a part of a continuing history: multimedia provides an essential link to the site's performativity. The camera becomes another investigative tool of/for the site, searching and recording the reactions of audiences and passers-by, the performance itself, backstage preparation and rehearsal, spectator/audience behaviour, spectators' reception and consumption of the event, and finally the site itself as an urban landscape. The film edit explores new relationships between the space, performers, and audience.

Spatial iteration takes on additional emphasis when combined with Judith Butler's argument (2011) for the construction of identities through social interaction (after J L Austin and Erving Goffman, among others). In particular, she discusses the role of context in the construction of meaning and how a particular context can privilege aspects of meaning. As performance in site-specificity undergoes a recontextualization that is at least partly conditioned by site, it is possible to test how meanings might be freed up, torn from the theatre venue, and remade in a new context. Because Butler uses a legal framework to demonstrate the importance of the linguistic in cultural production and the ascription of value, she can perhaps be useful in invoking the role of theatre in legislating for a particular kind of performance outcome for the audience, performer, and space. Newington Green itself was selected for this site-specific project because this public space provides a platform from which the value of Wollstonecraft's work can be viewed as public and historically significant. This exterior location adds value to the legacy, while attention is drawn to the epic scale of Wollstonecraft's contribution to human rights. The contribution made by Butler to the philosophical and linguistic debates surrounding the construction of identity helps to take the process of reviewing Wollstonecraft's legacy for a contemporary audience further. Butler argues that language is the site for the construction of identity and that it is through social interaction that identity is produced. The *Wollstonecraft Live!* project mobilizes site, costume (the box dress), audience, and local history to recalibrate gender constructions from a linguistic, visual, and embodied perspective and in this way engage with her legacy. As Wollstonecraft pushed the possibilities of a transformed future for humanity through her writing, Fragments & Monuments harnesses scenographic and dramaturgical languages to draw attention to the continued relevance of her arguments today. For Butler, 'performativity is [...] not a singular "act," for it is always a reiteration of a norm or set of norms, and to the extent that it acquires an act-like status in the present, it conceals or dissimulates the convention of which it is a repetition' (2011, p.xxi). The iterative and distributed aspects of the Fragments & Monuments project in themselves demonstrate where the repetition of the work itself has the possibility to interrupt the normative, taken-for-granted rehearsal of dominant power relations that Butler argues against.

The specific site is instrumental in altering the audience's relationship with mimesis since the shift from a location inside the theatre building to outside has shaped the work of Fragments & Monuments and the way that it is viewed. The audience is choreographed to travel around our performances and this entails physical movement, which in itself creates the possibility of an interactive experience. The logic of site-specific performance can generate a sequence of movements performed by audience, performers, and passers-by. This scenographic and dramaturgical score contributes to the overall concept and, through this embodied relationship to the site and performers, a gap in the Brechtian sense is created where an alienated experience invites the audience to look at the twenty-first century through the legacy of Mary Wollstonecraft.[12]

The form of this distributed work resembles a network which in itself is a reminder of, as Susan Leigh Foster puts it, the 'hyperlinked world that has emerged with the advent of new technologies' (2008, p.55).[13] In this way the content is communicated through a form of presentation which is site-specific (outside the gallery or theatre venue), mediatized, and distributed. Wollstonecraft was a social critic and an outsider – 'a hyena in petticoats', as Walpole dubbed her – so it is fitting to explore and celebrate her in this form or medium. As the beginning of printing was so important to Wollstonecraft and her circle in making their writing accessible to a mass readership, so is the capacity of technology to offer accessibility worldwide in the twenty-first century.

The combination of spaces (and, by implication, times) was well received by audiences. One audience member at *The Wollstonecraft Live Experience!* (2007) noted the following about the significance of the location:

> The outdoor experience gives a historical resonance where you see a history in the modern day and we can look back on it. It's really neat how you look at the screen and it cuts away to the road and you cut away and look at the road and a bus is going around the Green in the same place! [...] Events like this give a personality to the locality. Civil society started by people meeting in public places and it's very important to re-kindle this if we have any chance of surviving.
>
> (Richard Reiser, UK)

The specific site of Newington Green effectively provided a basis for the discussion of social and political change. By broadcasting this event from Newington Green, Fragments & Monuments made a local and global link between the Green, Wollstonecraft's legacy, and the wider social context. Designing performance materials for presentation outside the theatre building can foster a useful dynamism between audience, site, and performer.

The current phase of the project re-presents aspects of our performances and subsequent video documentation in a series of new sites, including outdoor cinema, streaming video using the Internet[14], further gallery and museum installations, and a book project. In the context of advancing digitization, this project provides a test case for how far the internet can support a site-specific theatre/performance project in producing a further life for the project and continued performance and film development. This trajectory is choreographed and tracked such that the original site is a starting point for a series of multimodal iterations. In this way the narrative produced through both performance and film is supported by a fragmented and distributed scenography and dramaturgy. This aesthetic choice challenges a single narrative and dominant version of biography[15], opening up provisional meanings and putting the audience/spectators in the role of meaning makers.

The documenting of this project points to a feminist interpretation of 'site'. The history of Wollstonecraft and her relationship to Newington

Green has been uncovered and bought to the attention of a new audience around the Green and beyond to help redress the balance of attention ascribed to male and female achievements from history. Early in 2007, Fragments & Monuments was invited to curate two exhibitions at New York's A.I.R. Gallery and then at the Ruskin Gallery, Cambridge, UK. The artefacts from *Wollstonecraft Live!* (2005), including the play script and films, were now reconsidered as elements of a gallery exhibition. The remnants or traces selected included the three dresses and tool belts worn by the Wollstonecraft performers; a redrafted and rewritten script; fragments of Wollstonecraft's writing from her published books; and letters presented as posters in the graphic style of Barbara Kruger's (2003) work. These items provided a link across two important periods of feminist practices in the eighteenth and twenty-first centuries. The films were looped to emphasize the replay dimension of the performance and installed as an integral part of the exhibition, providing an audio soundtrack from the films *VINDICATION* and *Wollstonecraft Live!* At the A.I.R. Gallery presentation and performance, a transatlantic connection was made between Newington Green, London, and the New York home of Tom Paine (1737–1809)[16], Wollstonecraft's friend and colleague.

The tools of site-specific performance and film – from which we have generated a performance archive – problematize both biography and monument, systems of representation that dominate western theatre. A site-specific performance continues to resonate in people's memories and in the material traces (the films, photographs, and costumes) that are left behind. The layering of these resonances and traces produces for the audience/spectators, artists, and community a transhistorical experience of an ongoing stake in the site. The aesthetic outcomes we develop drive the company on to the next stage; overlaying and revisiting our digital archives is a part of this. The process of filming a live performance and projecting that film back onto the site of the original performance offers a re-viewing of the digital archive and the possibility of producing a multilayered artefact. The ephemeral characteristic of live performance became a starting point for a continual remaking and revaluing of the performance site from various perspectives.

Two further interventions away from the Newington Green site demonstrate the shift in scenographic and dramaturgical terms from the local to the global. Image 8.1 was taken not on Newington Green but nearby at a pre-Olympic event, 'Inside/Outside Cinema', in which Fragments & Monuments designed a projection for a 2010 pre-Olympic cultural event in East London. Fragments & Monuments was invited to project its films on the inside and outside of the Portavillion bubble.

This gave us a new surface and new site to work with: *Wollstonecraft Live!* and *VINDICATION* were projected on the inside and the outside of the bubble. The nature of 'site' extended yet again through the overlay of locations when both films were screened at the same time. Image 8.1 was taken from the outside of the bubble and captures Mary Wollstonecraft (Ros Phillips) as cinematographer surveying Newington Green as she prepares to shoot the film of her life. This emerging multimodal scenography resulted in an invitation from the Hackney Museum, London, to develop a special exhibition on Mary Wollstonecraft. Artefacts resulting from our five-year project were once again selected and curated and this time presented alongside an original copy of *A Vindication of the Rights of Woman*, which was found in the Hackney Museum archive. Taey Iohe, lead artist with Fragments & Monuments, collaborated with me to produce a published artist's book entitled *The Wollstonecraft Live Experience!*, an account of the five-year *Wollstonecraft Live!* project. The dimensions of both the book and its cover replicate *A Vindication of the Rights of Woman*; a copy of *Wollstonecraft Live!* is now stored alongside Wollstonecraft's book in the Hackney Museum archive. The storage of the books together returns Fragments & Monuments to the printed page, the site where Wollstonecraft's voice was first heard.

Through the production of a series of ongoing artworks employing site-specific performance, film, still photography, and book publishing, the conceptual ideas around what a 'monument' might be continue to be interrogated. As a single version of reality, a monument represents a truth from one person's point of view, similarly the film biopic version of a person's life becomes the 'real' version. The *Wollstonecraft Live!* project invites the audience to create their own stories which, although partial and based on fragments, produce a contemporary engagement with the particular historical legacy of Wollstonecraft: her work is discovered and celebrated through the embodied participation of the twenty-first-century audience in both live site-specific performances and on film.

As this project has unfolded, the performance and film elements have undergone a progressive exteriorization away from the original site of performance, Newington Green. Subsequent iterations of selected elements of the project include exhibitions specially curated for galleries in the UK, the USA, and South Korea; these iterations suggest that the nature of the original 'site', Newington Green in this example, can be performed theatrically; its multimedia inflection provides it with a 'distance' that is nevertheless founded in the particularity of Newington Green. The combination of a site-based iteration and multimedia rethinks the scope of the history and geography associated with Mary Wollstonecraft and the liberation of both subjugated women and men.

Appendix: *The Wollstonecraft Live Experience!* chronology

2011

Mary on the Green: Celebrating Mary Wollstonecraft, The Gallery, Stoke Newington, Hackney, London. Fragments & Monuments's artists talk about their new book and about Strangers in the Neighbourhood, a collaboration between Anna Birch and Taey Iohe with Roberta Wedge, a Mary Wollstonecraft blogger. www.stokenewingtonliteraryfestival.com/

2010

Wollstonecraft Live! at Hackney Museum, London, UK, featured *A Vindication of the Rights of Woman* by Mary Wollstonecraft (1792) from the Hackney Archive and a specially produced companion volume and art book *The Wollstonecraft Live Experience!* by Anna Birch and Taey Iohe (2010). It was selected by *Time Out* for its critic's choice. www.fragmentsandmonuments.com

Wollstonecraft Live! at Portavillion Inside/Outside Cinema: specially curated projection for pre-Olympic cultural event, Gillett Square, East London, UK.

2009

Fragments & Monuments films on www.youtube.com

2008

Taey Iohe invited artist for Eonni (*Sister) is back* creates installation *Lure of the Lawn* featuring Newington Green, Hackney, London, UK and *Sleepwalkers,* Gyeonggi Museum of Modern Art, South Korea. http://www.gmoma.or.kr/eng/dis/dis_lastdis_view.asp?seq= 34&st= &sv= &st2=

Transhistorical Performative Lecture: Na Hye-Seok and Mary Wollstonecraft Live!, Anna Birch and Taey Iohe, International Federation of Theatre Research: The Art Center, the Graduate Center and the Law School of Chung-Ang University, Seoul, South Korea.

Strangers in the Neighbourhood is the artists' collaboration between Anna Birch and Taey Iohe: letter-writing, walking, workshop, tea party, websites, and conversations in London and Seoul.

2007

The Wollstonecraft Live Experience! (Isadora version) outdoor projection and live music at Newington Green, London, UK.

Wollstonecraft Live! a multimedia history of Mary Wollstonecraft Britain's first feminist. A.I.R. Gallery, New York, USA.

The Wollstonecraft Live Experience! at Ruskin Gallery, Anglia University, UK.

2005

SPICE Festival, Hackney, London, UK

Spit-Lit Festival, Hackney, UK

Wollstonecraft Live!, written by Kaethe Fine, conceived by Anna Birch and Kaethe Fine, and produced and directed by Anna Birch. Multimedia, site-specific performance in Hackney Unitarian Chapel and on Newington Green, London, UK, and short film *VINDICATION*, written by Kaethe Fine and directed by Anna Birch.

2002

Di's Midsummer Night Party (Keyworx version), screened the Cochrane Theatre, Royal College of Art and OMSK, London, UK.

2001

Di's Midsummer Night Party, outdoor projection of site-specific performance onto Clissold House, Stoke Newington, London.

2000

Di's Midsummer Night Party, exterior and interior site-specific performance at Clissold House, Stoke Newington, London. Mary Wollstonecraft is invited to a millennium party hosted by Princess Diana at Clissold House, Stoke Newington, Hackney, London, UK (walking distance from Newington Green).

Notes

1. There is now a plaque, unveiled on Newington Green on 8 March 2011, see Islington Council (2011).
2. Earlier versions of the discussion relating to Mary Wollstonecraft and Newington Green have appeared in Birch (2008, 2009, 2011).
3. Islington Greenspace is run by Islington Council as a part of their regeneration strategy to increase access to urban 'green' spaces.

4. This is from Kaethe Fine's unpublished script for *Wollstonecraft Live!* (2005).
5. The first night of *Wollstonecraft Live!* celebrated the completion of the regeneration of Newington Green and many tickets were complementary to thank the local community for their participation in the regeneration programme.
6. Mary Wollstonecraft was played by Katharine Vernez (Black British), Ros Phillips (White British), and Sadiqua Akhtar (Asian British) to reflect the local and culturally diverse demographic. This approach to integrated casting offered multiple versions of Wollstonecraft to challenge a single, dominant version of her story.
7. Performing 'site' as an act of resistance in the context of feminist performance studies is to explore how working outside traditional theatre and gallery venues can expand the gaze and the engagement for the audience/spectator. The use of multimedia facilitates the construction of Newington Green as a gendered site as well. Wollstonecraft's own writing works to triangulate the scenographic and dramaturgical vocabularies of this early twenty-first-century work. The box dress costumes were designed to critique the 'tea cup' shape of eighteenth-century skirts and the suppression of women through fashion and dress codes: Ferris notes that '[t]he actresses' skirts are the cages of Wollstonecraft's critique. Yet Wollstonecraft does not "plume herself." Instead, she works' (2006, p.79).

> Confined, then, in cages
> like the feathered race,
> they have nothing
> to do but to plume
> themselves, and stalk
> with mock majesty from
> perch to perch.
>
> (Mary Wollstonecraft,
> 1975, p.146)

The Mary Wollstonecraft performers wearing the box dresses continually formed and re-formed as they worked as film crew, making sculptural patterns of threes, twos and a single Mary, all contributing to the construction of a live and fragmented monument to Wollstonecraft herself.
8. *Wollstonecraft Live!* (2005) was repeated twice a night for four nights. The second audience waited to enter the chapel, viewing the performance and film projections on Newington Green, as well as the first audience who were now leaving the Green. The fast turnaround for the performers and the repetition of the show suggested a looped video recording that was never-ending, where the 'performers' included passers-by, the ticketed audience, the production's actors and Newington Green itself.
9. By harnessing multimedia, in this case photography, to capture a key image, the legacy of Mary Wollstonecraft is reproduced in a further iteration. This artefact facilitates the journey of the Wollstonecraft legacy beyond the site of Newington Green to a display in the exhibition at Hackney Museum (as discussed later in this chapter).

10. The publisher of *A Vindication of the Rights of Woman*, Joseph Johnson (1738–1809), also lived on Newington Green.
11. Dillon (2006) explores further the use of multilayering that the British-based photographer Idris Khan deploys.
12. See Birch (2006) for an analysis of the semiotic shift of meanings achieved through the recontextualization of theatre from new writing based in the theatre building to site-specific performance.
13. In 'Movement's contagion the kinaesthetic impact of performance', Susan Leigh Foster discusses how motor neurons seem to approximate the 'hyper-linked world that has emerged with the advent of new technologies'. She goes on to say:

> It likewise summons up the theories of performativity, such as those pro-posed by Judith Butler in her application of speech act theory in the 1990's. The perceiver no longer performs contact improvisation with the environment, but instead rehearses and simulates multiple roles, through his or her own actions as well as those of others. In the process of rehears-ing these roles, individuals formulate a self, not as an entity that will then perform an action, but rather as performance itself.
>
> (2008, p.55–6)

14. The global reach of the Internet links Newington Green to the rest of the world via a series of websites: www.wollstonecraftlive.com, www.fragmentsandmonuments.com, www.theperformancekit.com and www.youtube.com.
15. Cora Kaplan notes the difficulty of the process of biography and its impact on the Wollstonecraft legacy:

> Wollstonecraft is a key figure in late eighteenth century feminism – not then of course a movement, although there were other women with sim-ilar ideas. She was both original, bold and eloquent – and her ideas about women yoked to progressive politics more broadly. Although her influ-ence was felt throughout the nineteenth century her heterodox personal life, revealed by Godwin after her death, made even nineteenth century women like the feminist Harriet Martineau – who drew from her ideas wary of aligning themselves with her [sic]. The rise and rise of her rep-utation really belongs to various phases of the women's movement and feminist scholarship in the 20th and 21st centuries.
>
> (cited by Mary on the Green [2011])

16. Paine made a major contribution to the development of the American Con-stitution in the eighteenth century. Harvard University, which was originally founded as a dissenter's academy on Newington Green in the seventeenth century, makes a further connection with the USA.

9
Contemporary *Ekkeklemas* in Site-Specific Performance

Lesley Ferris

In Aeschylus' play *Agamemnon,* the door through which Clytemnestra leads her husband Agamemnon to a bloody death in a bath serves as a model for the theatrical space imagined and replicated in Western theatre practice. According to Froma I Zeitlin (1990), this infamous act of marital violence articulates stage conventions that map gender roles as spatially defined by outside and inside. Outside is the masculine world, a place where dramatic action unfolds, where choruses representing the male citizens of Athens pass judgement and offer advice to their leaders. Inside is the interior world of the home, the domain of the women, one that is unknown and potentially treacherous. Outside is public space; inside space is private, unseen, contained, and, as Agamemnon discovers, dangerous – fatally so.

Zeitlin offers a four-part analysis of Greek tragedy, examining the body, theatrical space, plot, and mimesis as the principal attributes or 'indispensible traits of the theatrical experience' (1990, p.71). I focus here on her considerations of theatrical space and how her analysis provides a framework for considering contemporary examples of site-specific performance and their gendered implications. She explains,

> If tragedy can be viewed as a kind of recurrent masculine initiation, for adults as well as for the young, and if drama, more broadly, is designed as an education for its male citizens in the democratic city, then the aspects of the play world I wish to bring into sharper relief [. . . are] all linked in some radical way with the feminine.
>
> (Zeitlin, 1990, p.68)

One of the principal means by which she makes her case is a rethinking of the use of the *ekkeklema,* the rolling platform used to transport bodies from the door of the stage facade. Using a feminist critical analysis of

135

Greek classical theatre may seem a stretch in terms of thinking about contemporary site-specific performance, but I bring three supportive threads to my argument. First, the Greek classical canon is the foundation on which Western theatre rests. For many, this male-only theatre represented a cultural high point that was indelibly linked to gender. As Goethe famously explained in his 1788 essay, 'The ancients, at least in the best periods for art and morality, did not permit women on the stage. Their plays were organized in such a way that either women could be more or less dispensed with, or else female roles were played by an actor who had prepared himself especially for them' (1993, p.48). While actual women were 'dispensed with' in Greek tragedy, Zeitlin demonstrates the prevalence of the feminine in the artistic and cultural practice of theatre.

Second, Greek theatre production is the 'original' site-specific work in the Western tradition with its history of written and performed extant texts. David Wiles explains the importance of the natural world and its relation to the Greek stage: 'Greek theatres were modifications of the landscape rather than impositions, and Greek architects always built their theatres with attention to the view, unlike the Romans who enclosed the audience within high walls' (2000, p.113). He argues the significance of the open, outdoor space in relation to the written texts which, in contrast to modern theatre's focus on interpersonal relationships, dealt with 'the relationship between human beings and their environment' (2000, p.113). Furthermore, the sheer scale of the Greek amphitheatre situated the human body in a physical correlation with the natural world. Wiles places theatrical space at the centre of Greek theatre: 'The topography of the theatre shaped the meaning of the plays' (2000, p.114).

My third reason to consider this particular reading of site-specific performance is informed by Rosi Braidotti's (1994) work on 'nomadism', wherein the 'nomad' is not an actual wanderer but a means of thinking about female subjectivity through a fluid, interactive exploration of identity. Such considerations include 'blurring boundaries without burning bridges' (Braidotti, 1994, p.4) because '[i]t is the subversion of set conventions that defines the nomadic state, not the literal act of traveling' (Braidotti, 1994, p.5). Here, the conventions are those of situated space.

I address three site-specific works that in their staging practice broke the boundaries of conventional theatre space, each in very different ways, but all linked to Zeitlin's understanding of theatrical space in Greek tragedy. These productions all employ variations on the *ekkeklema*. As Zeitlin explains, '[t]ragedy insists most often on exhibiting [the] body, even typically bringing corpses back onstage so as to expose them to public view' (1990, p.72). I read Zeitlin's articulation of the potentially destabilizing function of the *ekkeklema* in the context of Braidotti's 'nomadic subjects' to rethink the ways in which site operates in contemporary site-specific performances by women: the *ekkeklema* and the nomadic subject enable Zeitlin and Braidotti to argue for a border erasure that can undermine both literal and metaphoric boundaries. In theatrical terms, one of the most significant ways in which this is spatialized is through a shift in focus of the roles of – and boundaries between – actor and spectator. Fiona Templeton's *YOU – The City*, produced in New York City in 1988 and in London in 1989, was a radical reinterpretation of the understanding of site-specific performance at the time that incorporated an interactive relationship between the performer and the spectator. In the 1990s, African-American theatre artist Robbie McCauley created a trilogy of works in various locations in the USA that fostered powerful, fraught and poignant discussions on race. In 2005, the London-based British company Fragments & Monuments, committed to 'unearth[ing] and reactiv[ating] the stories of women's achievement' (Fragments & Monuments, 2005), produced *Wollstonecraft Live!* on Newington Green in North London.

In all three the conventional notion of a theatrical spectator as someone who is seated and static is transformed into a moving body, a disruptive *ekkeklema*, as it were. While for Braidotti (1994) the nomadic state is not the 'literal act of traveling', actual movement is required to provoke and transmute the silent spectator into an active traveller. Thus the spectator becomes a nomad, a roving, critically engaged eye whose presence gives new and startling meaning to the theatrical experience. I argue that a defining aspect of site-specific work is its ability to destabilize audience expectations and dissolve customary, time-honoured boundaries of theatrical space.

YOU – The City

Fiona Templeton's work played with the urban landscape in an intricate layered manner that confounded conceptions of stage space and performance. While most outdoor site-specific works perform to large numbers of spectators, *YOU – The City* played to an 'audience of one' (Templeton, 1990, p.ix). First created for New York City, the concept and the published poetic text was adapted and reconfigured for other urban landscapes. I was a 'client' (the term used by Templeton to describe the singular audience member) for the second iteration of the work in London as part of the LIFT Festival in 1989. The title of the work and the poetic monologues stress the one-on-one nature of the work as 'the "you" of the text is addressed directly to the client' (Templeton, 1990, p.vii).

The performance began in an office building in the financial district of London where a receptionist greeted me. From that point, I travelled by foot to various sites in the East End that included Spitalfields Market, Brick Lane, an empty basketball court, and what appeared to be a partially bombed-out church. At each site, and occasionally in the middle of the pavement, I encountered performers who approached me, singled me out, and spoke to me in a heightened poetic language that was inflected with the word 'you.' At one point a taxi drove me to a high-rise block of flats; shortly after I entered a small sweet shop. At this point I realized I was with a few other clients, which transformed the single-client experience into a small gathering of three or four people wondering what was next. Suddenly someone thrust a phone into my hand and asked me to take the call. The phone rang, and was answered, but the 'conversation' was confusing, out of kilter. The person on the other end of the line hung up. Following the sweet shop encounter, we were led to a ground floor flat. There the phone rang: we all looked at each other; I became the designated person to answer the phone, and hearing a confused voice at the other end, I realized that the call came from the sweet shop and that a fellow client, whose ticket was ten minutes behind mine, was speaking to me. The final stop was a pub, where other clients before me had gathered, and I was handed a program. Some of the actors who I had encountered earlier were present and there was a celebratory atmosphere and drinking a pint with the actors stood in for the customary curtain call.

In the years since I witnessed this work, I have mused on its revelatory force. I saw parts of the city that I had never encountered before and in the company of complete strangers who spoke directly at me without expecting me to answer. My role as a client forced me to question my definition of theatre while I simultaneously marvelled at my encounter with the 'you' that was 'me' and the 'you' that was the city. My physical presence, my motion, my mobility, in the primarily public space of London gave me a new awareness of the city's presence and particularly its relation to me. Indeed, I can now see that I was experiencing Braidotti's notion of the nomad as someone who 'has a sharpened sense of territory but no possessiveness about it' (1994, p.36). Braidotti continues, explaining that nomadism 'is not fluidity without borders but rather an acute awareness of the nonfixity of boundaries. It is the intense desire to go on trespassing, transgressing' (1994, p.36).

In a programme note, Templeton offers insight into her work:

'Why YOU? "You" – the pronoun of recognition, accusation, identification; beyond the visual, animate, returnable. "Yes, you".'

This ambiguous explanation of her work's theme goes beyond linking the 'you' to the urban landscape and plays with the word, the pronoun, as a moniker of the self, as a marker of identity, as a means of communication. One critic concurs with Braidotti's nomadic musing by describing Templeton's work as an exercise in 'reshaping and renaming' and suggests that a more convenient description of Templeton is not as a *metteur en scène* but as a *'metteur en rue'* (Duša, 1991, p.64). This critic continues to extend such 'renaming' by suggesting that she focuses on 'topography' instead of 'dramaturgy' (Duša, 1991, p.64). Instead of an audience encountering a conventional landscape of language and dramatic action, spectators experience a literal landscape, a city's surface of man-made features and surfaces.

Templeton's use of the urban city speaks to Zeitlin's gendered theatrical space. The stage of Greek theatre was identified as outdoors, in the public realm, the site of masculine presence and power. For Templeton the entire city landscape is a stage, and although she begins the journey in an office building in the financial district (in the New York performance it started in an office on Times Square), both beginnings are strongholds of masculine influence and authority. The singular clients, the 'Yous' so pointedly referenced in the work's title, are positioned in relation to the city's immense and overpowering geography. By moving the stage space to the city streets, Templeton holds up the public realm for scrutiny, an inquiry into the relationship between size, space, and the human form, whose diminutive vulnerable presence is transient, fleeting, ephemeral compared to the monumental solidity of the surrounding buildings. Despite their out-of-doors presence, Templeton's clients become feminized in relation to the monolithic cityscape, the masculine public world.

Yet at the same time as Templeton plays on the established and long-held binary of the stage space, she also renders it obsolete. As performance artist Tim Etchells says in relation to the London rendering of *YOU – The City*, 'The old dialectical separations between inside and outside, fiction and reality, self and other, audience and performer, were here exploited and blurred' (1994, p.119). My own response was a constant and troubling worry of not knowing what was 'real' and what was performed, fictional. At times I could not tell if my meeting with someone was intended or not. Was the street cleaner authentic or an actor performing a role? Was the man pulling rubbish out of a bin and giving me furtive looks followed by a smirking smile a homeless person or an actor in role? Stanton B Garner, Jr. describes the way the single client in the New York performance 'undergoes a series of encounters that explore the line between the personal and the anonymous in urban interactions: addressing a security guard, riding a cab, encountering a street person' (2002, p.105). He sees the work as a hybrid, providing 'an experience of the simultaneously private and public' (Garner, 2002, p.105). In notes to the published script, Templeton states, 'Like an analogue of the mind in the world and vice versa, the city is an experience of simultaneous interiority and exteriority' (1990, p.144). This simultaneity has an intriguing connection to classical Greek stage space's outside/inside boundaries. As Zeitlin points out, 'the arrangement of architectural space on stage [...] continually suggests a relational tension between inside and outside' (1990, p.71). Within this stratified, delineated theatrical world, the Greeks created a device – the *ekkeklema* – for bringing the inside to the outside. This rolling platform, the epitome perhaps of 'relational tension', delivered the dead bodies of those killed offstage, many of whom were, like Agamemnon, murdered by powerful and unruly women. Templeton's work does not use the *ekkeklema* per se, but the function of the *ekkeklema* – to connect the two worlds – is achieved nonetheless in perhaps a more profound way by the blurring of the inside/outside binary in terms of physical space and physical being. This boundary blurring, with its capacity to underscore issues of gender, permeates my site-specific examples; it is, I suggest, a defining characteristic of site-specific theatre in general.

Mississippi Freedom

African-American performer Robbie McCauley's *Primary Sources* uses the meaning and significance of geography to create 'an alternate public sphere' (Cieri, 2009, p.1), an approach that echoes Greek theatre's relationship between 'human beings and their environment' (Wiles, 2000, p.113). In McCauley's work, bodies are marked in invisible ways such that memory recalls various US geographic sites. The trilogy, on race relations in the USA, employed three crucial events in the 1960s and 1970s that took place in Mississippi, Boston, and Los Angeles (LA): the voting rights and desegregation struggle in the early 1960s (*Mississippi Freedom*, 1992); the school bus controversy a decade later

(*TURF: A Conversational Concert in Black and White*, 1993); and the conflict between the LA Police Department and the Black Panthers in 1969 (*The Other Weapon*, 1994). While Marie Cieri notes that artists have focused on such topics before, McCauley's 'approach to these themes has been unique within an American art world that has increasingly seen, supported and at times debated the merits of social-issue oriented subject matter developed in community settings' (2009, p.2). Cieri urges that McCauley's work – her collaborations with different communities and the trilogy's impact on local audiences – deserves renewed consideration because of the insights offered into 'the role theater can play within popular discourse on social issues' (2009, p.2). Using the theories of Claude Lefort and Nancy Fraser, she identifies *Primary Sources* as creating a site where genuine conversation on challenging topics takes place. I want to add another dimension by highlighting the connection between cites of history and sites of geography: *Primary Sources*'s site-specificity demands a rendering of performance space that requires multiple locations and a breaking down of traditional performance boundaries, particularly the dividing line between spectators and actors.[1]

I provide a brief analysis of the first work of the trilogy, *Mississippi Freedom* (1992), which revisited the places of the Freedom Rides in Jackson, Mississippi. The Freedom Rides were acts of civil disobedience involving activists who rode interstate buses into the segregated South with the express purpose of getting arrested under local laws that still upheld the 'separate but equal' doctrine despite the Interstate Commerce Commission ruling opposing it (1955) and the subsequent Supreme Court ruling which outlawed racial segregation in restaurants and bus terminals (1960). The first Freedom Ride began in May 1961 in Virginia with plans to continue throughout areas of the South. By the time the riders reached Jackson, Mississippi mob violence had broken out in Montgomery, Alabama, and the world news was inundated with images of police brutality and lawlessness. The governor of Mississippi agreed to a behind-the-scenes deal with the Kennedy White House to protect the riders from the violence by escorting them into Jackson under police protection and the National Guard. Once in the city, however, the riders were promptly arrested when they crossed the state-enforced racial boundary by entering white-only facilities. The Freedom Riders kept up the political pressure by ensuring as many arrests as possible to cause the local prison to overflow. The local authorities then placed the activists in the Mississippi State Penitentiary where they suffered extreme conditions and abuse.

McCauley's focus on this moment in the first part of the *Primary Sources* trilogy sets the stage for considering the site-specific nature of this work in what may seem an unorthodox manner. McCauley's work mirrors the geographic sweep of this particular civil rights action. The Freedom Rides themselves were engineered to spotlight the multi-sited presence of Jim Crow laws in a 'democratic' society. There was no solitary place that was the target; racism was endemic and everywhere in the segregated South. But the violence in Mississippi was particularly harrowing and the back-handed 'support' of the White House added another dimension to the challenges faced by the activists. McCauley's creative process required multiple site visits to Jackson as she met with local residents – both white and African-American – who had been involved in some way with the Freedom Rides.

Mississippi Freedom opened in 1992 at the Smith Robertson Museum and Cultural Centre in Jackson. This museum, part of the City of Jackson's holdings, has great historical significance. It was originally the Smith Robertson School, the first public school built for African-Americans in the city. While this building resonates with the past, McCauley's choice of location for her work cannot be bound by a single building, no matter what its cultural and historical significance. In an interview about creating this work, McCauley stresses the significance of her multi-sited process:

> I am drawn to Mississippi because I fear it. More an actor than anything, I long to confront that fear and talk out of it. Riding the roads here, I can't help thinking about Emmett Till, Goodman, Chaney and Schwerner, Fannie Lou Hamer. At night I think of the darkness. They were taken into the woods, the trees, basements of jails. I am overwhelmed by sadness and pain, but I can't cry. Riding the desolate trek from Philipp to Money, Mississippi, along the Tallahatchie River, where they dumped Emmett Till's body. [...] I am full of rage. I breathe into it, and know this, too, is why I had to come here.
>
> (1993, p.88)

'Riding the roads' with the ghosts of the Freedom Riders, McCauley finds herself immersed in memory. She takes the back roads of the state in order to witness the sites of past violence. Thus she passes through Money, the town where Emmett Till, the 14-year-old from Chicago visiting his family, was observed supposedly talking to a white woman, then on to Glendora where Till was tortured and brutally murdered, and finally to Phillip, where his body was disposed in the river (McCauley, 1993, p.96).

McCauley's creative process, infused with actual travel, intersects with Braidotti's nomadic concept. Braidotti argues that while 'the image of "nomadic subjects" is inspired by the experience of peoples or cultures that are literally nomadic, the nomadism in question here refers to the kind of critical consciousness that resists settling into socially coded modes of thought and behavior' (1994, p.5). Braidotti, simply put, refutes the Platonic model of a fixed, stable identity that still, to a large degree, holds sway in mainstream discourse. Instead she calls for fluid identities that embrace 'the construction of new forms of interrelatedness and collective political projects' (Braidotti, 1994, p.5). She describes her nomadic movement of the mind as 'a performative metaphor that allows for otherwise unlikely encounters and unsuspected sources of interaction and experience and of knowledge' (Braidotti, 1994, p.6). I see McCauley's project through the Braidotti lens as one of literal travel in which bodily movement is necessary, central to the work in order to deal with her autobiographical response to civil rights issues: she is afraid, she is angry, 'full of rage' (McCauley, 1993, p.88). Her personal encounter with the sites of racial violence in the state of Mississippi propel her to develop a way of working that can both interrogate and capture the multi-sited imperative of this experience.

In 1990 McCauley began her research for *Mississippi Freedom* by visiting the state, talking to numerous people about the work's subject matter and the goal of exploring the racial dynamics of the civil rights era. The mixture of fear and rage drove her need to articulate these feelings using performance as a public forum. During her early visits, McCauley chose 11 collaborators from the Jackson area with different backgrounds and ages who worked with her for about a year. McCauley was in residence in Jackson for about a third of the development time and in her absence the actor-collaborators worked to identify others in the state with personal stories to tell about the civil rights movement (Cieri, 2009, p.3). These residents were called 'witnesses' throughout the collaborative process and their interviews served as both the work's primary source material and the basis for dialogue between the actors and McCauley:

Nothing of what was exchanged between us in rehearsals was any more sensational than what happens in other black or white lives in this country, but it was all informed by the extremity of Mississippi's apartheid and historical isolation. The willingness of the actors to give up resistance to confronting that history, to engage in relentless dialogue about it, and to admit cultural secrets, made the work rich.

(McCauley, 1993, p.90)

The work's richness was further enhanced by her insistence that the actors play themselves as a means of asserting the present tense, the here and now moment of live performance. Cieri, the *Primary Sources* producer, describes the creative process:

Most of the cast's get-togethers with McCauley consisted of intense dialogues about race, class, politics, religion and sexuality, and there were many fights, tears and silences mixed in with reasoned conversation. With the cast's consent, a good deal of what went on in private became public as it was mixed with excerpts from the interviews and improvisational material in performances.

(2009, p.3–4)

McCauley describes the performances as 'a jazz-like, organized improvisation' and 'conversational music that reflects the language of ordinary people' (cited in Cieri, 2009, p.4). After opening in Jackson on 29 May 1992, *Mississippi Freedom* toured the state throughout the year. 'Talkback' sessions of 90 minutes followed each performance when the majority of the audience stayed on to continue discussions initiated by the performance. Cieri describes the way 'the audience played a large part in shaping the tone and content of each evening. McCauley and the cast set the drama in motion, and audiences were responsible for adding much of the unique content, analysis and emotion each night' (Cieri, 2009, p.4). The customary boundary between the performers and the spectators was overturned in three significant ways. First, the performance text was unstable, 'jazz-like', improvisational, and its transformations largely depended on its geographic location. Each performance location in Mississippi was a site of civil rights history that informed elements of what could be called an itinerant text. Second, the actors performed multiple characters, often themselves, as well as community figures who in many cases participated as audience members. Third, on a number of occasions spectators came onto the stage and gave witness to their own role in the Freedom Rides of the 1960s. These acts of witnessing blurred the boundary between acting, as in performing a role, and 'acting', as in articulating one's activism. This open-ended strategy underscored the significance of the itinerant text as constantly moving and shifting, always a nomad, never frozen in time.

Zeitlin writes of the central door in the Greek tragic stage's facade as an emblematic opening that is the threshold to inside/outside. The door 'continually establishes a symbolic dialectic between public and private, seen and unseen, open and secret, even known and unknown' (Zeitlin, 1990, p.75). McCauley's creative process moves back and forth over a threshold, a door if you will: on one side is the secret, hidden, and publicly unknown past; on the other is the era's official history. Using multiple geographical sites, McCauley is able to cite a multi-vocal history indelibly linked to place, location, site. Such a creative endeavour evokes Suzan-Lori Parks's belief that theatre is the place for 'making' history: 'because so much of African-American history has been unrecorded, dismembered, washed out, one of my tasks as a play-wright is to [...] locate the ancestral burial ground, dig for bones, find bones, hear the bones sing, write it down' (1995, p.4). By making 'the bones sing', McCauley insists on the secrets crossing over the threshold into a public sphere. From the actors' readiness to give up their resis-tance to confronting their own history, to witnesses telling their buried stories of their own fear and anger, the narrative threads of *Mississippi Freedom* designate the whole state of Mississippi as a site-specific arena that is charged with the bones of memory and a reclaimed collective history.

Wollstonecraft Live!

The inside/outside aspect of a performance is central to Anna Birch's *Wollstonecraft Live!*, a multimedia, site-specific work that begins inside the Unitarian Chapel on Newington Green in London. In the eighteenth century, this chapel was a hotbed of radical political views and intellec-tual debate. Mary Wollstonecraft (1759–97), who opened a school for girls on the Green in 1784, attended this chapel, which was led by the Reverend Richard Price. Price was infamous for his support of US inde-pendence and the French Revolution and his home in Newington Green became a meeting place for other leading British radicals. It was here that Wollstonecraft's reputation as an articulate, independent thinker started. In opposition to the tragic Greek stage space, where 'inside' stands for the private and the unknown, the chapel was a sanctuary where radical ideas were made public. Even the chapel's original name – Dissenting Chapel – proudly proclaims the importance of public speech and dialogue. And it is here that *Wollstonecraft Live!* resurrects Mary Wollstonecraft.

Fragments & Monuments, a London-based company dedicated to site-specific work charged with historical ghosts, produced *Wollstonecraft Live!*, which was conceived by Anna Birch, written by Kaethe Fine, and directed by Birch in 2005. The company's remit is to explore the dialectic between retrieved and ephemeral fragments of history and monolithic rock-solid monuments; the non-linear, fragmented script veers between eighteenth-century prose of Wollstonecraft's published works and con-temporary slang. The story that unfolds is as fragmented as its verbal text, swerving between full-blown period-style film projections, live actors, and a film crew.

The work provides manifold modes of storytelling framed by three different worlds. The first is the world of the play about Mary Wollstonecraft, with characters in period costume, a world initiated in the chapel with a screening of a short costume drama that identifies the main characters in Mary's story. The second is the world of a film being made of this play, with all the crew members, from Casting Director, Boom Operator, Camera Operator, and so on. The third, the world of the spectator, includes audience members with tickets alongside specta-tor characters – film extras – who hover, like the rest of the audience, on the fringes of the film set, watching the filming while commenting on its making. As the audience is already semiotized as 'film extras' by the Assistant Director, the difference between spectator and film extra is continually challenged: who is acting, who is not?

Like Templeton's work, the audience of *Wollstonecraft Live!* walks promenade-style to various locations, under the guidance of an Assistant Director and a film crew. From the initiating scene in the chapel, to out-doors, crossing the street to the Green, spectators find spaces to observe the unfolding narrative, which, once outdoors, transforms to the staging of a film company filming an event in Wollstonecraft's life. The sites of filming shift and change on the Green, as does the role of the audience. Once out of the chapel, the Assistant Director explains the importance of 'extras' to filmmaking, asking some of the spectators to assist when needed. The Green is full of activity: crew members are busily moving about checking their clipboards; the actors are fitted with sophisticated body microphones; board operators stand at the ready behind a fleet of sound and light boards; piles of film equipment cases litter the grass; and numerous photographers rove, ready to start filming.

These worlds overlap and collide, and the sense of doubling and simultaneity are core elements for the audience to negotiate. Enhancing the sense of multiplicity is the level of technology that is crucial to the story: a film is being made of this performance, but the performance of filmmaking itself is being filmed. Here we can consider Birch's use of projection screens. The performance started inside the chapel with a screening of the period-style film on a modest-sized screen hanging over the pulpit. Outdoors the visual presence is on a grander scale. A large prominent screen shows the casting reel tape of auditions for the role of Mary; the actor's audition text is from Wollstonecraft's letters. Other projections include real-time filming of the spectators themselves watching a scene. A spectator can watch live actors perform and with a redirected gaze see themselves on the screen watching the live scene. This playfulness overturns the inside/outside characteristic of film, where, for instance, screenings take place indoors. It also eliminates the separation between actor and spectator. In this world spectators *are* performers. These technologized scenes contrast the eighteenth-century world of Mary Wollstonecraft, but that contrast is central to the concerns of Fragments & Monuments. In the programme, the company describes its process, using live performance, installation, and digital technologies to investigate 'the interface between live and mediated performance, audience and performer, location and history' (Fragments & Monuments, 2005). The performance's engagement with the layers of history evokes Laurie Anderson's song *The Dream Before*, which pays homage to Walter Benjamin's angel of history, which in turn invokes Paul Klee's 1921 drawing 'Angelus Novus': 'She said: what is history?/And he said: history is an angel/Being blown backwards into the future' (Anderson citing Benjamin in Braidotti, 1994, p.280). This history has momentum, is a driving force; and this movement evolves through this work's multilayered performance strategies.

The entire performance pushes at, interrogates, and takes apart notions of authenticity; the site-specific location underscores and draws attention to authenticity while simultaneously questioning its veracity. It was here in Newington Green that for a period of time Mary Wollstonecraft lived. Is it possible to bring her back to life? If so, the only way perhaps to do so is through technology, the great giver of a second life.

And what a second life this is: it is by no means confined to a single actor playing the eponymous heroine of the work. When three women play the role of Mary Wollstonecraft, these triple Marys appear in the chapel, evoking a feminist trinity, demanding a multi-vocal presence in a space that is traditionally a male sphere of influence. This triumvirate combines with the local landscape of technological excess (cameras, screens, cables, boom microphones), a deliberate reconfiguration of Zeitlin's concept of inside/outside. The three women skew the conventional filmic concept of the singular hero/heroine. The visible and ever-present techniques meld with the Green, destroying the traditional, invisible role that cameras play. Technology is now firmly outside, no longer concealed out of sight. Echoing Zeitlin's explanation of the destabilizing potential of the *ekkeklema*, the stage device that delivers the dead to the public, outside space, *Wollstonecraft Live!* uses contemporary technology to deliver the dead while telling us, through performance, that history is always an act of reinvention. We can only have small pieces, snippets of a singular moment, a place, fragments of a life. And even those are moving too quickly, they are blurred by relentless time, or as the camera tracking shot moves in for a close-up. *Wollstonecraft Live!* stands as an example of Braidotti's 'philosophy of "as if" ' that allows for and encourages a 'politics of parody' (1994, p.5). Thus it is precisely through its parodic nature that *Wollstonecraft Live!* offers the mobile spectators the space for an encounter with a certain history that celebrates a collective feminist presence.

All three works overturn conventional expectations of the separation of the role of the actor and the spectator. In *Wollstonecraft Live!*, several actors play the roles of spectators and, functioning much like a Greek chorus, comment on the action; the film crew perform their roles outside, in the open space of the green, instead of their normally hidden 'behind-the-scenes' location; and actors appear simultaneously in film projections and in the flesh. The roving audience is at times part of the action if they happen to be near one of the scenes, and throughout their real-time images are captured and projected on the large outdoor screens. In *Mississippi Freedom* the actors not only play conventional roles, but their own lives become staged while the spectators transform into actor-witnesses during the course of a performance. *YOU – The City* undoes the clarity of role and actor by placing the nomadic performers amid a general unknowing public, confounding the spectators' ability to tell the difference between them. Those same spectators find themselves momentarily transformed into actors when they unwittingly answer a ringing phone. Transformations are made possible by the site-specific nature of each work.

While Zeitlin lays the foundation for my reading of theatrical space and site-specific performance through her analysis of the Greek stage, Braidotti's work on embodiment and her concept of the 'nomad' illuminates the ability of these three works to destabilize and challenge set conventions. Both Zeitlin and Braidotti employ an *ekkeklema*-like border erasure as a means of undermining both literal and metaphoric boundaries. It is through the site-specific nature of each of these works that the inside/outside element of theatre performance is overturned, undone as an all-embracing binary that confines stage practice to an implicitly gendered theatre space. Templeton, McCauley, and Birch expose and question these restrictions by imagining alternative routes to tell their stories: they use varying modes of 'as if' as site-specific performance strategies. Like Walter Benjamin's angel of history, as participants in this work we are 'blown backwards into the future' (cited in Braidotti, 1994, p.280).

Note

1. There is much to explore with McCauley's rich and provocative work, which examines issues of identity, race, and the notions of speaking out or being silenced, but this is beyond the scope of this chapter.

10
'Places, Like Property Prices, Go Up and Down': Site-Specificity, Regeneration, and *The Margate Exodus*

Louise Owen

In October 2006, conservative magazine *The Spectator* published a review of *Exodus Day*, a day of live events staged in the struggling British seaside resort of Margate, and part of Artangel's project *The Margate Exodus*. Opening her review, critic Ruth Guilding (2006) submits to her reader a piece of common sense. 'Places,' she writes, 'like property prices, go up and down. Margate, in the most northerly corner of Kent, is just beginning the uncertain journey upwards again' (Guilding, 2006). She imagines 'place', the project's organizing concept, as a volatile asset whose value might be represented as such on a line graph; poverty-stricken Margate currently languishes at the bottom of the scale. The imaginary graph's x axis, 'time', spans the 1700s to date: the critic's introductory sketch of the town name-checks the Regency period, J M W Turner, mass tourism, culture-in-regeneration, and immigration and asylum, topping the list off with the observation that: 'By southeastern standards, houses are still pretty cheap. Tracey Emin is Margate's only success story' (Guilding, 2006). 'This,' Guilding (2006) continues, 'is where that strange, magical organisation Artangel comes in. It aims to make art outside the gallery, matching up artists, contexts and audiences to get something relevant, democratic and unmediated.'

This critic's rhetorical move from property market speculation and local 'bad-girl-artist-made-good' to transformative 'relevance', 'democracy', and 'unmediated-ness' in art-making 'outside the gallery' is surprising, not least because Artangel's exceptional projects are 'born from an open-ended commissioning process with an artist offered the opportunity to imagine something extraordinary' (Artangel, 2011) whose result may not necessarily possess the attributes Guilding

specifies. Her narrative does bear a relation, however, to the principles of a governmental discourse of culture-in-regeneration.[1] Geared
jointly and reciprocally towards stimulating accumulation and building
'social' (or 'community') 'cohesion' (DCMS, 2003, p.9), this was a core
cultural policy rationale for the New Labour government and closely
connected to the production of 'social inclusion' (DCMS, 2003, p.32),
a term that euphemizes economic participation (Miles and Paddison,
2005, p.836). As the government framed it, cultural provision might be
deployed as an economically regenerative means in a labile economy of
'attracting companies and investment; having a role in cultural tourism;
adding to land values' (DCMS, 2003, p.21), thus functioning as 'a catalyst to turn around whole communities' (DCMS, 2003, p.3) – a claim
that resonates favourably with liberatory accounts of theatrical performance and 'its power to bring together divided communities of different
kinds' (Boon and Plastow, 2004, p.1). While John Gray defines the 'social
cohesion' that might characterize such transformed communities as 'a
general consensus on basic values, a lack of widespread alienation and
anomie and an absence of marginalized and disaffected social groups'
(cited in Cameron, 2006, p.397), Angus Cameron offers an alternative
analysis: 'inclusion as cohesion is achieved when specific social problems are removed or rendered invisible such that they no longer deviate
from, or threaten, the "reasonable" norms of national society' (2006,
p.397). These '"reasonable" norms' include 'morality, responsibility,
independence and competitiveness' (Cameron, 2006, p.401), the character traits of neo-liberalism's ideal subject, protagonist of the nominally
post-imperial, postcolonial scene of globalization.

I examine *The Margate Exodus*'s projects – a combination of photography, visual art, performance, and film – as instances of contemporary
site-specific performance responding to this context. Far from consti-
tuting examples of 'unmediated' action, I suggest that they intersected
in complex and often contradictory ways with the effects and apparatuses of global economic change – and in particular these constructs of
British governmental policy – as they manifested culturally in the seaside town. I draw on Miwon Kwon's understanding of site-specificity as
'a spatio-political problematic' (2002, p.2) where site-specificity is a rad-
ically contextual matter of performative logic: 'the cultural mediation
of broader social, economic, and political processes that organize urban
life and urban space' (2002, p.3). This insight applies to Margate, a place
that continues to seek to offer tourists a retreat from urban life. In recent
decades, this ambition has been overdetermined by Margate's reputation as 'that favourite symbol of seaside economic collapse' (Walton,

2010, p.2). A genteel scene of sea-bathing as both therapeutic and recreational practice in the eighteenth century (Pimlott, 1947, p.58), Margate prospered in the twentieth century as a lively venue of popular tourism, sardonically represented by Lindsay Anderson's Free Cinema short *O Dreamland!* (1953). Following the decline of domestic tourism – according to Richard Samuel, chief executive of Thanet District Council, 'by the early 1980s the area had been dubbed Costa del Dole' (2010, p.83) – it is now, in comparison with other resorts on the south coast, 'marked by its physical isolation and relative deprivation' (HCCLGC, 2007, p.3). A consequence of the high volume of private rental property available in the area – in particular, former guesthouses now functioning as 'homes of multiple occupancy' and the expedient promotion of this accommodation by landlords – has been the resort's implication in processes of immigration management (Shared Intelligence, 2008, pp.18–23). Though by no means the only story to tell about the resort's current circumstances, filmmakers have favoured Margate as a source and location for cinematic interrogations of twenty-first-century poverty, adversity, and British identity, dramatizing the effects of the unequal distribution of wealth with questions of race, ethnicity, and nationhood. Penny Woolcock's film *Exodus* (2007) – the ultimate outcome of *The Margate Exodus* – joins Pawel Pawlikowski's *Last Resort* (2000) and *Gypo* (2005), the first British Dogme95 film.[2]

While these films represent hardship and struggle, the discourse of regeneration pitches cultural provision as a 'post-industrial' economic solution – the rewriting of place narratives for economic advantage (hence Margate's 'uncertain journey upwards'). In Margate, such provision includes Turner Contemporary, a seafront gallery that opened to enthusiastic acclaim in April 2011. Dreamland, the town's currently closed amusement park, which boasts a Grade II* listed scenic railway,[3] was used as a location for *The Margate Exodus*'s events. A central figure for 'regeneration' is the individual tourist, whether seen in revamped dockside sites (Baltic, Gateshead; Tate Modern, London), former manufacturing districts (Northern Quarter, Manchester) or indeed dedicated sites for holidaymaking. This mobile consumer of experience, whose discerning attention and disposable income are solicited by authorities and businesses alike, practices what John Urry characterizes as 'tourism reflexivity': 'identifying a particular place's location within the contours of geography, history and culture that swirl the globe, and in particular identifying that place's actual and potential material and semiotic resources' (2002, p.142). The establishment of Turner Contemporary represents one kind of deployment of 'actual and potential material and semiotic resources'; the staging of *The Margate Exodus*'s temporary performance projects, five years before, another. I argue that *The Margate Exodus*'s various modellings of 'site' – a significant category for Artangel's commissions – engaged in unexpected dialogue with the representational logics of 'inclusion', 'cohesion', and 'exclusion' and the subjects and forms of social action they imagine. Taking account of the productive effects of discourse in and for artistic practice, and the theatrical production of aesthetic 'immersion' which foregrounds and accentuates the individual audience member's active role 'in place', my analysis examines the limits and politics of the project's putatively 'unmediated' communication.

'In a different place, at a different time'

Artangel strongly asserts the importance of site, in the widest sense, to its commissions: whether located in the street, a vacant shop, a storage unit, or even gallery or theatre, 'the choice of environment irreducibly shapes the final work, making uprooting or relocating often impossible' (van Noord, 2002, p.11). Each work's 'immovability' entails that, from Jeremy Deller's participatory re-enactment of *The Battle of Orgreave* (2001) to Michael Landy's mechanized, conveyor belt-assisted destruction of all his possessions in *Break Down* (2001), acts of travel to witness the work *in situ* or understanding its context or environment are integral to its effects. For Claire Bishop (2002, p.26), Artangel works reflexively offer 'the "experience of experience" ': 'the whole experience of visiting each work acquires a purposive character comparable to that of a pilgrimage. You need your London *A-Z* and your wits about you' (Bishop, 2002, p.25) – an observation which enacts an interesting slippage between the morally impelled religious expedition and the pleasurable frisson produced by visiting somewhere new as a tourist. The mobility of the spectator reflects that of the artwork itself. Artangel co-director James Lingwood writes that Rachel Whiteread's *House* (1993), a famous commission located in Mile End, 'could have been made elsewhere, in a different place, at a different time; perhaps with another cast list and chorus' (1995, p.7). Whiteread's audacious concrete sculpture, a cast of the interior of a Victorian terraced house, attracted considerable controversy on-site and in the press. *House*, Lingwood writes, 'laid bare the limits of language and expectation which afflict the contentious arena of public art' (1995, p.8). His assessment resonates with Richard Serra's similarly controversial *Tilted Arc* (1981), which sliced uncompromisingly across Federal Plaza in New York. As Miwon Kwon argues (following Rosalyn Deutsche), Serra's sculpture (like *House*) represented a model of site-specific art 'without obvious utilitarian payoffs, one that critically questions rather than promotes the fantasies of public space as a unified totality without conflicts or difference' (2002, pp.79–80).

Ten years on, *The Margate Exodus* staged a series of works, some of which offered an aesthetic address quite different to *House*'s challenge to 'unified totality', reflecting new dominant popular and governmental understandings of the 'work of art' in the public realm. The project was made in collaboration with a range of funders and partners, including Creative Partnerships Kent. Director Anna Cutler's intention for this branch of the national arts education programme, sited initially in targeted areas of deprivation, was to work with artists of the highest quality, 'raising the quality of work in schools and in the community as well as increasing the capacity of arts practice in Kent' (2007, p.196). During a conversation in 2002 with Artangel co-director Michael Morris, she discussed a short-term education project; ultimately,

> what actually arose from this conversation, and a follow-up visit from Michael, was the decision by them in agreement with Channel 4 to work on a film commission with Penny Woolcock for the summer of 2006. This film was to involve the entire local community in a contemporary re-telling of the epic *Exodus*. This shifted the project from a stand-alone education project within schools into a significant piece of art in the public domain that impacted on the community at large and fed in to the ongoing regeneration of the area.
>
> (Cutler, 2007, p.197)

Penny Woolcock's filmmaking, an innovative variant of social realism, utilizes documentary methods in the creation of both documentary and fictional works – in the latter case, often working with non-actors in their places of residence (in her Tina films, council estates in Leeds).[4] *Exodus* (2007) – a project that a promotional flyer advertised as 'the biggest community feature film ever made in the UK' (*Margate Exodus*, 2007) – would be the final outcome of a four-year process in Margate, incorporating *Towards a Promised Land* (2005–6), a photography and public art project made by US photographer Wendy Ewald with young people arriving in Margate who she encountered in schools, the Nayland Rock Induction Centre, and a facility for 'unaccompanied' children; Antony Gormley's *Waste Man* (2006), a giant temporary sculpture made entirely from waste materials and burned spectacularly in the grounds of Dreamland, Margate's amusement park; and *Plague Songs* (2006), a concept album featuring songs by, among others, Rufus Wainwright, Imogen Heap, and Brian Eno. With the participation of local residents, the works would reflect on Margate's engagement in global processes of migration and the experience of social marginality. Woolcock's film narrativized the contemporary situation by directly (and rather awkwardly) transposing the Exodus story to contemporary Britain. The film rendered the oppression of the Hebrews as the confinement of an expansive group of 'recidivist criminals, travellers, the mentally ill, the long term unemployed' (*Exodus*, 2007) to a shantytown – metaphorically called 'Dreamland' – whose set, built in collaboration with local schools and artists, was also in the amusement park grounds.

Less concerned with the perceptual 'ghostings' such sites might produce (Carlson, 2001, p.134), the performative naming of the fictional shantytown addressed the 'real' site's semiotic potential as a source for producing fiction. Thematically, the film's metaphoric and ironic citation of 'Dreamland' commented on the status of 'excluded' characters corralled within it, the imagined 'others' to tourists in search of escape. However, the seaside resort's resonance for this project as 'a perfect place to explore issues of identity, tolerance and social equality' (*The Margate Exodus*, 2011) was more directly connected to immigration, an issue that (the project's website asserted) has 'never been more meaningful than it is today' (*The Margate Exodus*, 2011) – a debatable claim that gestured implicitly towards local controversy. Acts of violence in Margate became more numerous in the late 1990s (Thanet Refugee Access, 2007), inflamed by bigoted statements in the media such as the *Dover Express*'s notorious 1998 article 'We want to wash dross down drain', which described 'asylum seekers' (along with 'illegal immigrants', 'bootleggers', and 'scum of the earth drug smugglers') as 'a nation's human sewage' (cited in Robinson, Andersson, and Musterd, 2003, p.16). In 2000, a National Front march on Margate's seafront prompted the *Isle of Thanet Gazette* to launch a detailed series of awareness-raising articles to explode 'urban myths' about 'asylum seekers' being automatically 'given council houses, mobile phones, free food, free taxis' (Anon., 2000). In common with other ongoing arts projects and anti-racism campaigns (Kidd, Zahir, and Khan, 2008), *The Margate Exodus* sought to challenge racism of the sort evidenced in 2006 by the graffito 'Go Home Kosovans', sprayed on a seafront car park wall (Aitch, 2006, p.22).

Towards a Promised Land refused stereotypical understandings of Margate and its newer residents, working with 'a group of children in Margate uprooted from wherever they called home, a group whose common emotional experiences might cut across the divisions of race, faith, politics and circumstance' (Morris, 2006b, p.16). Some participants were living in Margate having fled situations of conflict in places as far-flung as Northern Ireland, the Democratic Republic of Congo, and Afghanistan. Others, more prosaically, had moved because a parent had changed jobs, or to be closer to other family. With an aesthetic similar to Dorothea Lange's photographic documentation of migrant workers in 1930s America,[5] Wendy Ewald's bold, monochrome portraits of the young people were staged as large-scale outdoor banners in Margate in 2005 and in 2006. During the course of *Towards a Promised Land* in 2006, a person arriving in the town from elsewhere would be greeted by the contemplative gaze of a young white boy, whose gigantic image appeared on Dreamland's cinema tower.[6] As if part of an adventure tale, this handwritten legend curved around the boy's face: 'It happened that we had to leave our lovely city.' The writings on other images ranged between optimism ('I helped mum pack. I hoped for luck and success'); wonder ('I didn't believe it – me, in Europe? No, it's not me!'); mundanity ('I feel the same really except I drink tea') and exasperation ('I didn't like English. It gave me a headache'), to complex effect.[7] The autobiographical relation suggested between the statements and the images invited imaginative projection while at the same time being vulnerable to reductive discourses of 'reality': assertions of Margate as located in 'Europe', and difficulties encountered in learning another language, complicated narratives of nation, cultural homogeneity, and 'integration'. The enormity of the images had a peculiar scalar effect: from a distance, they were the only perceptible detail of the buildings, which now seemed almost miniature; up close, they towered over the spectator and dominated the buildings. The hypervisibility and longevity of the project, called 'monumental' (Ewald and Morris, 2006, p.144) by the artist, asserted the continued 'presence' of the young people in the town, eliciting questions and comments from passers-by during the installation process, and, once the images were in place, an angry objection from one local couple: 'We know there are asylum seekers, and we've accepted that, but we don't want it rubbed in our face' (cited in Cutler, 2007, p.215). Others replied with physical violence to the symbolic confrontation the photographs staged, repeatedly burning a portrait of a Muslim girl from South Africa that was displayed on Margate's sea wall. The project directors attributed these particular actions to the coincidence of the images' public installation and the London bombings of 7 July 2005, which further politicized an already contentious project (Cutler, 2007, pp.215–17). For one commentator, the project's exposure of the images of the young people to such actions was deeply problematic.[8] Others praised the project and its various elements[9] as brave and informative (Cutler, 2007, p.217). If acts of destruction signalled an 'antipathy toward immigrants and strangers who represent the involution of national culture' (Gilroy, 2004, p.97), the project showed that, as Paul Gilroy insists, '[i]t is the workings of racism that produce the order of racial truths and not the other way around' (2004, p.116).

Ewald's project thus tested 'the limits of language and expectation' (Lingwood, 1995, p.8) attending Margate. Media treatment of *The Margate Exodus* as a whole, meanwhile, broadly and decisively invoked a scene of cohesive integration – quite unlike the debate that had raged in the press regarding *House*. Articles ranged from local stories in *The Margate Exodus*'s media partner *Isle of Thanet Gazette*, to broadsheet commentary and magazine diary listings, including possibly the first appearance of information about a community arts project in *Vogue* (Anon., 2006c). Coverage favoured tropes of breaking down barriers, cultural recognition and ethnic mix, in a project that 'would involve people from all walks of life' (Cotton, 2006, p.21). 'Community cohesion' was represented as an item on a job description: *The Guardian* reported that Woolcock's assistant casting director and outreach worker on the project was the 'person with most responsibility for bringing about community cohesion' (Aitch, 2006, p.22). Resonating with the governmental construction of 'cohesion', this integrationist narrative ran with and alongside another, of competitive excellence. Michael Morris's words in *Thanet Extra* reflect these principles:

> The *Waste Man* is a very strong image and it will be remembered forever. But the real legacy is in the communication between people who live in the same town, who live next to each other but don't know each other. All the way through we have been making alliances between people at the top of their game with people who have never had any opportunity to show their talents.
>
> (cited in Denham, 2006)

Author of the blog *Turneround Margate*, a participant in the project, vouched for the beneficial effects Morris describes for local cultural production (Anon., 2007). Nonetheless, recruiting participants in advance of the project, several article headlines in the *Isle of Thanet Gazette* appealed to readers' sense of celebrity, now largely in relation to the film itself: 'Your chance to be a star' (Anon., 2006d), 'Be a star in movie of town' (Bailes, 2006), 'Chance for all to shine with film project' (Anon., 2006b), 'Your invitation to create an art legend' (Anon., 2006e).

These contrasted with Antony Gormley's articulation of the *Waste Man's* intended meaning. It represented 'the displaced and disadvantaged everywhere, exclaiming: "I want to be recognised! I want to belong! I want to be part of this world!"' (cited in Chater, 2006).

'Immersive cultural experiences'[10]

These discursive moves rehearsed then-dominant ideologies of art-making: participation as a means to producing inclusion and cohesion, and the desirability of 'excellence' in artistic practice. But, as in Ewald's project, the greater complexity of the social situation was made apparent on *Exodus Day*, which took place on 30 September 2006, a few days into the seven-week film shoot. I attended this event, catching the midday train to Margate from Charing Cross. (Supplementing the scheduled train departures was a dedicated National Express coach, the Exodus Express, running from London to Margate.) Lyn Gardner's preview encouraged anticipation of a day of theatrical performance:

> Artangel is responsible for some of the most stupendous live art events of the last decade, and this two-day performance, taking place as part of the filming for Penny Woolcock's film, should be a genuine marvel [. . .] a fiesta of performances, speeches, songs, processions and even plagues.
>
> (2006, p.38)

An hour and a half later I disembarked onto a train platform thick with people. Beyond the doors of the station, where one of Wendy Ewald's pictures was displayed behind glass, a representative of the Margate Town Centre Regeneration Company approached and handed me a leaflet, encouraging me to subscribe to their text messaging service. Unsure of which direction to take next (the crowd had by now dispersed into the streets beyond), I followed the road down towards the clock tower on the seafront. An encounter with a T-shirted guide provided a *Margate Exodus*-branded map of the town bearing a schedule for the day, and a similarly branded stick of rock. Thus equipped, I made my way towards the shopping precinct where the first staged piece would take place.

En route, the first signs of the performance began to appear. In the recess of a doorway were two homeless people, and a garish neon election campaign poster featuring actor Bernard Hill as fascist leader

Pharaoh Mann – the legend 'NOB' scrawled across it – was posted on a doorway just above. As the fiction-effect of the poster registered – and a moment's indecision regarding the status of the people beneath – I recognized that the town was being imagined as the immersive site of the film's action, and its visitors, its characters. Approaching the entrance to the precinct, a narrow covered arcade, I waited for a woman with a pram to come through, and, while waiting, read the full text of a sign displayed at the opening of the arcade's passageway (Image 10.1).

The 'crowd release notice' is a standard supplement to acts of filming in confined, quasi-public places (Light Honthaner, 2010, p.274). In the context of *Exodus Day*'s address to its audience as a live event, its simultaneously theatrical and economic implications were thrown into relief. If the event's framing of the town theatrically hypothesized its visiting spectator as 'character', this pre-emptive staging of the shopping precinct, a zone now discursively partitioned or enclosed from the surrounding environment, promised swiftly to divest the 'actor' of rights to the image that their public 'performance' – mere presence – might produce.

Within, a more explicit form of 'character' asserted itself: a line of uniformed actors performing as military police secured the interior

Image 10.1 Crowd release notice for *Exodus* filming, Saturday, 30 September 2006. Courtesy of Louise Owen.

of the precinct. A large podium festooned with posters would accommodate Woolcock's character, Pharaoh Mann. Following a brief wait characteristic of a film set, the crew shot Bernard Hill's rendition of Mann's election speech, a torrent of fascist rhetoric, before its live audience of 'real' people. The speech concluded with the news that Mann had won the election and a celebratory explosion of streamers popped into the air; their ungovernable distribution prevented the scene from being re-staged. Like the staging of Moses's and Aaron's speech from the belly of Gormley's *Waste Man* and the sculpture's burning later that day, this was filmmaking in a definitively 'live' mode: there would be no second takes of this moment. During the shoot, however, after a particularly incendiary passage of fictional hate speech, a member of the crew called 'cut' and took to the stage, assuring the assembled audience 'this is just a film, we don't endorse any of these views' – Bernard Hill interjected, 'Particularly me! Especially me!' – 'we love everybody, we're peaceful people' (Palmer, 2007), which received a gale of laughter. The scene complete, Mann and his entourage left the podium, and the crew invited the audience to follow the victorious politician towards Dreamland, some carrying placards bearing his election poster. Walking down the street outside, I passed a woman being interviewed for a local radio station, testifying to the dynamic benefits of the day for Margate. As the crowd made its way, the 'police' would seize and assault 'dissenters', placing the holiday atmosphere in what felt to be uncomfortable dialogue with the acts of staged and filmed violence being perpetrated in the immersive environment of 'the street'.

Maddy Costa's disappointed review of *Exodus Day* appeared in *The Guardian* the following Monday, her critique based largely on her sense of listless inaction during 'great expanses of time when it's clear that we are just sitting on the sidelines of a film set, waiting, bored, for the cameras to roll' (2006, p.36). She describes the burning of Gormley's sculpture as the day's high point:

> an awe-inspiring spectacle, a lifetime of Guy Fawkes Nights all rolled into one. What it all means, though, is anybody's guess. And that's the problem with *Exodus Day*. It is not designed as a piece of integrated street theatre, so audiences have no narrative to follow, no sense of how each scene fits in with Woolcock's story [...] the common cry, heard throughout the day, is: 'I'm confused.' The day needed more cohesion, more activity – more theatre, essentially – for audiences truly to feel involved.
>
> (Costa, 2006, p.36)

If the day's disparate proceedings lacked an intentional and unified narrative construction, what she suggestively calls 'cohesion', they did not lack theatre. Costa's implicit definition of theatre as a representational procedure which materially organizes space and ideas is similar to the definition Sophie Nield offers in her discussion of the production of 'border' space and its relation to the theatre: it is 'not one of the imitative to the authentic, of the "fake" to the real, but rather is contained in a series of shared concerns around space, appearance, disappearance and representation' (2006, p.65). It enables a precise understanding of the ways in which 'site' made its appearance on *Exodus Day*. At the most straightforward level, the staging of the journey from London to Margate both cited and materially performed a model of tourism – the day trip to the seaside – whose participants did not only consist of pleasure-seeking city-dwellers intent on a day at the beach, but a group including myself whose (professional) interest in common was *The Margate Exodus* as art. More than this, the immersive sense of the 'town-as-set' was the work of theatrical production. *Exodus Day*'s immersive staging of the town is a familiar gesture in contemporary installation and performance, but its basis here was the representational imperative of making a film in the realist mode. Trading on the site as aesthetically 'real' in order to produce the film, a work explicitly challenging authoritarian politics, its liberal makers also intervened to acknowledge the multiple and competing political positions present in the 'really real' public space of Margate's shopping precinct by confirming Pharaoh Mann's fascist rhetoric to be 'theatre'.

Iain Aitch commented about *Exodus Day* that '[a] story about migration is perhaps the most controversial tale Artangel could have chosen to tell in Margate' (2006, p.22). Though the theme of *Exodus Day*'s events was unquestionably 'violence to achieve political ends' (Morris, 2006a), its now ubiquitous immersive representational logic, deployed here to produce a piece of cinematic realism, also reflected the kind of 'place-making' semiotic activity that creates tourist sites: the theatrical construction of 'real' venues for spectacular consumption. The re-staging of this 'real' with signage and speech dramatized the contingency of such constructions. Wendy Ewald's *Towards a Promised Land*, meanwhile, disclosed conflict that would rupture such consumption, providing evidence of social problems that the (insistently reiterated) discourse of cohesion, as Cameron argues, is concerned to 'remove' or 'render invisible' (2006, p.397).

The Margate Exodus witnesses a particular historical moment in cultural production, a moment that has now passed. Creative Partnerships, an institution central to the project, was axed immediately following the coalition government's Comprehensive Spending Review in 2010 (Woolman, 2010). To conclude, I draw attention to an unexpected instance of interruption to the scene of immersion on *Exodus Day*. As the crowd progressed towards Dreamland, we reached a crossroads. There I noticed a set of other placards competing for attention with those of Pharaoh Mann – handmade fluorescent orange signs wielded by a group of protestors. These read:

ACTION NOW! WE NEED YOUR SUPPORT

HOUSES HOUSES HOUSES HOUSES

WHERE'S THE DOCTOR, DENTIST, HOSPITAL AND WATER?

The protestors, from an association called Save Thanet, had chosen to hijack the public events to advance their cause, a fight against a planning authorization for 4000 houses in the Thanet area. This was not a spontaneous incident of protest: Save Thanet had launched its intervention with an announcement in *Kent News* about their plans the day before *Exodus Day*:

'We know the film-makers are planning some spectacular public events for Saturday in Margate, and we aren't going to spoil the fun,' said organiser Norman Thomas,[11] 'but we are going to make our voices heard. After all, the theme of Exodus is all about people looking for a promised land. The problem for Thanet is that our land has been promised away to be built over – and we are not prepared to accept this. All over Thanet housing developments are springing up. We have to say enough is enough ... Thanet depends on tourism and visitors. Who's going to want to come and visit a huge urban sprawl?'

(Anon., 2006a)

At this moment in 2006, in the midst of the housing boom (Haurant, 2006), the demand the placards made for investment in public services strategically asserted the Thanet area as a site of settlement whose economy is based on acts of travel, instead of property speculation in search of quick profits. On location, the demonstration also had the effect of denaturalizing the fake placards, disclosing the public, a site of struggle

over the terms of social life and its material shaping, having characteristics akin to the dual representational logic of theatre.[12] Like Ewald's
photographs, it dramatized 'site' not as commoditized parcel of land,
nor as theatrically produced 'experience', but as a question of culture
engaged with social and economic change – distinctly at odds with Ruth
Guilding's understanding of place as asset.

Notes

1. I use culture-in-regeneration as a catch-all term here. Graeme Evans and
Phyllida Shaw's (2004, p.5) research report identifies three models: 'culture-
led regeneration' (exemplified by stand-alone capital projects such as Tate
Modern, London and the Lowry Centre, Salford), 'cultural regeneration'
(cultural provision well integrated into local planning), and 'culture and
regeneration' (culture as add-on). *The Margate Exodus* represents a mix of
the second and third models.
2. Dogme95 was a movement in experimental cinema that staged a playful
challenge to the Hollywood blockbuster. Dogme's *Vow of Chastity* (1995),
authored by the movement's founding directors Lars von Trier and Thomas
Vinterberg, set out a series of conditions to which makers of Dogme95 films
should adhere – location-only shooting, hand-held cameras and 35mm film
stock only, no special lighting or effects, and so on – effectively recommend-
ing the production of a certain sort of site-specific and logically naturalistic
film. The first Dogme film was Vinterberg's *Festen* (1998). The movement's
'official' life was brought to an end in 2002 as a consequence of its having 'almost grown into a genre formula, which was never the intention'
(Stevenson, 2003, p.291).
3. Since the beginnings of its gradual closure in the early 2000s, Dreamland has
represented an important focus of struggle regarding the future of tourism in
Margate. A locally organized campaign to save Dreamland was launched in
2003. In 2009, the campaign successfully negotiated a grant of £3.7 million
from the government's Sea Change fund for the site's redevelopment as a
heritage visitor attraction, which was consolidated in 2011 by the upgrad-
ing of the scenic railway from Grade II to Grade II* status, – a category of
'particularly important buildings of more than special interest' (English Heritage, 2011). For exhaustive documentation and regularly updated details
of the Save Dreamland campaign, see Joyland Books, 2011. For details of
the development of the new Dreamland project, 'a living breathing tourist
attraction, with many thrilling historic rides', see Dreamland Trust, 2011.
For more information regarding listed buildings and their status, see English
Heritage, 2011.
4. *Tina Goes Shopping* (1999), *Tina Takes a Break* (2001) and *Mischief Night*
(2006).
5. Thanks to Steve Farrier for drawing attention to this similarity.
6. The Dreamland Cinema (opened in 1935) is the last remaining cinema of
three built in the Art Deco style in Margate in the 1930s. Designed by cinema

architects W F Granger and J R Leathart, its style was informed by northern European modernism, in particular the work of Dutch architect William Dudok (Prince's Regeneration Trust, 2009, pp.40–1). It was given Art Deco Grade II listed status in 1992, and upgraded to Grade II* in 2008 (Prince's Regeneration Trust, 2009, p.46).

7. For images and other documentation, see Anna Cutler (2007), Louise Neri (2006) and Ewald's portraits, published on Artangel's website (2011).

8. Caroline Blunt writes: 'As much as these acts may trigger a variety of responses of disgust, sympathy, surprise or lack of it, it does not seem to me that the destruction and defacing of children's pictures are acceptable casualties in a process of changing minds and raising consciousness' (2006, pp.28–9).

9. The project also staged an audio walk around the town, featuring spoken recordings of the young people's reflections, and two exhibitions – one at the Outfitters' Gallery in 2005, and the second at Margate Library in 2006, which featured Woolcock's portraits and the young people's own work.

10. This heading quotes Michael Morris (2006a) where he uses this phrase in his description of contemporary performance practice in a piece published about *The Margate Exodus* after Exodus Day.

11. Norman Thomas is a Thanet-based filmmaker and campaigner. He ran for the European Parliament in 2004 as a representative of RESPECT. A recent film project, *Are Refugees the Problem?* (2009), is a documentary challenging racism in Thanet.

12. Tracy C Davis examines 'theatricality' as a historical problematic connected to the public sphere as a construct. Her definition characterizes the representational effect I describe here: '*Theatricality: n. A spectator's dédoublement resulting from a sympathetic breach (active dissociation, alienation, self-reflexivity) effecting a critical stance toward an episode in the public sphere, including but not limited to the theatre*' (Davis, 2003, p.145; original emphasis).

Part IV

Site-Specificity and Theatrical Intimacy

11
Ambulatory Audiences and Animate Sites: Staging the Spectator in Site-Specific Performance

Keren Zaiontz

Whether they find themselves holding props, touring an IKEA showroom, or knocking on a stranger's door, spectators often perform a unique set of roles in contemporary site-specific performance. The novelty of their role play hangs upon the challenge to cross into the space of the artwork as participants in three key ways. First, the involvement of audiences in site-specific performance reconfigures interpretation as an act where meaning is made through a visible 'doing'. Second, as collaborative participants, site-specific spectators often function as both the 'sight' of artistic attention and the physical 'site' of the performance (in some productions and events, spectators often serve as the equivalent of an 'animate' *mise en scène*). Third, as a corollary of being propelled into the spotlight, audiences regularly take on roles within the performance as facilitators and co-creators. In short, these site-specific performance contexts compel spectators to perform 'double-duty': audiences retain their role as interpreters and witnesses of the stage action, but they also labour as role players and aides to the performance. In what follows, I outline some of the working conditions in which doubled spectators find themselves, and how these conditions make demands upon audiences to reassess how they value objects, relate to strangers, and treat marginalized others. Within these scenarios, I consider how their bodily encounters with things and strangers produce binding ethical relationships with the other. To conclude, I situate audiences within a performance ethnography whereby otherness is negotiated and made representable through participatory practices.

The working audience

My examination of how spectators work within the ephemeral terrain of the performance event occurs against a backdrop of interest in the aesthetic potential of audiences as well as other subjects that do not typically 'belong' on stage. There is an emerging interest in the ways in which spectators perform 'double-duty' as witness-participants, whether as 'delegated performers' or 'experts of the everyday'; audiences frequently support the aesthetics and embody the politics of the event, largely through performative acts.[1] The productions documented here exemplify this drive to realize the possibilities of spectatorship for performance, showing what spectators can do (or are made to do) by companies at the forefront of site-specific practices. While the projects and approaches of the companies described here are disparate, the ways in which they put the audience to work – particularly through mass movement and physical contact – point towards a common preoccupation with how to transform the literal presence of audiences into a vital point of play.[2]

Unpacking the ways in which spectators labour for their artwork raises questions about how artists constantly remap the dynamics of reception. How, for example, does a spectator get 'cast' into the action – become a 'doubled' subject – in a way that not only comments upon but constitutes the performance event? What does immersion as witness-participants signal within the context of a given performance, site, or to those subjects simply passing by? What does being 'part of the show' add to the piece and, by extension, the experience of reception? And what kinds of communities (however temporary) are forged in the process of participation? Other questions directly concern dramaturgy in 'spectator-specific' contexts. How do artists choreograph conventionally immobile spectators into a portable collective? How can the 'bodied space' of the audience dramatize the theatrical worlds of artists? And how can the 'bodied space' of the audience be used to rattle the binaries of subject and object, self and other?

Three companies working in urban Canadian centres help address these broad questions about spectatorship. Since the late 1990s, Radix Theatre Society (Vancouver-based), bluemouth inc. (based in Toronto and New York City), and Toronto-based Mammalian Diving Reflex (MDR) have developed and staged original productions in disused warehouses, barbershops, parks, run-down hotels, boiler rooms, local diners, city intersections, subways, elementary schools, big box stores, and conference rooms.[3] Rarely conforming to the conventional uses of these places, the companies have repurposed walls into projection surfaces for images, used countertops as places to dance, recorded soundscapes using the acoustic elements of the site, and travelled to intersections, homes, and strip malls to interview strangers and collect 'material' for shows. These performance practices prioritize a collision between art and site that is facilitated by spectators who are scripted as assistants to, and participants of, artistic creation and production.

Contact and content: the uses of the spectator in performance

The collision that audiences help to enable within artistic production necessarily changes the boundaries of spectatorship. By coming into contact with the discourses that are being dramatized – which in this chapter includes consumerism, authenticity, and the threat of the other – spectators navigate the artwork through what Gilles Deleuze and Felix Guattari (1987) call a 'smooth space', a space perceived through direct physical engagement. Laura Marks explains that smooth spaces are necessarily experienced at '[c]lose-range' and 'navigated not through reference to the abstractions of maps or compasses, but by haptic perception, which attends to their particularity' (2002, p.xii). Spectatorship at 'close range' aptly characterizes how audiences make contact with, and join themselves to, the performance; in some cases, they share in the expression of the piece by acting as a sensory stage environment. To illuminate how the role of spectator diverges to become an animate *mise en scène*, I examine how the binaries of self and other, and container and content, are challenged in two bluemouth productions: *How Soon is Now?* (2007) and *American Standard* (2001). The construction of animate environments in these works reveals space, and specifically theatrical space, to be far from absolute. Rather, theatrical space proves to be a site of mutual production where performers and participants are not distinct from the stages they occupy but through physical contact are shown to produce those stages.

The audiences' immersion in site-specific events as interpreters and objects of artifice has an additional, portable dimension in the work of bluemouth, Radix, and MDR, since these companies 'choreograph' the movement of audiences through performance sites. As bluemouth's co-artistic director Lucy Simic observes, this movement is often intertwined with the twists and turns of the performance proper: 'By directing their [the spectators'] movement through the performance, we are asking them not only to travel through the site, but to travel through the content of the piece as well' (cited in bluemouth, 2006, p.161). There are several ways that a company can choreograph the movement of audiences as they 'travel' through a piece, and by extension, through an indoor or outdoor site: an audience can flow *en masse* from station to station in a single site; their movement can be dispersed so that they surround the action; they may be asked to sit for one scene and then stand in the next; or they may be called upon to do a combination of all of the above.[4] As audiences take on the portability of crowds and travel through a site, they themselves become objects of display as their movement occurs within the shared space of art. Radix's *The Swedish Play* (2002) and MDR's *Home Tours* (2005–6) demonstrate how this movement, specifically indoor travel, is used to produce cultural criticism about the instrumental role prefabricated objects play in everyday life.

Ambulatory audiences, part I: 'shelving units might contain our salvation'

Radix describes the movement of spectators in *The Swedish Play* as 'invisible theatre', because in critic Andrew Templeton's words, it 'involve[s] performers and audience members moving [silently] through the "performance space" during store hours' (2005, p.4). This restriction means that performers in the IKEA showroom are not permitted to speak and/or disrupt the flow of commerce. Instead, spectators don headsets, which both enables a theatrical space within the flow of the showroom and links them to the world of the performers. The headsets themselves do not relay any one recording, rather spectators tune into a low-band radio station that alternates between broadcasting 'comedy' and 'tragedy' tours. The soundtracks are deliberately opaque and consist of 'a collage of sounds and samples, including discourses on theatrical forms, post-modern theory and sound clips from old movies' (Templeton, 2005, p.4). The privileged position of standing outside the work, something that audio tours usually enforce in institutional contexts such as museums and galleries, here situates the audience as 'spectators' who are as much a point of curiosity for those shoppers passing by as the performers who occupy the displays. While *The Swedish Play* does not announce itself as play – 'regular shoppers [...] have no idea that a performance is taking place right before their very eyes' (Radix Theatre Society, 2002) – the claim to 'invisible theatre' does not hold. The headsets, mass movement of the audience throughout the showroom, and living room scenes draw a line around the show in a way that marks it as anything but invisible.[5]

In *The Swedish Play*, spectators follow the path choreographed by the store, which is designed so that shoppers experience a series of utopian interiors that encourage fantasies of domestic tranquillity. However, the movement through the model sets did include one crucial alteration: audiences assess rather than fantasize about the furniture. This assessment occurs through a theatrical display that involves abstract vignettes and a soundtrack that functions as a commentary on the experience of consumerism. In the words of *The Swedish Play* sound designer and Radix collaborator Andreas Kahre, 'The "strategy" employed was to overburden the dynamics of browsing by superimposing its faux fantasies [...] with a meta-text that acknowledged them to be a ruse – employed simultaneously by us and by IKEA' (Kahre and Taylor, 2008, p.311). The net effect of the audio tour and showroom vignettes is a disruption of the sensible where IKEA is revealed to be as much (or more of) a symbolic medium of escape than the Radix performance. These alienating strategies are used to encourage the audience to, in Templeton's words,

> consider the artificiality of the showrooms and, hopefully consider the processes at work below the surface of consumer culture. It is fair to say that companies like IKEA are selling lifestyles as much – if not more – than practical products. The messages contained are loaded with implied criticisms of the individual and the notion that shelving units might contain our salvation.
>
> (2005, p.5)

As Templeton (2005) argues, *The Swedish Play* reveals that the way in which we secure our 'salvation' lies not in our encounter with one another but in things.[6]

Occupying the doubled role of spectator and shopper, audiences facilitate the company's commentary on our compulsion to endlessly collect things, and in doing so they reveal the illusory power of 'practical products' in our everyday lives. In helping Radix stage their cultural criticism, the doubled spectator doubly objectifies IKEA as a site of multiple and overlapping forms of conduct. The showroom is a space where one literally *acts* as a consumer who follows the correct codes of looking, desiring, and buying, but, in this instance, it is also a space where subjects query their social world through critical acts. By engaging in both types of conduct, the audience helps to unsettle the space of the IKEA showroom and re-situate the store as a site of theatrical representation: IKEA in quotation marks.[7] Fidelity to consumerism now jostles alongside a performance of those things that inaugurate a new form of conduct in the showroom, one where contact with shelving units is exceeded by the face-to-face encounter staged in the showroom.

Ambulatory audiences, part II: 'Ask for a quick peek'

Home Tours, an event organized by MDR, can be said to begin its curious ambles where *The Swedish Play*'s audio tour ends. Its spectators tour those sites where the frozen domestic settings of IKEA have been installed – in actual homes. The company circulates an email in which they invite 'audience/participants to walk through random neighbourhoods, knock on random doors and ask for a quick peek' (O'Donnell, 2006a, p.62). Throughout 2005 and 2006, MDR and its participants strolled through neighbourhoods in Toronto and Calgary in search of homes to do domestic walks. The movement of outdoor rambles indoors repurposed the inside as places that could be toured,

Image 11.1   Mammalian Diving Reflex, *Home Tours*. Toronto participants tour through the Annex neighbourhood in 2005. Courtesy of Mammalian Diving Reflex and David O'Donnell.

potentially recasting the inhabitant as a tour guide and the home a tourist site. The reception from residents who greeted anywhere from two to ten MDR participants was far from uniform. Home dwellers in the Mount Royal neighbourhood in Calgary lodged complaints with the host theatre, Alberta Theatre Projects; while home dwellers in the Annex neighbourhood in Toronto, which includes a large population of student renters, were more hospitable and, in one case, residents gave participants basil from their backyard. In those instances where a home tour was provided, the trajectory through the premises was determined by the dweller (see Image 11.1).

Because it occurs in a domestic space, the movement of the audience in *Home Tours* constitutes a more vulnerable engagement with subjects and sites than *The Swedish Play*. While the Radix audience can revel in the ironic subversion of the IKEA 'thing-world' because they are intervening into a commercial site that belongs to the global marketplace, in *Home Tours* the audience intervenes in a site that belongs to a person, and they experience that space through a roving encounter with him or her. This form of domestic display, which, to some, clearly felt like a home invasion, points to the unparalleled level of responsibility that is required of audiences who 'double' as cultural tourists. Since the felicitousness of the tour relies almost exclusively on conduct between resident and roving audience (host and guest), the exhibition of the home is made in and through the intersubjective contact between these parties.

The encounter between home dweller and audience is tied to a performance ethnography that brings together strangers to re-stage scenarios that resemble everyday cultural practices with a difference. By 'blanketing' what artistic director Darren O'Donnell calls 'traditionally non-artistic activities' (2006b, p.33) as performance (i.e. strolling through a neighbourhood), MDR engages different social groups in artistic production. The object is to form what Nina Möntmann calls 'hybrid "experimental communities"' that bring 'together individuals with different knowledge and experience in a collaborative process' (2009, p.14). A community that is founded on difference – particularly one that embodies cultural practices that largely reconfigure, and parody, the everyday – sets the stage for a potentially charged encounter (as noted by residents who refused to provide tours). In his art-activist manifesto *Social Acupuncture*, O'Donnell (2006b) argues that if contemporary art goers desire a more crucial comprehension of the other then they must be willing to feel uncomfortable, and experience socially awkward moments.[8] While courting difficult and even risky intersubjective scenarios is a staple of a broad range of relational works, including *Home Tours*, the particular issue of concern is the kind of social formation produced in the private space of a home. How do we measure if touring someone's place is a respectful way of knowing the other, particularly if the structuring assumption of the work is discomfort or antagonism? While on tour, are we supposed to imagine ourselves as home dwellers in the style of empathetic ethnographers, or are we there to have a taste of the other? Ultimately, the desire 'to knock on doors and take a quick peek' suggests that any site can be made representable, and any subject a site of display. *Home Tours* is interesting for the way that residents are interpellated as dramatic subjects (or subjects of dramatic interest), and points to an insatiable appetite in relational and site-specific performance to mine even our most private spaces for aesthetic merit. Here again, conduct is inseparable from how we experience the site, since the way in which home dweller and audience act shapes the kind of community that is formed. Gaining entrance onto a domestic stage is not easy, but for all its difficulties, *Home Tours* highlights a desire for an experiential spectatorship that, through a tenuous form of participation, offers a different way of engaging daily social practices.

Audiences as animate sites: Contact and co-presence

As we have seen thus far, the role of the audience is figural to the cultural criticism that site-specific artists stage as well as the communities they bring together. But in addition to their role as roving witnesses and travellers, spectators may find themselves in altogether different working conditions as the very material of the event. bluemouth exemplifies this material use of the audience, which is bound up in one of the key thematic concerns of the company: to dramatize mad, even threatening, others. In bluemouth productions, the other rarely encounters the audience in an intact or integrated state. From their 2001 premiere production *American Standard*, a collectively created one-man show about seven American 'archetypes' which includes the figures of a terrorist and immigrant; to *Lenz* (2001), which centres on a homeless man suffering from mental illness; to *What The Thunder Said* (2003/2006), which stages squatters, tramps, and dispossessed family members; to their 2007 production *How Soon Is Now?*, which adapts the tale of Peter and the Wolf into a parable about the village scapegoat, the company's repertoire can be viewed as an extended meditation on otherness. In all of these productions the 'bodied space' of the audience highlights and complicates the conditions of these characters.

Two examples, from *American Standard* and *How Soon is Now?*, are especially pertinent because of the unique placement of the performers and
spectators. In both instances, the audience can be said to function as
the characters' theatrical environment. In *American Standard*, the terrorist archetype, performed by Stephen O'Connell, does not perform
in front of, or amid, the audience, but hangs above them from a harness directly outside of the performance space, as a wall-sized screen
projects images in the background. His face with ghostly white make-
up, his body dangling from what appears to be a noose, the terrorist
speaks to the audience 'below' as core member Richard Windeyer accom-
panies this direct address with a persistent drum beat. In the 2005
re-mount of *American Standard*, performed in a warehouse in downtown
Toronto, spectators were positioned along the perimeter of the performance space. The terrorist engaged the audience in a series of questions,
and opened by asking, rather casually for a man in a noose: 'Excuse me.
Do you have a minute? Do you have some spare time?' (bluemouth,
2005, p.11). This exchange quickly unfolded into a darker, more violent
set of queries: 'Would you rob a bank if you needed the money? Would
you kidnap a child if you had nothing to lose?' (bluemouth, 2005, p.12).
In asking the audience if they think themselves capable of becoming the
threatening other, the terrorist expresses what the scenographic arrangement makes all too clear. Sitting as an immobile group while the terrorist
hangs above them like a spectral presence, audience and terrorist dramatize 'us' versus 'them' through the placement of their bodies. This
mutual production of theatrical space illustrates the construction of the
'other', or as Michael Taussig puts it, 'alterity is every inch a relationship,
not a thing in itself' (1993, p.130).

As audience and terrorist show, us and them may be divided but they
are not static. Through the use of live feed and a newspaper, both sides
labour together to construct these positions. As the terrorist speaks, his
movements are projected onto the back of a paper held by an audience member.[9] A live feed (operated by a company member) projects the
image of the terrorist, which serves to instantiate him in two places at
once. By making contact with the terrorist through his image, the audience's space in turn functions as the terrorist's space. In other words,
the material presence of the spectators affords the terrorist access to the
'real' space of the audience. Our contact with his spectral appearance
is what gives him his terroristic reality. His material lack thus illustrates
how the threatening other is in part the creation of the self's fearful
imaginary. The spectator who labours as a stagehand helps to show
that it is the internalization of the threatening other into our collective

imagination that manufactures his presence as everywhere and ever present.

The ubiquity of the terrorist archetype – dramatized through his multi-sited appearance – creates a ripple effect. One cannot reframe the self/other divide without it fanning out to other binaries, such as container and content. In this divide, space is typically understood as autonomous from those subjects who occupy it – a distinction anchored in the assumption that the stage is an empty vessel for the art. However, if a stage subject – such as the terrorist – is simultaneously in more than one location, then the container overflows, so to speak, its contents dispersed everywhere. This dispersal of the subject into every space implies that bodies are not distinct from their containers: quite the opposite. Bodies produce their containers. Henri Lefebvre questions the division imposed between bodies and spaces when he asks: 'Can the body, with its capacity for action, and its various energies, be said to create space?' (1991, p.170). He answers that 'each living body *is* space and *has* its space: it produces itself in space and it also produces that space' (Lefebvre, 1991, p.170; original emphasis). Here we can expand Lefebvre's statement to include mediatized bodies *as* space and as those which produce space.

The digital body of the terrorist archetype stands in contrast to the all too 'real' body of the wolf in bluemouth's 2007 production *How Soon is Now?*[10] The figures of terrorist and wolf are useful to compare because they insinuate the audience (as a theatrical environment) into the plight of the threatening other in almost oppositional ways. While the audience in *American Standard* is used to construct an innovative theatrical world that is underpinned by appearance, spectators in *How Soon is Now?* are implicated in a theatrical scenario underpinned by materiality. This shift from appearance to materiality changes the role of the audience from docile stagehands who prop up newspapers to that of co-creators who interact with the performer.

bluemouth sets the conditions for an animate *mise en scène* in the third scene of *How Soon is Now?* when spectators enter a cloistered, pitch-black room, single file (which necessitates ducking through a low entry way). As they stand immobile in the dark, shoulder-to-shoulder, dangling from a harness just above their heads is the wolf. A work light illuminates the performance space to reveal him hanging upside down. Unshaven, bare-chested, arms suspended above his shoulders, the 'savage' body of the wolf is initially still. Resembling a meat carcass, strung up and cellared, he is remarkable for his presence as flesh-and-bone. Contrasted against the terrorist, who hangs right side up, wolf and terrorist effect different relationships with the audience who in turn facilitate different 'spatial' stories about the threatening other.

Right side up, the terrorist tells a story of acting upon innocents, of wilful destruction, and uses the space of the audience as a site to be infiltrated. The terrorist's movements oscillate between static, angular gestures that have the quality of electric shock to arms and legs in full motion, walking at full speed but going nowhere fast. Upside down, the wolf tells a story of mock accusation and treats the space of the audience as a site of contact. When he first releases his upper body into the mass of people below there are audible gasps and expressions of surprise as spectators do not expect the locus of the action to be taking place both above and within their midst. Through a series of non-sequiturs – 'gray skies, winter skies [...] small town, cold town' – he stitches together events and images that bear the quality of a dream or, to be more exact, a nightmare. His body, suspended and bound, is nonetheless unpredictable, shifting from still and hanging to curious (he holds the gaze of those spectators immediately around him) and violent (he swings back and forth in the grip of the harness, yelling). Clearly desirous of contact, his arms and fingers, which are curled around his head, frequently stretch out to touch the audience. An audience member in turn responds by holding his hand, and, in some instances, spectator and wolf touch one another's faces. The intimacy of these gestures is not confined in their affect to novel interaction between performer and audience; rather the gestures have an ethical dimension within the story. In the scene following the wolf's monologue, the audience sits in judgement of him, positioned as jurors and witnesses. Throughout the mock trial, black and white images of a bloodthirsty crowd are projected onto a large screen, drawing an unsettling link between community and mob. The sensuous contact made between wolf and audience alters the view of the other so that those threats that circulate around him, and those accusations that are thrust upon him, are drained of their potency.

In place of the threats and collective paranoia is contact. Contact with the wolf – whose very physical position is at odds with his larger community (those spectators who will soon be cast as jurors) – overturns paranoia. It transforms fear of the other into mutuality by taking those binaries encoded in space, such as container and content, and challenging their division. Rather than being a purpose-built site, the container in *How Soon is Now?* is situated as an unindividuated mass (the audience) that envelops the wolf. The audience is a sensate container, a group witness to the wolf's fragmented tale. But this container also functions as the content of the theatrical scenario. Here, Walter Benjamin's image of the animate site in 'Convolut M' of *The Arcades Project* is useful for the way it proposes that 'space winks at the *flâneur*' (1999, p.419). In *How Soon is Now?*, space not only winks but touches back. The audience's space, rather than treated as 'flat' – a site lacking a physical dimension – is acknowledged as a space composed of bodies. Moreover, these bodies have a formal function within the performance. The gestures of 'winking' (looking, gazing at one another and the wolf) and touching which make up the scene point towards Stephen O'Connell's observation that 'space', and specifically within the work of bluemouth, bodied space, 'can create a beginning, middle, and end' (2007).

O'Connell's comment demonstrates that, for artists, much of the pleasure of staging site-specific events arises from highlighting, with the facilitation of audiences, how distinctions such as self and other are established. For audiences, much of the pleasure of participating in site-specific events arises not only from the ability to recognize how these distinctions are being established, and ultimately challenged, but from their ability to adapt – and contribute to – the theatrical worlds that the companies stage. Here, spectatorship represents a badge of theatrical acuity that may in part explain why audiences, rather than shrink from the 'doubled' position of witness-participant, often energetically embrace the challenge to perform.

In assessing how spectators are put to work, I want to focus briefly on the attraction of alterity in these site-specific performances. The works described here place audiences in direct contact with the other, which we know ranges from contact with threatening others, as compellingly staged by bluemouth; contact with quotidian others in the domestic environs of *Home Tours*; and contact with objects and consumer others in events like Radix's *Swedish Play*. These experiences of alterity, which audiences willingly facilitate and co-create, overlap with what Hal Foster calls 'pseudoethnography' (1995, p.304).[11] Such an approach describes those artists – as well as critics and historians – who collaborate with communities in ways that ultimately prove limiting due, in large part, to inadequate institutional support, which places temporal and financial constraints on the kind of work artists can do outside the gallery or theatre. Foster postulates that these conditions set the stage for the spectacularization of the other who serves as a projection of the artists' (and sponsoring institution's) imaginary. '[T]he artist, critic, or historian projects his or her practice onto the field of the other,' notes Foster, 'where it is read not only as authentically indigenous but as innovatively political!' (1995, p.307). If the pseudoethnographic impulse (that is, the method of projecting authenticity onto subjects and sites) is indeed enacted in the works discussed here, what do we make of the audience's involvement as fellow travellers? Are they too pseudoethnographers who project their dreams of authenticity and subversion onto the other? In these works, alterity is more than a play of projections. The willingness of audiences to other themselves as the site of performance and the sight of attention speaks to a potential turn from pseudoethnography to sensory ethnography, where alterity is not 'out there' but co-extensive with how one physically encounters subjects and sites. The challenge of performance, for artists and audiences alike, may lie beyond rattling distinctions and performing with theatrical acuity, but also in the being aware of cultural differences *as* differences rather than exotic sites of display. The question remaining is how these performances might set up the necessary parameters for a sensory ethnography wherein difference is troubled rather than consumed. The answer – and entry point – begins by assuming two core ethical principles of contemporary ethnography: reflexivity and dialogism. The experiential draw of site-specific performance necessitates that we discuss, and account for, how artists attend to such principles in the formation of their work. This requires that we not only account for the ways in which site-specific artists vividly re-imagine place, but query the effects that these re-imagined places have upon audiences as witnesses and participants of artistic production.

Notes

1. For a discussion of 'delegated performance', see *The Double Agent* (2009), co-edited by Claire Bishop, Silvija Jestrovic, Nicholas Ridout, and Silvia Tramontana. See Bishop (2009) for a genealogy of the delegated 'non professional' performer. Additionally, Eva Behrendt provides a valuable description of how companies like the Berlin-based Rimini Protocol outsource their performance expertise to what they call 'experts of the everyday' (2007). See also Erika Fischer-Lichte (2008) for a historical overview of audience roles within Western avant-garde performance.
2. Representative publications in English-language Canada alone that devote attention to participatory art practices include *Public*'s special issue on 'New Communities' (Möntmann, 2009); *Canadian Theatre Review*'s special issues on Site-Specific Performance (Houston and Nanni, 2006) and Performance Art (Levin, 2009); *The Dance Current*'s special issue on 'the ART of participation' (2007–8); *Fillip*'s Fall 2009 issue on participation in contemporary visual art (Podesva); Darren O'Donnell (2006b); and Carl Wilson (2007).
3. For information about the companies' mandates and production histories visit their websites: radixtheatre.org, bluemouthinc.com, and mammalian.ca. At the time these productions were first staged, the co-artistic directors of Radix Theatre Society were Paul Ternes and Andrew Laurenson;

the co-artistic directors and associate members of bluemouth included Ciara Adams, Stephen O'Connell, Sabrina Reeves, Lucy Simic, and Richard Windeyer; the producer of MDR was Naomi Campbell and the artistic director, Darren O'Donnell.

4. See Mike Pearson and Michael Shanks (2001), specifically their description of site-specific scenography, 'performance and the manipulation of space' (2001, pp.20–1) for the myriad ways in which the spectator–stage relationship can be reconfigured.

5. In 'The Aesthetics of Disappointment', an interview with Heidi Taylor and Andreas Kahre, Kahre describes why *The Swedish Play* was too visible to be 'invisible' theatre: 'Their [Radix] desire to accommodate larger audiences shifted the critical balance between the "witness" and the "witnessed," and all but obliterated the chance of discovering the poetic nexus – observing real shoppers making real choices against a field of auditory events invoking a state of epistemological crisis' (2008, p.311).

6. Michael Taussig's observation about the commodity fetish, which he makes in line with Marx, supports this viewpoint. He writes that:

> For [Marx] such fetishization resulted from the curious effect of the market on human life and imagination, an effect which displaced contact between people onto that between commodities, thereby intensifying to the point of spectrality the commodity as an autonomous entity with a will of its own.
>
> (Michael Taussig, 1993, p.22)

7. The specificity of Radix's encounter with IKEA in *The Swedish Play* resists engaging with 'brandscaping' (Klingmann, 2007, p.55), or the advertisement of a homogeneous, global 'lifestyle'. While a discussion of this concept in the context of site-specificity is beyond the scope of this paper, work on this area would be a useful development to the discourses of site-specificity.

8. O'Donnell speculates:

> I wonder if there might be [...] a way to induce encounters between individuals where we bring the aegis of art out into the world and use it to blanket traditionally non-artistic activities – activities in which power differentials are at least tacitly acknowledged and the artistic manoeuvre [sic] is to either reverse or erase them temporarily in a gesture of antagonism that contributes to rising social intelligence.
>
> (2006b, p.33)

9. The company took the same material they used to project images onto the wall-sized screen and put it onto the back of a newspaper.

10. Core and founding member Stephen O'Connell plays both characters. The collaborators for the 2005 remount of *American Standard* included Jeff Douglas, Kevin Rees, Lucy Simic, Richard Windeyer (sound design), David Duclos (lighting design), Heather Schibli (costume design), and Vicki Fausz-Quinsac (make-up). The devisors for the 2007 production of *How Soon Is Now?* included Stacie Morgain Lewis, Daniel Pettrow, Lucy Simic, Sabrina Reeves, Richard Windeyer, David Duclos (space and lighting design), Rachel Jones (costume design), and Laura Nanni (site and production coordinator).

11. Pseudoethnography is obviously as much a critique of community-based art practice as it is a descriptive term. Ethnography shifts course to 'pseudoethnography' when artists and institutions fail to fully engage with the communities they represent. However, pseudoethnography also points to those artists that engage in a comic vision of ethnography by parodying assumptions about the authority of the cultural specialist, querying our desire to experience difference, and assessing the relationship between what Anthony Downey calls 'ethnographic authority' and 'artistic authorship' (2009, p.597).

12
Immersive Negotiations: Binaural Perspectives on Site-Specific Sound

Bruce Barton and Richard Windeyer

BB⌕ One of the most compelling aspects of site-specific theatre is the potential for heightened immersion within a specific environment. Increased mobility (on the part of the performance and its audience), combined with the inevitably performative architecture of a hosting site, makes possible a pervasiveness of sensory stimulus unattainable in conventional theatrical contexts. While these conditions appeal to the full range of the senses, some modalities contribute to this experience with significantly more intensity than others. Yet beyond this cross-modal competition, site-specific sound design – particularly that which incorporates the binaural properties of headphone listening – regularly also explores the often contentious interplay between what Paige McGinley, among others, distinguishes as 'soundscapes' and 'soundtracks'. The soundscape – 'the "acoustic ecology" of a given place or environment'[1] – she suggests 'is concerned with the local spatial environment, the sounded knowledge of a particular place' (2007, p.58). By contrast, the soundtrack, as a performative intervention, 'offer[s] emotional and thematic cues, creating – and documenting – a journey' (McGinley, 2007, p.58). The soundtrack is understood as a 'mobile soundscape', one that 'accompany[ies] everyday life, but also perform[s] an aesthetic intervention that shapes one's daily experiences' (McGinley, 2007, p.58). The terms are instructive: while 'scape' suggests a broader field of undetermined options and co-existing dynamics, 'track' evokes a particular, predetermined path, one defined by active guidance and/or historical intention. Engaged in an inevitably unstable negotiation of meaning and experience, these two terrains mark site-specific sound design as already and overtly fraught, a realm of choice rather than resolution.

The structure and graphic design of this chapter are inspired by this multifaceted relationship between soundscapes and soundtracks: at times complementary but more often ambiguous, elusive, suggestive, partial and/or contradictory. In this study of Canadian sound artist Richard Windeyer – his solo practice and his work as a member of the performance troupe bluemouth inc. – we seek to enact a 'stereophonic collaboration' between the contextualizing perspective of the dramaturge (**BB**) and the reflective practice of the artist (**RW**). At times moving in parallel, at others intersecting, our aim is to examine, articulate, and evoke some of the characteristics and possibilities of sound design in site-specific performance. Taking its cue from the various sites of perceptual tension explored herein, this chapter also grasps towards the embodiment of an agonistic, practice-based, aurally fixated negotiation, with only black lines on a white surface (and one photograph) at our disposal.

[SFX: face slap (far left)]

In the case of listening-in-readiness, the 🖉**RW** listener's background activity scans incoming patterns (right hemisphere), seeking a match with one deemed to be of significance. If a close match is found, the listener's attention is re-directed to the sound and a close analysis is made (left hemisphere) to determine its 'fine structure' as an indicator of specific information (e.g. is that really the friend's footsteps, and what details indicate the person's mood or purpose?) (Truax, 2001, p.63).

Formed in 1998, bluemouth inc. is a Toronto-based, Canadian performance collective that creates original, dynamic, and immersive performance events for audiences in alternative spaces (bluemouth, 2011). The artistic mandate of any bluemouth project is to collectively create a uniquely site-specific experience, in which a variety of different artistic disciplines – including choreographed movement, spoken word performance, creative writing, immersive sound design, original live music and video, experimental film techniques, and environmental installation – are brought together to inform, animate, and cross-fertilize one another in a cohesive, multi-sensory experience. The various themes, issues, and subject matter of a bluemouth performance are often multilayered but always strive to form a relevant and vital witness to our particular time and place.

BB Working with and observing bluemouth[2] has altered my understanding of what a theatrical collective can be and what theatrical collaboration can mean.

From an audience member's perspective, the performances of bluemouth are essentially non-narrative. Traditional conventions of story/character resolution are intentionally subverted in exchange for works that are capable of encouraging and supporting multiple interpretations. Ideally, there are as many interpretations of narrative as there are participants in the creative process. In performance, we try to encourage the spectator to participate as a witness, constructing resolutions of character conflicts and situations based on the imagery and content presented.

bluemouth's approach to creating site-specific work is a challenging and multivalent one that does not always fall entirely within the conventional definitions of 'site-specific'.

There is always an underlying tension between the company and the site in both the creative process and performances. While a site is usually chosen for both its 'cool factor' (a barbershop, a burnt-out boiler room, a run-down porn theatre), and for its relevance and potency as a means of framing the central themes of a performance (porn theatre = sexual ambivalence; run-down hotel = mental illness; barbershop = male stereotypes), the influence of the site on the creative process – from writing to staging to sound design and *mise en scène* – varies from project to project. While *The Fire Sermon* (2003) (porn theatre = sexual ambivalence) was created for the most part in studio, and then adapted to the site, much of *Death By Water* (2004) was developed and shaped in a downtown park during the height of winter. By contrast, the (then) run-down conditions of Toronto's Gladstone Hotel[1] and its residents held a quietly profound influence on the creative evolution of *LENZ* (2001), as we often found ourselves delicately padding across creaking wood floors and resonant vaulted corridors to collect film footage and sound recordings, rehearse choreography, and so on. It is this dynamic – the many levels of influence that a particular site or environment exerts on the design process – that continues to attract the company and myself to site-specific performance.

[SFX: lobby desk bell struck once loudly (close left)]

BB In what ways and by what means does sound design play such an important role in generating site-specific performance's 'immersive' experience? 'Immersivity' has regularly been proposed as a definitive quality of aural perspective and, as Ross Brown has observed, 'is often described as the opposite of visual perspective' (2010, p.1). Descriptions of the physiological, cognitive, and aesthetic bases for this distinction – only some of which will be considered in the following pages – are complex, varied, and rarely harmonious. Nonetheless, most share a common perception – to draw on Salomé Voegelin's evocative terminology – of aurality's immediate, generative 'phenomenological doubt', which is held in diametric opposition to the reductive 'certainty of the image' nourished by the 'visual "gap"' between the seer and what is seen (2010, p.xii). 'Stability,' Voegelin asserts, 'is the object minus the action of perception, a state that does not exist but is assumed and pretended by a visual ideology. Sound by contrast negates stability through the force of sensory experience' (2010, pp.11–12).

For Brandon LaBelle, 'sound's relational condition can be traced through modes of spatiality' (2007, p.ix). This leads, LaBelle proposes, to a set of realizations that effectively and inevitably locate the subject within an interactive environment: 'sound is always in more than one place'; 'sound occurs among bodies'; and 'sound is never a private affair' (2007, p.x).[4]

This direct association of sound and spatiality is hardly surprising. As Brian O'Shaughnessy reminds us:

> The evolutionary rationale behind the sense of hearing determines that our minds should be concerned with the place of the sound-maker, knowledge of which must have important survival value [...] The ultimate purpose of perception is to lead the mind beyond itself, maximizing the available data as it does, outwards onto the objective and often significant material realities in the environment. (2009, p.125)

Yet, despite the undeniable 'survival value' associated with sound's fundamental spatiality, it is also inherently restless, unreliable in its assertiveness. As Gabor Csepregi observes, '[s]ounds [...] detach themselves from their source and pursue us [...] The acoustic sphere entails an element of possessiveness; we are seized by sounds and delivered to their influence' (2004, p.172). The resulting paradox of sound's refusal to adhere to the source that it is, ostensibly, tasked with announcing gives rise to what Pierre Schaeffer

[SFX: measuring tape being extended (moving close right to far left)]

terms 'acousmatic' situations, in which 'we hear sounds without seeing their cause' (cited in Chion, 2009, p.465). The same paradox, hardly by coincidence, is a critical element of potential within site-specific dramaturgical strategies.

To no small degree, the contemporary strength of this paradox, if not its root cause, is associated with the transition to transmission – that is, the emergence of recording and playback technologies. The radical dislocation of sound from a specific, material spatial context towards a virtual sphere of transient performance has generated myriad consequences, the articulation of which is clearly beyond the scope of this chapter. But as the sources of mediated sound continue to diversify and proliferate exponentially, the overwhelmingly immersive nature of intrusive electronic ambient sound has facilitated the dramaturgical possibility of what Peter Salvatore Petralia calls 'headspace' – that is, 'the notion of *sound and physical presence being re-located to within a viewer's brain* through the use of headphones in live performance' (2010, p.96; original emphasis). Yet while Petralia draws on models of embodiment based in contemporary cognitive science to explicate his desire 'to shift the location of the performance into the third space of the head' (2010, p.108), we draw on related sources to posit an understanding of auditory embodiment that remains, squarely and intentionally, 'immediately here and there, out of and in my own body' (LaBelle, 2007, p.230), at the constantly negotiated intersection of internal and external spatiality.

My approach ✑**RW** to designing soundtracks for site-specific performance stems from long-held interests in environmental sound ('soundscapes')[2] and the interdisciplinary study of acoustic communication and acoustic ecology. In light of the growing body of knowledge around the cognitive, social and technological relationships between humans and their sonic environment, I have tried to push theatrical sound-recorded design ('soundtracks') beyond the conventions of pre-recorded sound-effects and incidental music cued under and around scripted stage action. I have often employed the techniques and aesthetics of contemporary cinematic sound design – in particular, the confluent roles of diegetic and non-diegetic sound in immersive auditory experiences.

BB ✑ I found this comment of Richard's both instructive and provocative, particularly in terms of the type of perceptual experience he was aiming for.

The process entails a great deal of time spent recording and documenting the soundscape of the performance site. Sonic gestures and textures are then rendered from these recordings through computer processing and manipulation. Often the goal here is to frame and feature specific, discreet sounds of the site, and to transform them digitally over the course of the performance. These sounds are reintroduced to the performance site as 'keynotes' or 'soundmarks' (Truax, 2001, pp.66–7), and are given a life of their own, evolving and morphing over time. In a sense, the central aim of my approach to sound design is to let the naturally occurring soundscape of the site speak more dynamically and expressively, ideally to the extent that the site itself becomes a clearly defined character within a larger, immersive performance experience.[3]

[SFX: coins dropping on wood floor (far left)]

BB The relative virtues of attending a movie as opposed to a live performance have been argued since the first films were produced. However, recent scholarship that applies emerging understandings of human cognition to cinematic spectatorship provides new tools for appreciating the distinctions to be made, especially as they relate to the experience of sound in the two contexts. Further, when brought to bear on Richard's practice, these observations shed light on his distinct combination of often mutually exclusive, media-specific strategies.

Particularly significant is the near exclusive preoccupation with visual perception in most cognitive analyses of film viewing. In terms of spatial assessment (Levin and Wang, 2009) as well as character comprehension, proposed as a process of visual analysis, identification, and empathy (Bacon, 2009), perception is understood as ocular recognition via a combination of instinctual and conditioned responses. On a more fundamental level, Francis Crick and Cristof Koch have suggested that 'conscious awareness [for vision] is a series

[SFX: water lapping against side of wooden rowboat adrift in choppy water (close right)]

LENZ, Death by Water, and *Still Ringing* are three site-specific works that share this particular sonic design feature. In each one, a cinema-like framing of an environment is created for the audience through the use of headphones and binaural sound recording technology. This particular recording technique involves two microphones, one mounted in each ear of the recordist. This method exploits the of static snapshots [. . . and] that perception occurs in discrete epochs' (2003, p.122).[5] Of particular relevance is the assertion that because these snapshots are static, movement is the product of perceived difference *between* perceptual moments and is, thus, inferred rather than actually observed. The correspondence of this understanding of visual perception with the basic mechanisms of film projection and reception is, of course, striking.[6] Extending this perceived similarity even further, Yadin Dudai has drawn upon the Working Memory model of cognition proposed by Alan Baddeley, among others, as the basis for the assertion that '[t]he human mind has adapted cinema so rapidly and successfully because the human brain has a neural system [. . .] which almost called for cinema to be invented once the technological elements became available' (2008, p.22).

Formulated upon both the centrality of carefully controlled viewing conditions in film spectatorship and the extreme compatibility between visual perception and cinematic processes, watching a movie is presented in these arguments as a largely unidirectional and unilateral experience[7] – one capable, under certain conditions, of prompting a partial surrender of individual agency (Dudai, 2008, pp.28–30). Moreover, with only a few exceptions[8], the perception of sound as articulated within these cognitive approaches to film experience is interpreted as the

fact that we are able to hear the physical location of a sound by virtue of our ears being located on either side of the head. The brain registers slight differences in time, phase, and intensity of sounds as they strike each ear. The microphones pick up these differences, including any colouration of the sound produced by the pinnae (the fleshy parts outside the ear) (Truax, 2001, p.151). As a result, binaural recordings can replicate both the spatial movement of sounds and the acoustic 'signatures' of a space (produced when sounds interact with the many reflective surfaces, resonances, reverberent qualities of the physical space), in a manner that is virtually identical to the way our ears actually perceive them.

When the recording is heard through headphones, the effect is striking – especially if listened to in the same physical space in which the recordings were made. Here, a potentially profound 'slippage' of perception can occur: the listener experiences an aural deception or *trompe l'oreille* whereby they cannot be entirely certain if the sounds they are hearing are from the recording or from the outside world. Since the acoustic 'signatures' of the actual space and those on the recording are virtually the same, the brain cannot completely distinguish largely supporting and reinforcing complement to these vision-oriented processes – a contemporary version of the 'added value' (Chion, 2009, p.466)[9] of Michael Chion's 'audiovisual illusion' (1994, p.5) – without that writer's assertion of sound's key, under-detected contributions. One might initially expect to find a quite different scenario, for a broad range of reasons, within the context of live performance. Yet, as Philip Auslander asserted so provocatively in his 1999 treatise *Liveness* (and again in the 2008 second edition of that volume), all forms of popular expression participate in a 'cultural economy' that involves relative emergence and recession, dominance, and subservience:

between the naturally occurring sounds on the recording and those in the site. As a result, the ear is effectively tricked into thinking that these sounds are actually occurring in the room (and not necessarily through the headphones). The triggering of this response in the listener is often strongest with the use of sounds that signify the presence of another person, such as footsteps, the jangling of keys, or the opening of a door, which may effectively activate deeper environmental sensing and processing faculties in the brain (environmental monitoring, surveillance and sensing, and so on) (Truax, 2001, pp.57–8).

The resulting experience 'blur[s] the line between experienced reality and narrative fiction' (Cardiff, cited in Traub, 2007), infusing the audience experience with a subtle yet relentless tension – the soundtrack's seemingly controlled (composed) aural frame is continually expanding to embrace the largely uncontrolled and unpredictable soundscape of the surrounding performance site. The listener's ability to distinguish between the two sound worlds is constantly being tested and (re)negotiated.

> Initially, mediatized events were modeled on live ones. The subsequent cultural dominance of mediatization has had the ironic result that live events now frequently are modeled on the very mediatized representations that once took the self-same live events as their models. (Auslander, 2008, p.11)

While the subtler limitations of Auslander's now familiar argument have become apparent over the past decade, so too has its enduring general relevance. Mainstream theatre productions increasingly emulate the familiar (and thus familiarizing) practices of film and television: miked performances, celebrity personalities, adaptations of mainstream Hollywood films and television shows. In the process, they also intentionally pursue a similarly unidirectional and unilateral 'delivery' of standardized and repeatable fare.

In many ways, however, site-specific theatre operates as a direct refutation of this pattern of 'cinematic' familiarization. Andrew Houston has suggested that to create site-specific and environmental theatre is 'to be perpetually working between the absence of what we imagine the space to be and the material evidence of its proper and present uses' (2007, p.vii). If we adapt Nick Kaye's (2000) formulation (itself based upon Michel de Certeau's terminology) for site-specific art, it is possible to understand contemporary popular (that is, commercial) expression as a primary 'place', a dominant 'ordering system', that the 'space(s)' of site-specific performance set out, inevitably but also intentionally, to trouble: 'Space, as a practiced place, admits of unpredictability. Rather than mirror the orderliness of place, space might be subject not only to transformation, but ambiguity' (Kaye, 2000, p.5). Contrary to the relatively unidirectional delivery of stimuli that characterizes cinema spectatorship – and, arguably, much of the mainstream theatre activity that emulates commercial mediation – site-specific theatre regularly involves the total immersion of spectators and capitalizes on the accompanying sensory ambiguity that results. In this context, the roles and functions of sound are increased and assume heightened autonomy.

LENZ is a site-specific performance event that ⌀**RW** occurred simultaneously in three separate rooms of the Gladstone Hotel.[4] In the play, two of the rooms contain single live performers, while the third room contains a 20-minute film that introduces a third character whose ghostly presence haunts the characters portrayed in the other two rooms. The film is projected onto the hotel room's bed while the audience listens to its soundtrack though pairs of headphones placed around the bed's perimeter. The film's soundtrack is designed to evoke and support this character's past and his place within both the narrative threads and the site of the hotel: bilingual narration, environmental sounds common to a late nineteenth-century urban environment, and fragments of music. Much of the hotel's existing soundscape – creaky wooden floors; hissing furnaces; whirring ceiling fans; battered doors; voices and sounds (including radios and televisions) wafting into the hallways from occupied rooms; resonant wood and plaster acoustic signatures – were recorded binaurally and incorporated into the film's soundtrack.

One particular highlight of the soundtrack's design is a scene in which the coroner's report from Michel Foucault's dossier *Moi, Pierre Rivière, ayant égorgé ma mère, ma sœur et mon frère...* (1975, pp.54–5) is read (in French). The sound design of this scene was achieved by the sound recordist (me) lying on the floor in the position described by the coroner while wearing binaural microphones. The activities of an actual crime scene – measuring tapes stretching, camera shutters snapping, feet stepping around and across the body, faces breathing in close proximity, backgrounded conversations, and so on – were then acted out and recorded binaurally from the perspective of the corpse (though somewhat regretfully, we did not insist that audience members lie on the floor in the same position while listening to this recording).

BB The general understanding of auditory perception is also demonstrating similar acceleration in contemporary research and, in fact, has been the focus of cognitive analysis for an extended period. In a related development, bypassing the roadblock experienced in earlier psychological research, the study of...

In designing the sonic experience of *LENZ*, my initial goal was to immerse the audience in both the soundscape of the hotel and the fictionalized soundscape of our show simultaneously.

Ideally, the listener's...

... attention ...

RW ... would continually slide between light and shadow; between the actual, naturally occurring sounds, resonances, and reverberations of the hotel and those embedded within the sonic contructions of the performance – so that the sounds of the real-world hotel live within the fictionalized world of bluemouth's characters, and vice versa.

... has recently been **BB** revitalized, and with it the awareness of the distinct yet inter-related processes of visual and auditory perception (among the other modalities). Yet, as Elizabeth A. Styles has observed, while a commonsense perspective

Admittedly, a number of the sound design elements for *LENZ* – including pre-recorded music, voices, and sound-effects – were imported to the performance site from the studio. Yet all of it was subsequently enveloped by a larger soundscape constructed from sounds recorded within the rooms and hallways of the hotel during the production...

holds that '[e]veryone knows what attention is', there is little agreement among researchers. We do find, across multiple definitions, a belief that 'attention is characterized by a limited capacity for...

...process...

BB✎ ...ing information and that this allocation can be intentionally controlled' (Styles, 2006, p.1). However, the factors determining this 'limited capacity' are quite different for visual and auditory perception.

...✐**RW**

The selectivity of visual perception stems first from its unidirectional nature, and is thus in part imposed and unavoidable. By contrast, Chion observes, '[t]here is always something about sound that overwhelms and surprises us no matter what – especially when we refuse to lend it our conscious attention' (1994, p.33). As a result, auditory selectivity and comprehension require additional neural activity – we have to work harder at it because it is an almost entirely internal process and is, thus, a 'wholly cognitive act' (Scharf, cited in Styles, 2006, p.121). By extension, the nature of auditory distraction is in many ways more complex (and, thus, for the sound artist, more fertile) than visual distraction.

[SFX: ball-point pen clicking (close centre)]

In complex auditory environments, auditory perception attempts 'auditory streaming' (Styles, 2006, p.129) to segregate and group different sounds according to a variety of common characteristics, such as location and pitch, which are analysed in 'mutually reinforcing' assessments of one's surroundings. Contemporary analyses

In exploiting the ✐**RW** *trompe l'oreille* effect of binaural recording, the required use of headphones – especially those having a 'circumaural' design with pads that surround the ear – enable the sound designer to focus and restrict the audience's aural attention by attenuating also suggest that auditory perception in many ways parallels visual perception in its ability to compensate for omissions and interruptions or override contradictions (Warren, 2008, pp.150–73). However, the 'omnidirectionality' of hearing fosters distinct cognitive strategies of particular relevance to this discussion.

In the revised edition of his significant study *Acoustic Communication* (2001), Barry Truax proposes two modes of listening that, while not mutually exclusive, call upon distinct levels of neural processing. In 'listening-in-search' mode, '[d]etail is of the greatest importance, and the ability to focus on one sound to the exclusion of others (an ability termed "cocktail party effect" when it occurs in fairly noisy situations), is central to the listening process' (Truax, 2001, p.22). Conversely, 'listening-in-readiness [...] depends on associations being built up over time, so that the sounds are familiar and can be readily identified even by "background" processing in the brain' (Truax, 2001, p.22).

Truax's two categories have affinities with what Chion (building upon the earlier work of sound pioneer Pierre Schaffer) calls 'active' and 'passive' listening, which Chion further subdivides into three interacting modes: *casual* listening – listening to a sound to gain information about its cause or source (2009, p.471); *semantic* listening – listening to sound as a code or language to interpret a message (2009, p.489); and *reduced* listening – which focuses on the qualities of the sound itself as the object to be considered, independent of its cause or meaning (2009, p.487; see also Chion, 1994, pp.25–8). Overlapping and working in combination, these modes reflect the listener's attempt to locate, comprehend, and respond to the soundscape – an explicit recognition of what Truax also terms the 'survival value' implicit in the ability to interpret information about the environment and one's interaction with it, based on the detail contained within those physical vibrations (Truax, 2001, p.16).

much (if not all) of the outside world. Even the simple, physical act of putting on headphones leads the spectator to *assume* that their listening experience is about to become a very intimate and singular one, in which the outside world is effectively shut out. Ironically, this same use of headphones can also be very effective in cultivating a heightened sensitivity of the listener to the auditory world of both the performance and its site. Similar perhaps to the focusing of binoculars onto a landscape, headphones can mediate the perception of an immersive and performative environment through amplification, augmentation, and distortion.

However, all of these orientations rely upon what Truax calls 'hi-fi' environments with 'maximum signal-to-noise ratio[s],' which are 'by definition, balanced and well "designed," whether the design is intentional or the result of natural causes' (2001, p.23). By contrast, Truax asserts, 'lo-fi' environments 'encourage feelings of being cut off or separated from the environment. The person's attention is directed inward, and interaction with others is discouraged [...] Feelings of alienation and isolation can be the result' (2001, p.23).

[SFX: male voice speaking French in hushed tones (moving far left to close right)]

The implications of these observations for site-specific theatre are significant, to say the least. Hearing, itself, like site-specific performance, is immersive. Listening, like site-specific attendance, is an act of survival in a constantly swirling sea[10] of stimulus: reaching for and clinging to the 'objects' that flow towards one from all sides, making intuitive and instinctual selections, rapidly assessing potential, testing qualities, estimating utility, and interpreting significance. By contrast, in the isolated, insulated, unidirectional context of the cinema, the soundtrack of a popular narrative film is a 'high-fi' environment, 'balanced and "well designed" ', with a 'minimum signal-to-noise ratio.' The mainstream film soundtrack thus sets out to 'mirror the orderliness of place'. It is an environment specifically created to offer minimal resistance to conditioned auditory perception to facilitate a specific emotional, psychological, and intellectual response through the strategically 'limited capacity for processing information' that is the spectator's attention. In site-specific

While not ✐**RW** an official bluemouth performance project, *Still Ringing* (2005) is a sound installation which was conceived in the wake of *Death By Water*. In this work, a single viewer sits on a designated bench and dons the pair of headphones resting there. Through the headphones, the soundscape surrounding the bench can be clearly heard, fed to the headphones by binaural microphones mounted directly beneath the listener under the bench. In this experience, sound and vision are fused together in natural and complete synchronization. Gradually, however, the soundscape is filtered and attentuated while time-delays are introduced, forcing the synchronization to begin drifting imperceptibly. While sound separates from its source, further processing is applied to the audio feed, emulating the effect of hearing loss (the reduced perception of different ranges in the audio spectrum, such as high-pitched sounds) and the performance, however, a space that 'might be subject not only to transformation, but ambiguity', the soundscape and soundtrack regularly combine to crack open unidirectional reception and embrace the immersive co-mingling of found and created sound as a direct challenge to the capacity of auditory perception.

accumulation of resonant ringing frequencies (which are often diagnosed as a form of tinnitus). This accumulation builds to the point of complete (though simulated) deafness and then recedes, returning the listener to their original audio-visual state. The overall effect of this work is that – through the wearing of headphones – the listener's experience of their surrounding environment is initially reinforced but then dramatically reduced and refocused. Electroacoustic mediation is introduced with a level of transparency akin to a hearing aid or perfect prosthesis. Only then does it gradually betray the listener and then reposition itself as a portal through which the listener can rediscover their surrounding acoustic environment.

The use of binaural recordings has become increasingly popular among sound artists, perhaps most famously in the guided audio walks of Janet Cardiff and Georges Bures Miller. Cardiff's walks are designed to guide a mobile listener through a physical environment. The artist's own voice serves as an ever-present personal guide, speaking directly to the listener and exacting focus on specific sites and sounds along the route. The listener's participation is acknowledged at all times by the narrator, resulting in an experience that feels intimate, personalized, and secure.

By contrast, the use of binaural recordings in bluemouth's work is often designed for a stationary listener in a fixed physical position. Physical movement through the site's soundscape is instead recorded by the microphones, providing the listener with a kind of virtual movement. Narrative voices speak with an emotional distance that avoids the kind of direct address found in Cardiff's audio walks. The listener is more of an anonymous witness than a participant. The listener is, in a sense, set adrift in this convergence of the virtual recorded soundscape with the actual physical one and left to their own navigational devices to (re)negotiate their place within it.

BB A case in point: Cardiff's project *The Paradise Institute* (2001) makes for a enlightening comparison, especially with bluemouth's *LENZ (room 3)* and *Death by Water*.

BB Cardiff's performance is set up as follows:

In this installation, '[v]iewers approach a simple plywood pavilion, mount a set of stairs, and enter a lush, dimly lit interior complete with red carpet and two rows of velvet-covered seats. Once seated, they peer over the balcony onto a miniature replica of a grand old movie theatre created with hyper-perspective. This is the first in a series of illusions orchestrated by Cardiff and Miller. Viewers then put on the headphones provided and the projection begins. [. . .]

At least two stories run simultaneously. There is the 'visual film' and its accompanying soundtrack

RW The similarities between these works are compelling. *The Paradise Institute*, *LENZ*, and *Death By Water* all make use of binaural recordings and headphone playback to create a personal 'surround sound' listening experience couched within a movie-going pretense. In all three works, the audience engages visually with headphones on. In particular, both *The Paradise Institute* and *Death By Water* place the audience in a small, specially constructed viewing structure. As noted, in the case of *Death By Water*, the audience sits in a small wooden shed (with a large plexiglass window) in the middle of a city park in winter (Image 12.1). It is here that these works begin to diverge. In *The Paradise Institute*, the experience of sitting in a miniature replica of a grand old movie theatre reinforces the pretense and conditions of a movie-going environment: that it is a safe, insulated, and single-focus environment. Binaurally simulated 'intrusions' (mobile phones, whisperings, body sounds, and so on) provoke and reinforce the listener's awareness of the site, yet these do not ultimately distract the viewer from the main focal point (the movie); instead they help to reinforce its presence and that of the theatre

Image 12.1   *Death By Water*, Brooklyn, 2008. Courtesy of Ania Gruca.

that unfolds before the viewers; layered over this is the 'aural action' of a supposed audience. The film is a mix of genres: it is part noir, part thriller, part sci-fi, and part experimental. What is more particular about the installation is the personal binaural 'surround sound' that every individual in the audience experiences through the headphones. The sense of isolation each might feel is broken by intrusions seemingly coming from inside the theatre. A cellphone belonging to a member of the audience rings.

as an environment. In the bluemouth shows, the listening audience is left considerably more exposed to their physical surroundings and to the unpredictable nature of the live performers (something which is generally not an element in Cardiff's work). As the audience sits in a heated shed for the wintery *Death by Water*, they are kept intensely aware of the cold weather. Even more significant is how the overall physical positioning and trajectory of the live performers is one of moving ever closer to the shed, to the point where it is entirely conceivable that a performer could walk right into the shed, breaking the fourth wall completely and (perhaps ironically) letting the cold air of 'the real' into the fragile warmth of the shed.

In *LENZ* there is the potential (even expectation) for a live performer to burst into the room. The binaural experience continually draws the listener into the soundscape

A close 'female friend' whispers intimately in your ear: 'Did you check the stove before we left?' Fiction and reality become intermingled as absorption in the film is suspended and other realities flow in' (Cardiff and Miller, 2001).

of both the film and the surrounding hotel site simultaneously. It is important to note here that each audience member experiences the three rooms in one of three possible orders. Therefore, some audience members will experience the film first, while others will experience it last or as the middle segment. For audience members witnessing the film first, its soundtrack (perhaps unknowingly) provides them with a taste of the hotel's actual soundscape. I continue to wonder what effect this may have on the audience's experience of the hotel's actual soundscape, once they leave the room – haunted imaginings and thick resonances forming and gathering energy with each step through the site. For audience members having already experienced one or both of the other two rooms, the acoustic signatures of the hotel's soundscape on the soundtrack may serve to punctuate or reinforce their prior experience of that same soundscape. Indeed, each of these experiences plays an important role in creating and intensifying the *trompe l'oreille* effect.

[SFX: television sounds, behind door (close left)]

BB🔍 Finally, in response to Douglas Kahn and Gregory Whitehead's suggestion that '[t]he human ear offers not just another hole in the body, but a hole *in the head*' (1992, p.ix; original emphasis), we may now offer the contrary observation that the ear is not only another hole in the head, *it is a hole in the body*. The most free-flowing conduit of perception, audition is *the* site of performative embodiment, at which internal and external experience is confronted, negotiated, experienced. What I find so exciting about Richard's work is the degree to which he is able to employ the 'hi-fi' strategies of film soundtracks to utterly undermine the familiarity and perceptual apathy that they normally evoke. The comparison with Cardiff is particularly instructive here. As Seth Kim-Cohen has noted, some critics of Cardiff's work have questioned the degree to which participants in her performances can actually explore the environments through which her carefully planned forays are set. Yet, for Kim-Cohen, the primary experience of these performances is 'not a greater awareness of what is real, but of the absolute contextual constitution of perceived reality' (2009, pp.228–9). *The Paradise Institute* effectively pries open the insular experience of cinematic identification by manifesting (and thus juxtaposing) the spectator's immediate exteroceptive and proprioceptive experience; yet these are, ultimately, folded back in to construct a unified, self-contained logic – a perceptual consensus, if you will. In Cardiff's own words: 'The virtual recorded soundscape has to mimic the real physical one in order to create a new world as a seamless combination of the two' (cited in Petralia, 2010, p.106).

By contrast, Richard's work in performances such as *Still Ringing, Death by Water*, and *LENZ (room 3)*, deeply confounds an audience member's desire for such a consensus, even while his meticulously 'balanced' and conspicuously 'well "designed"' orchestration of auditory input implicitly promises the same. Rather, audience members are immersed – indeed, submerged – relocated and then effectively abandoned. They find themselves not only in a space of ambiguity, but also in a site of constant, ongoing, agonistic negotiation of virtually indistinguishable components drawn from both the found, unpredictable, and incidental *and* the recorded, composed, and premeditated. Confronted with their own vulnerability (physical, emotional, psychological, phenomenological), they become adversaries (as opposed to enemies)[11] of the company and of the space. They are required to witness and weather the perceptual debate. In the process, they must recognize, exercise, and potentially expand their auditory competences – that is, if they want to stay afloat.

Notes

1. McGinley here relies on Steven Feld's (2005) terminology.
2. I worked as dramaturge on the development of bluemouth's *Dance Marathon* in 2008–09.
3. I first employed Mouffe's (1999) concept of agonistic pluralism in relation to bluemouth (Barton, 2008, p.xv).
4. Extending this perspective, Alan Licht suggests that:

   > [s]ound also connotes companionship; part of the appeal of radio and records is simply that a voice is speaking or singing to the audient and engaging them in some way. Likewise ambient sounds remind the listener of his own presence in a living world, rather than an empty void. (2007, p.15)

5. Admittedly, these 'snapshots' are not understood to be uniform, like photographs or frames of film. Rather, each visual percept

Notes

1. Within a year of the bluemouth inc. performances of *LENZ*, the Gladstone Hotel was renovated into an upscale boutique hotel.
2. Two excellent introductions to this interdisciplinary field of research are Schafer (1994) and Truax (2001).
3. A further extension of this process – one that remains largely unexplored – is to introduce theories of acoustic communication and ecology into the development process around the characters portrayed in a performance.
4. *LENZ* was subsequently performed at the Ye Olde Carlton Arms Hotel in New York City in October 2006.

must include a huge amount of parallel and mutually influencing neural activity that must cross a certain threshold of intensity to result in a 'perceptual moment'.

6. For a detailed discussion of this correlation, see Konigsberg (2007, pp.7–11).

7. Even watching other forms of media, such as a television, seem to involve higher levels of apparatus – and thus self – awareness (Levin and Wang, 2009, p.43–8).

8. Two notable exceptions to this visual 'myopia' can be found in (Branigan, 2010) and (Fahlenbrach, 2008).

9. Chion defines 'added value' as follows:

> A sensory, informational, semantic, narrative, structural, or expressive value that a sound heard in a scene leads us to project onto the image, so as to create the impression that we see in the image what in reality we are audio-viewing. Added value is a common phenomenon; its effect tends to go unnoticed. (2009, p.466)

The concept of 'added value' takes on heightened relevance in the context of Casey O'Callaghan's (2006) discussion of cross-modal influence:

> What I'm suggesting is that a convincing explanation of the cross-modal effects requires appeal to a dimension of perceptual content shared across the modalities. If that's right, then any snapshot that arrives within a specific modality is itself already a multi-modal photo infused with information shaped by and gleaned from the other modalities. There is no separating off without remainder the purely auditory content or even the purely visual content. Even the content of vision itself cannot be thoroughly understood in complete isolation from the other modalities.

10. Ross Brown has noted that the immersive nature of auditory perception is often 'conveyed in acquatic tropes of oceans, bathing, drowning, swimming, floating and so on' (2010, p.1).

11. Maria Lind offers this gloss on Mouffe's distinction between adversaries and enemies:

> 'Agonistic' relationships involve struggles with an adversary rather than with an enemy, as in antagonistic relationships. An adversary is someone with whom you share a common ground but with whom you disagree on meanings and implementation of basic principles – disagreements which simply cannot be resolved through the deliberation and rational discussion celebrated by 'third-way-politicians' and defenders of the 'post-political' alike. (2007, p.19)

13

My Sites Set on You: Site-Specificity and Subjectivity in 'Intimate Theatre'

Helen Iball

The first decade of the twentieth century saw the opening of August Strindberg's Intimate Theatre in Stockholm on 26 November 1907, its diminutive stage (6 by 4 metres) and small auditorium designed to intensify the theatre experience.[1] The first decade of the twenty-first century ascribed new meaning to 'intimate theatre' as a face-to-face interaction between performer and audience, at its most concentrated in one-to-one dynamics.[2] In reviewing the 2009 Edinburgh Festival Fringe, Lyn Gardner re-invoked the term 'intimate theatre', acknowledging that, while the participatory experience that she categorized was not new, its new 'widespread availability' (2009, p.22) was noteworthy.[3] Gardner also voiced concern that such 'intimacy' placed 'audiences in situations they would never encounter in a traditional theatre' and that this raised 'ethical issues – both for those making and watching the work' (2009, p.22).

In pockets of 'intimate theatre' practice,[4] there is evidence of UK-based practitioners using site-specific strategies for an ethical imagining of audience participation. As artist Adrian Howells suggests, this is based on the recognition that 'place/space, combined with mode of address, is significant to potential genuine exchange' (2007). My motivation towards an ethics of 'intimate theatre' research is equivalent to the recognition from practitioners working intimately with audiences that such work necessitates a particular responsibility. It is for this reason that I use my own audience experiences as examples here. I do this to contain the risks of embarrassment and vulnerability and to sidestep the dangers of interviewees feeling misrepresented or exposed as a result of sharing intimate information about personal anxieties and insecurity. My research also responds to the need to re-evaluate methods for considering audience response. As Helen Freshwater argues in her consideration of *Theatre and Audience*, 'intimate theatre' is a field of theatre where habitual scholarly practices are rendered, perhaps, even more unsuitable:

> why, when there is so much to suggest that the responses of theatre audiences are rarely unified or stable, do theatre scholars seem to be more comfortable making strong assertions about theatre's unique influence and impact upon audiences than gathering and assessing the evidence which might support these claims? [...] Could this apparent aversion to engaging with audience response be related to deep-seated suspicion of, and frustration with, audiences?
>
> (2009, pp.3–4)

In 'intimate theatre', to a greater extent than in other forms of theatre, no response is easily dismissed as inappropriate, over-sensitive, or shallow because there can be no grounds to be frustrated with audience response.

Phenomenology can assist in rethinking the terms of audience response. As Steen Halling suggests, phenomenology is 'concerned, above all, with doing justice to the ambiguities and nuances of human experience' (2008, p.13). The phenomenological process of horizontalism[5] is particularly useful in counteracting the tendency to dismiss personal responses because of value judgements that predetermine what is valid and what is trivial. Horizontalism, as Phil Joyce and Charlotte Sills outline, is used in Gestalt therapy as a means of 'trying to stay as close to the client's experience as possible' (2009, p.16). In the 1970s and early 1980s, director and playwright George Tabori was using Gestalt techniques in actor training.[6] It seems an apt moment for a renewed interest in Gestalt as a beneficial approach towards a nuanced facilitation of audience participation by theatre-makers and students, and I suggest ways of applying its methods later in this chapter.

Anthony Giddens's views on the democratization of personal life published in 1992 also resonate with 'intimate theatre' practice in the 2000s/2010s: 'intimacy should not be understood as an interactional description, but as a cluster of prerogatives and responsibilities that define agendas of practical activity' (1992, p.190). Recognizing the usefulness of considering theatre's accountability in these terms, I ask three questions in this comparative study of Adrian Howells's *The Garden of Adrian* (Gilmorehill G12 Theatre, Glasgow, 15–20 June 2009) and Sylvia

Mercuriali's *Wondermart* (toured internationally since 2009):[7] in terms of prerogatives and responsibilities, how has the practitioner prepared the ground for 'intimate theatre'? How does the participant interrelate with site in light of the practitioner's preparations? And, given the relational focus of these site-specific 'intimate theatre' practices, what phenomenological methods are useful towards an ethics of 'intimate theatre'? These questions facilitate an analysis of the practitioners' manipulation of site towards scenography, through the imposition of role upon spectator.

The Garden of Adrian

Adrian Howells's *The Garden of Adrian* transports its participant into an intercultural, interfaith sanctuary. Minty Donald's scenography overlays the shed, conifers, and potting table of a British back garden with the stones, water, and meditative objects of a Zen garden. In some ways it does not seem to be site-specific performance, because it is easy to assume that the venue presents the 'blank slate' of a theatre studio, but this is not the case. *The Garden of Adrian* is housed in the Gilmorehill G12 Theatre, a building that is now a theatre studio but was formerly a Christian church, and whose stained-glass windows and architectural features testify to its origins. These features both inspire and become incorporated into the design. The site is also a 'set' constructed in the space as a response to the architecture. It has a wooden walkway through it, specifically for the purposes of the journey. An existing lift provides the entrance and its confines are echoed in the shed that has been installed to function as a waiting room: this is something of a compression chamber intended to prepare the participant for the experience. On leaving the dark shed, one meets the expanse and the spreading light of the church, the whole space visible from this vantage point as an overview of the journey through which each person is guided. Participants have each of their five senses directed towards objects at stations along the path by Howells as (spiritual) guide. There is an invitation to intimacy in his reassuring gaze and touch, as he proffers contact to the participant: hands and forearms to be bathed; mouth to be fed strawberries; body to be spooned. This is my recollection:

> *The width of the boardwalk means that Howells walks slightly ahead, holding me by the hand as I follow him. The dominance of the stained glass window on the far wall is both the destination and, in a detail with a*

border of sunflowers around it, provides the motto: 'he that soweth/ to the Spirit shall of/ the Spirit reap life/ everlasting.' In its vicinity, this message presents itself as the source of inspiration for a potting table from which, in a small act of gardening (alone and behind a conifer hedge, out of Adrian's sightline) I select a seedling to take away and nurture. There is a sense of relay, of Adrian passing his role and demeanour on to me.

Wondermart

Wondermart happens in public but covertly,[8] with the aid of an MP3 player and headphones. Scrutiny of site is at *Wondermart*'s gently mocking centre, with creator Sylvia Mercuriali recognizing that '[y]ou think of the supermarket as just a place to shop, but really it's a highly stylised environment that subliminally guides people to behave in a certain way' (cited in Power, 2010). A critique of globalized consumer capitalism, the site can be any large supermarket – a loaded comment in itself. The minimalist content of *The Garden of Adrian* is the antithesis of the laden supermarket aisles from which participants are asked to select items at various points in the performance. Into this environment they arrive equipped with the 30-minute audio and cluttered with (or clutching) socio-cultural baggage. The participant listens to the following audio track as they negotiate the presence of 'ordinary' shoppers and employees, and their own self-consciousness in diverging from consumer behaviour:

> Concentrate on the humming of the fridges (*sound of humming on audio track*) [...] Open one of the fridges. (*Sound of icy winds underscoring the following*) [...] Look at the white wall in the back of the fridge, get close to it, touch the back wall of the fridge [...] Feel the temperature. Turn towards the fridge door. Notice the condensation on the glass. With your hand, make a peephole (*sound of hand wiping condensation away*), look through it.[9]

The participant needs to overcome anxieties about appearing foolish or suspicious in a public space. The ubiquity of headphones in contemporary life provides some cover as they hear this:

> The store is designed to appeal to everyone and you'll find a wide range of people inside. Perhaps people with headphones on like you, travelling through this public space in their own private world [...] Remember, you aren't breaking any rules.[10]

Preparing the ground

While very different performances, *Wondermart* and *The Garden of Adrian* share key approaches that bridge site-specificity and 'intimate' audience participation. Anticipation can breed uncertainty and audience participation can feel daunting, even threatening. To compare Sara Ahmed's phenomenological description of establishing oneself in a new home – when 'the work of inhabitance' is 'a process of becoming intimate with where one is' (2006, p.11) – with theatre's very different ecology, is to recognize that to encourage the participant to *inhabit* a site-specific event is to risk *inhibitions*. I investigate one such scenario later, reading my own experiences as participant in *The Garden of Adrian* through Gestalt models of applied phenomenology borrowed from psychology and psychotherapy, fields equipped for describing the experience of psychological boundaries. Ahmed describes phenomenology as 'a way of thinking about orientation which points to how the bodily, the spatial and the social are entangled' (2006, p.1). In their different ways, Mercuriali and Howells use theatre to encourage such thinking. Reviewer Liza Power describes that during *Wondermart*:

> [T]he [supermarket] aisles you've wandered hundreds of times before begin to look different. The tin of green beans you've hitherto plucked absent-mindedly from the shelf and placed in your trolley beside milk and toothpaste becomes, well, more than a tin of beans. It becomes a cultural artefact. (2010)

In her Introduction to *Intimacy* (2000), an edited collection that seeks to 'further ongoing conversations in the humanities' about 'the modes of attachment that make persons public and collective and that make collective scenes intimate spaces' (2000, p.8), Lauren Berlant notes that 'intimacy builds worlds; it creates spaces and usurps places meant for other kinds of relation' (2000, p.2). When Berlant's observation is applied to theatre practices, one perceives opportunities that are in the gift of site-specificity. If Howells is the creator of spaces, then Mercuriali is the usurper of places. To build their intimate worlds, the practitioners use their insight into human perception and feelings. Both performances demonstrate their makers' understanding that intimacy can be a quality of the relation between participant and site, rather than the privilege of participant–performer relations. I recall:

> *After being introduced to Adrian and his garden, I am invited to join him in contemplating the first station along the path. The corner of the*

walkway creates an L-shaped frame for the white freesia flowers that stand out beautifully against the rich black-brown of the compost. They are displayed under an elegant glass cloche that Adrian removes, leaving a circular indentation in the compost like a subtle frame.

In *The Garden of Adrian* the resonance of small objects is harnessed for contemplation. Gestalt has its basis in Field Theory, thus the process of contact, as Frederick S Perls, Ralph Hefferline, and Paul Goodman describe, is in 'the forming and sharpening of the figure/ground contrast' (1994, p.73). As an area of Gestalt psychology, Field Theory, in Joseph Zinker's definition, recognizes that 'as we experience the environment visually, we choose a particular focus of interest, which stands out for us against a fuzzy background. That which stands out is called figure and the rest is ground' (1978, p.92). This figure/ground phenomenon provides a useful model by which to approach *The Garden of Adrian* because of the constant shifting and sometimes reversibility of figure/ground: the church architecture is my first focus, then my lips round a strawberry, then how small I am and my sense of how the ceiling soars. The participant, in becoming intimate with the site and with Adrian's inhabitance of that site, shares in and, through personal response, extends its resonances, so the piece becomes more than the sum of its parts. The experience is meaningful because of the memories and projections each one of us brings to the *Garden*. In their Introduction to the edited collection *The Senses in Performance* (2007), Sally Banes and André Lepecki recognize performance practices as offering 'privileged means' to investigate 'sensorial-perceptual realms, alternative modes for life to be lived' where 'the corporeal meets the social' and 'imagination meets the flesh' (2007, p.1). From an understanding that 'perception informs and is informed by subjectivity' and given that 'subjectivity is always embodied perception' (Banes and Lepecki, 2007, p.6), *The Senses in Performance* provides numerous performance examples from different socio-historical contexts to demonstrate that there is affective advantage in the multiple perceptual fields that are available through the theatrical sensorium. Exploring phenomenology and affect, Eve Kosofsky Sedgwick identifies the liminal sensory register of texture and asserts the need to discuss texture across the senses (2003, p.16). She describes how the title of her book, *Touching Feeling*, 'records the intuition that a particular intimacy seems to subsist between textures and emotions. But the same double meaning, tactile plus emotional, is already there in the single word "touching"; equally, it's internal to the word "feeling"' (2003, p.17). My two examples demonstrate that in 'intimate theatre' there can be an 'easing in' that works back through emotion towards affect. The field has to be established before the process of singling out figure from ground can occur, both sharpening and shaped by the affective focus.

Wondermart and *The Garden of Adrian* both orientate their participants with an overview of the site early in the proceedings. In *Wondermart*, the participant is advised: 'Now you have two minutes to wander around freely. Go everywhere, familiarize yourself with the space.' It is, of course, a wry instruction; it is likely that the participant has been in this supermarket many times before or ones very much like it. In *The Garden of Adrian*, the participant enters the main space at height and has the opportunity to survey it in its entirety before descending the staircase to meet Howells, who is waiting with a welcoming hug. In both pieces, the spectator is encouraged to participate because they witness demonstrations of an established intimacy between practitioner and site. These practitioners 'prepare the ground' by making evident their prior knowledge of site. There is no pretence that this is as new for them as it is for the participant – a contentious strategy employed in some 'intimate theatre', as I turn to shortly. Rather, the strategy is one of openness about the knowledge/power imbalance in the performer–participant relationship.

Both Mercuriali and Howells use their prior knowledge as the 'groundwork' for the acclimatization and orientation of the participant. Intimate knowledge of the location enables the practitioner to act as tour guide. Indeed, this is a role that site-specific theatre has borrowed frequently, for example in Wrights & Sites *Mis-Guides* (founded 1997) or Forced Entertainment's *Nights in this City* (1995). As well as providing playful opportunities for misinformation and subjective redefinition facilitated by the tour-guide role, demonstrations of being at home with the chosen site can provide a way of engaging the participant's trust and compliance. This is important given the 30-minute duration of both of the chosen examples, which, in Howells's one-to-one performances has been described as 'an accelerated friendship/relationship between two initial strangers' (Howells, 2009). Not only does the tourguide role enable the dissemination of prior knowledge of site, the proffering of a recognized role by association with the site cushions the process of enrolment for his participant. This form of orientation draws on the shared experience of cultural recognition. In *The Garden of Adrian*, the participant is offered the site – the converted church – as a sanctuary. This inculcates performative responses: the participant recognizes the role prompted by the site and thus site chaperones role, inviting the participant to ease into an appropriate demeanour. In one-to-one theatre, the participant is likely to mirror and complement the demeanour of the practitioner whose persona and dress may evoke the profession associated with the location: doctor, nurse, priest, therapist, beautician, masseuse, and so forth.[11] Howells takes on a mantle somewhere between spiritual guide and holistic therapist. My recollection is that:

> In relation to the site, I am mindful of a role in the vicinity of parishioner, client, novice monk, cherished companion. I behave with reverence towards the space, towards Adrian and towards the experiences he offers me. A friend wonders later what Adrian would have done had she chosen to run down the boardwalk or rushed from one experience to the next.

Equal playing fields

Performative strategies such as instructions and role play orientate the participant and establish the relational tone, simulating[12] connections vicariously as a means of accelerating the feeling of inhabitance. These connections function as a portal through which the participant forms their personal relation to the performance. In both *Wondermart* and *The Garden of Adrian* there is transparency – maybe even blatancy – about this process. By comparing these performances with one that has acquired some notoriety, and by situating them in relation to the counter-reactions it provoked, the use of site-specific strategies offers the opportunity for an ethical and contextualized reimagining of 'intimate' audience participation. Lyn Gardner's review (2009, p.22) cites the key examples of 'intimate theatre' from the 2009 Edinburgh Fringe as Adrian Howells's *Footwashing for the Sole* (premiered at The Arches, Glasgow, 2009) and Belgian theatre company Ontroerend Goed's *Internal* (premiered in Ghent, Belgium, 2007). As Howells's title suggests, the former was inspired by religious traditions of foot washing and by massage therapies. The latter, *Internal*, borrowed its intimacy from speed dating and group therapy. It sparked anecdotes about traumatized participants and personal repercussions.[13] Further accounts of 'intimate theatre' experiences have accrued online and in journalism, particularly since the *One-on-One Festival* (BAC London, July 2010). Indeed, *Internal* has become a notorious paradigm for other pieces similarly conceived or, sometimes, unintentionally manipulative by accident of misguided good will and lack of forethought. One response that expresses some of the most common objections is Dominic Cavendish's criticism of 'intimacy' that he finds 'coercive' and 'bogus' (2009). In a review of what has become a landmark for 'intimate theatre', the 2009 Edinburgh Festival Fringe, Cavendish observes that 'for all the aspiration' to 'create a proximity that feels true to life' it is 'not an equal playing field' when 'the performer is not only primed as to what's happening but can fall back on rehearsed techniques' while 'the requirement is on the audience member to act "naturally"' (2009).

The deliberate or accidental exploitation and potential vulnerability of participants has become a concern to the degree that it has mobilized proponents of a more ethical approach to 'intimate theatre'. At the time of writing, the main account of this position appears in the online discussion compiled by theatre practitioners who were involved in the British Council's *Connected* event in Tokyo (1–4 March 2010). *Connected* was billed as 'a showcase of interactive performance from the UK' (Connected, 2010).[14] James Yarker pinpoints the issue: 'Often it seems artists get so excited by the new situations that they put people into that they don't stop to consider if they should' (2010). *Connected* is evidence of a substantial commitment to an ethics of interactive theatre from key figures in the field. Their work is evidence of their commitment to finding creative solutions that address key concerns. For example, it was the inherent imbalance of power in audience–actor dynamics that prompted Rotozaza, a London-based group with core members Ant Hampton and Silvia Mercuriali,[15] to create the *Autoteatro* series, 'whereby audience members perform the piece themselves' (Rotozaza, 2008b)[16] and of which *Wondermart* is an example. Matt Trueman tags his experience of Rotozaza's strategy as a 'thought implant' (2009). Given that this is the case, the mental hijacking that occurs leaves me little opportunity to respond to my own inhibitions. Mercuriali is intrigued by responses to Rotozaza's use of instructions:

> It's strange. At first there's a resistance, like 'hold on, I have a free will,' but then it's very liberating. For a while somebody else has written your lines and you just have to say them. Whatever happens is not your fault.
>
> (cited in Power, 2010)

While in *Wondermart* the one-to-one dynamic is mediated through the pre-recorded audio, in *The Garden of Adrian* it is a private journey shared by Howells and his participant. In *Wondermart*, the audio-guide format means that the practitioners do not need to be there in person and that their absence concentrates the central relation between participant and site. In *The Garden of Adrian* the performer's retreat from the 'limelight' is also, though by a different means than in *Wondermart*, a key premise and the meditative walk is guided by an almost silent, contemplative Howells.[17]Indeed, Howells comments: 'With *The Garden of Adrian* I was aware that I was an integral part of the environment, that the piece was more about people being guided through a whole series of different garden locales'.[18] My thoughts return to Howells's artist's statement, quoted at the beginning of this chapter: 'place/space, combined with mode of address, is significant to potential genuine exchange' (2007).

Nevertheless, even in such sensitive approaches, the devil is in the participant's personal daemons, whose idiosyncrasies practitioners cannot predict but whose manifestations might be accommodated...

The 'cycle' shed

I am sitting in the shed waiting to be invited to open the door and join Adrian in the garden. Having taken off my shoes, I don't have anything to do but sit and wait. I realize that this is intended to be a soothing period of acclimatization, a bridge from the outside world to the sanctuary of the garden, but I am on tenterhooks by this point. Before entering the shed I have been given an instruction by the usher: 'when you hear Adrian call your name, open the shed door and go through it.' So I worry. Did Adrian already call my name? What if he did and I failed to hear him? If so, will he call it again? How terrible would it be to pop my head around the shed door and check? What would he think of me if I did that?

This section applies a Gestalt psychotherapeutic model to my recollection of waiting to be invited into *The Garden of Adrian*. The Gestalt Cycle of Experience, sometimes also called the Cycle of Awareness, is a useful tool for reading 'intimate theatre' experiences. It provides a means of dividing those experiences into smaller parts, and thus, to return to my earlier discussion, a way of charting shifts from affect to emotion (from 'I' to 'me'). The cycle enables this process to be plotted as sequential and as subject to interruptions. A key benefit is that such detailed content provides specific evidence for the general observation expressed by Erin Hurley that emotion is shaped by 'expectations forged in experience and cultural norms' (2010, p.19). A further benefit is that the fundamental principles of the cycle are sufficiently robust as a stand-alone model, though this must be qualified by urging recognition of the rigour and integrity of Gestalt as a professional psychotherapeutic method, and acknowledgment that such practice is distinguished from the proposals set forth here. In terms of my argument, the Cycle of Experience provides a way of framing and describing aspects of participant

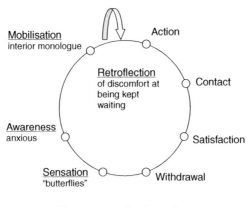

The gestalt cycle of experience
Applied to waiting in Adrian's shed

Figure 13.1 The Gestalt Cycle of Experience applied to waiting in Adrian's Shed.

experience as outlined: first, while the participant can be enrolled to participate, the assimilation will not be seamless; second, in encouraging the participant to *inhabit* the site-specific event, the experience of specificity is also subjective and this is bound up with *inhibitions*. In Gestalt terminology, these are described as 'interruptions to contact'. This diagram (Figure 13.1) illustrates the following description of the anecdote described above:

> The **sensation** probably originated as butterflies in my stomach, but rather than permitting myself the **awareness** of excited anticipation, I fall into an habitual pattern that recognizes the butterflies as anxiety, not relaxing with the radio and birdsong that twitter gently in the shed. Having taken off my shoes, I have no further outlet for my mobilized energy. I turn my anxiety against myself in an interior monologue. 'I should follow instructions carefully' is one of my introjects; those shoulds, musts and oughts I internalized earlier in my life. Another introject is that 'I must not be late or keep anybody waiting'. So, I have turned around the discomfort and uncertainty produced by the fact that Adrian is keeping me waiting and directed them at myself, an activity that Gestalt therapy calls retroflection. Somewhere between **mobilizing** my energy and putting that energy into **action**, the wheels of self-doubt spun. I could not bring myself to make **contact** by calling Adrian's name or opening the shed door to check whether he had called me.[19]

As soon as I do hear my name and, following the usher's instruction, leave the shed, the cycle is complete. The anxieties disappear. Although, for me, the shed and the call are not a relaxing way to begin an experience of audience participation, they do not have an adverse effect on my engagement with the rest of the event. Nevertheless, I would venture, based on this experience alongside similar ones that I have had and have heard about, that a key consideration for 'intimate theatre' makers is how the solitary nature of the five or ten minutes in a waiting or acclimatization space might impact on some participants. As I discover weeks later, my inhibitions have a bigger impact on my visit to *The Garden of Adrian* than the shed cycle. The fact that I do not like foot massage imposes significant limits on the affect of the performance, even though, as it turns out, this inhibition is irrelevant. I recall that:

> During **The Garden of Adrian** I am aware of the choice I've made to keep my socks on, and I imagine the consequences that this has in relation to particular phases of the event. I realize that what Adrian intended as wonderful experiences – the feel of rich soil between my toes, for example – are not at all sensuous and are even slightly ridiculous in socks. This is ok with me. It is worth the sacrifice because I know that I would very much rather Adrian bathe my hands than my feet.

Had I not seen the DVD recording made for the archives, I might never have known that Adrian washed each of his participant's forearms, whether or not they were wearing socks. The bare feet were to feel the changing textures of the journey, to make contact with the soil and bark and turf. From this rather mundane story comes an ethical and practical point about being indiscriminate when providing details and descriptions, because all or any of them could help specific participants give informed consent. Here, Gestalt's phenomenological strategy of horizontalism, when applied by practitioners and arts administrators, might provide support for participants towards their inhabitance of 'intimate theatre'. Had I been given the reason for going barefoot, I would have done so without hesitation.

One-to-one to 1:1 (some conclusions)

I have explored the imposition of role upon spectator, using myself as a test case, to consider the ways in which practitioners manipulate site towards scenography; the site becomes scenographic by being perceived as the performance environment in the practising of that place through the participant's inhabitance. This practising is, potentially, unpredictable. The unpredictability is, in turn, tempered by socialized behaviour and managed with detailed instructions; to be subjected to rules can be, paradoxically, freeing. Nick Kaye observes that site-specific work 'tests the stability and limits of the very places it *acts out*, at once relying on the order of the sites it so frequently seeks to question or disrupt' (2000, p.57; original emphasis). In tuning the embodied experience of its participants, *Wondermart*'s overlaying of life with art is a seductive intervention into the everyday that relies on the order of the supermarket as a means to unsettle its habitat. *Wondermart* has a mischievous eye on the opposite goal to Howells. Whereas in *The Garden of Adrian* site chaperones role, accelerating the closeness between Howells and his participant, *Wondermart* uses the participant's engrained familiarity with social role as a challenge. As blogger Matt Trueman suggests:

> For all that *Wondermart* succeeds as an eye transplant, it doesn't rid us of deeply felt obligations to the conventions of social behaviour. When it asks us to reach to the back wall of a freezer, to circle our trolley aimlessly or to abandon it half-filled in the aisles, we do so gingerly, awkwardly, even reluctantly. We never totally step outside the norm. [...] Though *Wondermart* makes us see the odd patterns of conformity, it never manages to entirely unshackle us from them. Not, of course, that it's trying to do so. (In fact, it preys upon precisely this when it asks us to consider stealing an arbitrary item. Hold it, it teases; feel it; notice the cameras and security guards; perhaps put it in your pocket; imagine leaving. Now, feel the sweat pricking at your skin). (2009)

Given that a primary focus of 'intimate theatre' is the participant's experience (and particularly when the performer retreats, in order to help liberate the participant's experience, that is, the move from inhibition to inhabitance), this disturbs the assumption that 'audience participation' refers primarily to exchanges between performer and audience member. Thus it is possible to consider participation in broader terms, overriding clear distinctions between interactions with people and interactions with things, to dislodge hierarchies of the *mise en scène* that privilege the performer over scenic property. It is on this basis that there is fluidity in the concept of one-to-one theatre, between quantitative categorizations (1 practitioner + 1 audience member) and their equivalents in the qualitative dynamics of intimacy. These are expressed in Mel Thompson's notion of personal identity, where 'what it is to be me is a process of creating and using a map scaled 1:1' in which 'the map we construct is superimposed by our minds full-scale over the universe' and is 'a constant process of referencing new experience against what we've experienced before, accessed by a process we call memory' (2009, pp.81–2).

In describing relations between theatre and perception, of which Howells and Mercuriali are clearly well aware (evidenced by the humane and imaginative nuance of their practice),[20] I am playing catch-up. It is my hope that this chapter participates in, as well as commentates upon, ethical approaches to 'intimate theatre' practice. The 'intimate theatre' dynamic, situated on the scale of one-to-one (the meeting of practitioner and participant) and/or 1:1 (the meeting of memory and site), intensifies the site-specific experience by giving the impression of being tailored to and realized by the sights that are set on me or you as the individual participant.

Notes

1. For a detailed discussion of the Intimate Theatre, see *Strindberg on Drama and Theatre* (Tornqvist and Steene, 2007).
2. For reflections on being an 'audience of one' see Rachel Zerihan (2009).
3. Gardner links the 'widespread availability' (2009, p.22) of such work to the popularity of the immersive audience experience of Punchdrunk's *The Masque of the Red Death* (BAC, London 2007).
4. 'Intimate theatre' is being used as an umbrella term taken from theatre journalism, as discussed here. It is not being taken to represent a defined genre or organized movement.
5. Horizontalism is 'creative indifference', that is, bracketing out assumptions and expectations to grant all aspects of the phenomena equal importance. The process is one of description rather than interpretation.
6. Tabori drew on his direct experiences of Gestalt therapy and John O Stevens, *Awareness: Exploring, Experimenting, Experiencing* (1989), and Frederick S Perls, *Gestalt Therapy Verbatim* (1969). For further details, see Antje Diedrich (2002).
7. *Wondermart* is by Silvia Mercuriali in collaboration with Matt Rudkin and Tommaso Perego. Details of touring are available at www.wondermart. co.uk.
8. The participant is alone but there is a version for pairs of participants.
9. This is my transcription of an audio tour extract made for the purposes of this chapter and to which I have added the parenthetical descriptions of sound.
10. This is my transcription of an extract from the audio tour.
11. It is no coincidence that one-to-one theatre often echoes appointments or brief encounters between the individual seeking support/advice/blessing/ comfort/release/relief or some other form of personal overhaul from a

priest/doctor/date/prostitute/therapist/hairdresser/masseur. Notably, these are dynamics in which the client's self is the focus of the transaction.

12. For discussion of simulation and stimulation of audience response, see Erin Hurley's summary of the application of recent neuroscientific discoveries, such as 'mirror neurons' (2010, pp.30–1, 36–8).

13. Examples from newspaper journalism include: 'One couple were said to have split up over a performance ("You weren't the reason," the woman told Devriendt [an actor in *Internal*] "you were just the catalyst.") while a previous participant became so besotted with one of the actors he was cautioned against stalking her' (Crawley, 2010). Lyn Gardner notes: 'There are stories of artists being stalked by audience members who believe there was real intimacy' and of 'theatre-goers being left genuinely distressed by their experience' (2009, p.22).

14. The *Connected* artists are Andy Field, Adrian Howells, Billy Cowie, Blast Theory, Coney, Duncan Speakman, Gob Squad, Hide&Seek, Melanie Wilson, Rotozaza, Stan's Cafe, Stoke Newington International Airport, Third Angel, and Tim Crouch.

15. Rotozaza describes itself as 'a group based in London making innovative, live artwork: theatre, performances, installations, happenings and more' (2008a). The name comes from an interactive sculpture (1967) by the Swiss artist Jean Tinguely.

16. Along with *Wondermart* (2009), the other pieces in the *Autoteatro* series are, to date: *Etiquette* (2007), *Guru Guru* (2009), *The Quiet Volume* (2010), *The Bench* (2010), *And the Birds fell from the Sky* (2010).

17. Howells created this piece during his AHRC Creative Fellowship at the University of Glasgow (September 2007–June 2009). The influence of his research and, particularly, the advice of the University Ethics Committee are evident in the detailed information provided to participants on the flyer about what will happen during the performance. In relation to his 'most radical project to date', *The Pleasure of Being, Washing, Feeding* (BAC, London July 2010), in which Howells invites his participant to be 'bathed naked, cradled and fed', Howells 'admits this is "really pushing the form," and emphasises that audience members can stop the performance if they are uncomfortable'.

> It's really important that they have agency, because even more in a one-to-one show people feel that they have to go along with things in case they sabotage the piece. It's about creating a safe space.
>
> (cited in Mansfield, 2010)

18. Howells in conversation with participants during a three-day interdisciplinary workshop in the Workshop Theatre, School of English (University of Leeds, May 2010) exploring the ethics of one-to-one theatre, funded by the British Academy as part of my ongoing research project *Theatre Personal: audiences with intimacy.*

19. For examples of the Cycle of Experience in therapeutic practice, see Joseph Zinker (1978).

20. This observation invokes an aspect of Carol Becker's discussion of 'the artist as public intellectual' in *Surpassing the Spectacle* (2002).

Part V
Site-Specificity and Politics

14
Siting the People: Power, Protest, and Public Space

Sophie Nield

I begin with three 'theatrical' events. On 21 June 1887, after almost 20 years away from public life, Queen Victoria travelled in an open landau through the streets of Westminster to Parliament Square and Westminster Abbey, escorted by her Indian cavalry and accompanied by rows of brightly uniformed soldiers. The streets were packed with well-wishers and spectators, arrayed on ten miles of specially erected scaffolding, who had gathered to see as much as they could of this glittering imperial pageant. This moment marked two things: the shift from actual to symbolic power of the monarch, and the beginning of Britain's reputation for unparalleled pageantry. By the time of her Diamond Jubilee ten years later, Victoria was able to write, '[n]o-one, ever, I believe, has met with such an ovation as was given to me passing through these six miles of streets' (cited in Cannadine, 1983, p.134).

On 15 February 2003, one million people marched through the streets of Westminster, passing Parliament Square and the Houses of Parliament, to protest the imminent attacks on Iraq. This was one of many demonstrations around the world on that day: an estimated ten million people mobilized in 60 different countries. The London march started on the Embankment, and most of the marchers were still weaving their way along a 3.5-mile route through the gridlocked city when the speeches were wrapping up at Hyde Park. The march had been a long time in the planning, with the Stop the War coalition, Muslim Association of Britain and the Campaign for Nuclear Disarmament (CND) working with international partners and domestic law enforcement. No disruption was reported: the march passed by peacefully.

On 24 November 2010, a protest against planned rises in university tuition fees organized by the National Campaign against Fees and Cuts and the University of London Students Union gathered in Trafalgar Square, and made its way down Whitehall towards Parliament Square.

At 1pm, as the protesters reached the southern end of Whitehall, near the Houses of Parliament, police formed a cordon of riot police, creating a 'kettle', or containment. Adam Gabbatt and Paul Lewis (2010) reported in *The Guardian* that at around 6pm, police on horses moved in from the north side to push back the protestors, which compressed people into a smaller and smaller area. Some of the protestors broke away, but around 200 people were held, so they said, without access to food, water, or toilet facilities until 10pm that evening. Some of those who were unable to leave when they wanted to have mounted legal challenges to the legitimacy of the 'kettle' as an effective tactic of public order policing.

The first account conjures a nation united under a monarch, who is herself thrilled to see so many of her subjects there to greet her. The second represents the orderly expression of dissent by the people against the policies and actions of their elected government as it takes the country to war. The third episode is a spontaneous occupation of public space by people angered by changes in public policy, followed swiftly by police action restraining the occupation on the grounds of public order. All present different iterations of nation, public, and state, and raise questions about spectacle, witnessing, and participation. They are all expressed through symbolic or theatrical performance; and they all took place on the same site.

In this chapter, I unpick some of the ways in which we read and interpret site-specific theatre, and some of the dominant critical tropes that have been used to model it, by looking at a very specific site and a series of events which have taken place there. These are, evidently, not 'theatre' events, yet they are certainly 'theatrical'. As Elizabeth Burns noted in her influential study *Theatricality: A Study of Convention in the Theatre and in Social Life*, we can claim an event as theatrical 'when we suspect that behaviour is being composed according to this grammar of rhetorical and authenticating conventions that we regard as theatrical'; when we feel we are in the presence of 'some action which has been designed to transmit beliefs, attitudes and feelings of a kind that the "composer" wishes us to have' (1972, p.33). The actions described above are all concerned with the relationship of a state to its 'people': they occupy a site at the geographical heart of the nation, and stage competing narratives of control, belonging, and ownership. Through interpreting some of the ways in which these events work in conjunction with 'site', this chapter opens up some new ways of thinking about the relationship of more formally understood theatre events with their places of performance. In particular, I want to trouble the metaphors of writing, and of ghosting, which are often invoked when describing and interpreting site-specific performance, proposing instead the idea of the 'horizon of meaning' described by the French philosopher, Henri Lefebvre.

Westminster has been the site of the administration of the English, and more recently British, state for almost a thousand years. Already the place where the coronations of English monarchs were staged, it was William the Conqueror in 1066 who began the practice of using the Palace at Westminster as the principal royal residence. Westminster forms a rough triangle with two other key sites: Buckingham Palace (the official royal palace since 1837), and Trafalgar Square, the geographical centre of London and a favoured site for popular protest since its inception in 1843. These sites are linked by two grand roads: Whitehall, upon which the great offices of state are lined up like Medici palaces; and the Mall, widened from a fashionable promenade into a 115-foot-wide processional route in 1911. Despite this being unquestionably the ceremonial centre of the capital city, as we shall explore, it was not consolidated as such until the turn of the twentieth century. Although the great offices of state had congregated here for almost 200 years, as David Cannadine notes in his study of civic pageantry, 'even the most ardent champion of the "infernal wen" conceded that it could not rival the careful planning of L'Enfant's Washington, the venerable ruins of Rome, the magnificence of Haussmann's Paris' (Cannadine, 1983, p.113). Now these streets, thronged with tourists and hurrying civil servants, and lined with statues of warlords and soldiers, are infused with a sense of government in action. They are where power speaks: but what kind of power? Only totalitarian states generate the kind of spaces which permit no ambivalence. Here, we see the articulation of a democratic state, albeit one which retains a constitutional monarchy. The balance of authority between its powers – crown, government, and people – is reflected in the different aspects of this ceremonial/governmental geography. And the historical and political struggles staged between these forces also take place here, in the form of performances which cannot help but be specific to this most resonant of sites.

Site-specific theory returns frequently to the idea of the palimpsest as a model for understanding the relationship of place and performance. This metaphor, based in the history of writing itself, positions the 'site' as a scraped-out document, its previous meanings and inscriptions rubbed out but still vaguely legible, onto which the performance will write a new text. Fiona Wilkie (2008, p.94) notes that both Mike Pearson and Cathy Turner (2004) use the analogy, envisaging the site not as *tabula rasa* but as something already replete with meanings and uses, which the performance may overwrite but cannot (and does not seek to) erase. Certainly, these ceremonial spaces are containers of this sort, although they are perhaps more explicitly developed with the idea of 'message' in mind than more quotidian venues such as disused factories or office blocks. They are specific to their urban (and national) context, and so not generic in the way that, for example, a law court might be – in that it could stand in for other law courts, or even the 'law' in the abstract. In fact, unlike even the most specific of theatre performance sites, such as the Crumlin Road Gaol used for Tinderbox's 2000 'Convictions' (Tinderbox Theatre Company, 2009), or the old Harland and Wolff engine shed in Glasgow, which was the setting for Bill Brydon's 1990 'The Ship' (The Glasgow Story, 2004), these are sites which are deliberately intended to be read in their own right: an interesting complication to which I will return.

A second central metaphor in site-specific analysis is perhaps Mike Pearson and Cliff McLucas's powerful metaphor of the 'host' and the 'ghost'. This figures the performance as a 'ghost' invented and produced by the theatre-makers, which, for a short period of time, haunts the host site. Importantly to the metaphor, the host remains visible through the transparency of the ghost – always already preceding and succeeding the temporary presence of the event (see extended discussion in Kaye, 2000, p.125). Pearson develops the thought elsewhere, differentiating between 'those (narratives and architectures) which pre-exist the work – of the host – and those which are OF the work – the ghost' (1997, pp.95–6). Again, it is clear how this metaphor speaks clearly and strongly to ceremonial space. It is built out of symbols explicitly designed to invoke a sense of history, and meanings that appear, at least, to be grounded in the deepest antiquity. This construction of a sense of historical continuity is, as we shall see, part of the ideological work of the space. The careful recreation and repetition of the forms of ceremonies from year to year and decade to decade (the Remembrance Day service and parade, for example, or the State Opening of Parliament), all contribute to the impression of shades of past kings, queens, soldiers, and people standing alongside participants and spectators in the present.

Yet it seems that within the host/ghost interpretive model, there is a troubling temporal hierarchization: the site precedes the performance, which is fleeting, evanescent, almost mystical. It is present for a short time and then it is gone, leaving the site deserted and abandoned, much as it was by its original inhabitants. Part of this derives from theatre's myth-making about itself, and the ways in which it has dealt with its own status as a time-based medium. It is also a troubling model in relation to social and political space and the performances, particularly of protest, which take place there. Demonstrations and occupations are often dismissed for precisely their time-limitation and described as temporary 'tactics' in the face of a dominating and dominant power which controls and determines space. The host/ghost framework cannot help but contain the assumption that the performance disappears at the end of the 'haunting' of its temporary site. I propose instead a strategy which suggests that the resonances of a performance remain after the event itself is over, and form part of a differently configured relationship between site and event: the idea of a 'horizon of meaning' provides a way of understanding the relationship of performance to site.

To develop this proposal, I turn to the work of Lefebvre (1991) and his now famous treatment of the 'production' of space. He argues that, rather than being a neutral void in which social life is merely situated, space is in fact a product of the events and activities that take place there. Space, he writes, is 'social morphology: it is to lived experience what form itself is to the living organism' (Lefebvre, 1991, p.94). This reciprocal relationship (what Edward Soja (1989) and others would later call 'the socio-spatial dialectic') means that 'any activity developed over (historical) time engenders (produces) a space, and can only attain practical "reality" or concrete existence within that space' (Lefebvre, 1991, p.115). Space is not separate from what it contains: it is formed by social relations and activities, and then sustains itself by restricting or permitting those activities. It does not precede the activities. Moreover, if the activities change, the space will change too. This offers an approach in which site is not simply haunted by the performance, nor is it temporarily animated or overwritten by performance. We begin to see more of a mutual process of construction – action determining space, which reciprocally determines action. This approach allows us to make two related proposals: first, that 'site' may not be the stable, 'found' entity which a performance temporarily haunts. Second, the importance of the performance itself in producing (rather than occupying) site may allow for a re-temporalization of its work, and, perhaps, restore something of its potential political force.

As we have seen, it was at the end of the nineteenth century that the ceremonial spaces of London were consolidated. Victoria's long absence from public life after the death of her consort Prince Albert in 1861 had eroded popular support for the monarchy. This, combined with shifts in both the balance of popular power (particularly following the extension of the franchise in 1884), and Britain's expanding reputation as an imperial power, prompted a broad rethinking of the relationship of governmental and sovereign power, and re-emphasized the importance of London as imperial centre. The Queen was repositioned as the figurehead of nation, and, following her styling in 1886 as Empress of India, of Empire. This was the point at which, according to Cannadine, 'national prestige was seen to be threatened' and 'action was taken, converting the squalid, fog-bound city of Dickens into an imperial capital' (1983, p.127). Between the 1880s and the completion of the Victoria memorial in 1912, the ceremonial centre of London was transformed from a series of accidental geographical coincidences into a coherent whole. The greatest expansion of Whitehall came in Victoria's reign, and these buildings are, to a great extent, echoes of the oldest edifice on the street: the Banqueting House, built by Inigo Jones after 1619 and the first in London in the classic Italianate tradition. Lewis Mumford observes that the kind of spatial perspective at work in the ceremonial vista first appeared, 'not in the actual city, but in a painted street scene in the theatre by Serlio' and that many early monumental city designers, such as Inigo Jones, were scenic designers (1961, p.433). In the early years of the twentieth century, Buckingham Palace was refaced in Portland Stone and the Mall was widened into a formal processional route. Admiralty Arch, which stands at the junction of the Mall and Trafalgar Square, was completed in 1912, and, although the configuration of the streets remains somewhat awkward (royal carriages must take a sharp right turn onto Whitehall from Horseguards Parade, and another at Parliament Square to arrive at Westminster Abbey), the overall effect is unquestionably grand.

Although Lefebvre has very little to say about theatre or 'theatrical' space (assuming it to be two-dimensional and essentially superficial), his outline of a 'monumental' space offers some very useful perspectives here:

> [Usually] space was *produced* before being *read*; nor was it produced in order to be read and grasped, but rather in order to be *lived* by people with bodies and lives in their own particular urban context. In short, 'reading' follows production in all cases except those in which space is produced especially in order to be read. This raises the question of what the virtue of readability actually is. It turns out on close examination that spaces made (produced) to be read are the most deceptive and tricked-up imaginable. The graphic impression of readability is a sort of *trompe l'oeil* concealing strategic intentions and actions. Monumentality [...] always embodies and imposes a clearly intelligible message. It says what it wishes to say – yet it hides a good deal

more: monumental buildings mask the will to power and the arbitrariness of power beneath signs and surfaces which claim to express collective will and collective thought. In the process, such signs and surfaces also manage to conjure away both possibility and time.

(1991, p.143; original emphasis)

Monumental space is not just a space that contains monuments: it is a space which is itself monumental, in that it embodies and describes a projection of political realities. It is designed to be legible; to produce a readable surface which will appear to be the whole 'message' and work of the space. The offices of state on Whitehall echo both classical and Renaissance architectures in a deliberate strategy to harness historical authority; the impossible scale of the Sovereign's Entrance to the House of Lords, with its lions rampant, forces spectators to crane their necks upwards to encompass it. These effects are carefully considered for their psychic and physical impact. Monumental space not only mystifies, it makes the individual tiny in relation to the architectural grandeur, the scale of the ceremonial avenue or building, the soaring ceilings of the cathedral. And in this way, it becomes much more than a text whose signs can be read, like architecture. Monumental space makes power *felt*.

Yet state power (which tends to be the 'author' of these ceremonial spaces) is much more provisional, much less authoritative than the narratives of its monumental spaces might want to suggest. For this reason, monumental space (and its successful maintenance) is vital to the continuation of power: the spaces in which it expresses and projects its narrative of its own authority must be coherent, for they not only disguise its actual provisionality, they replace it. They 'conjure away,' as Lefebvre has it, 'both possibility [of things being different] and time' (1991, p.143). Cannadine notes that the sense of antiquity which adheres to British ceremonial space and performance is in part due to the huge changes which transformed the European political landscape in the wake of the First World War. Between 1910 and 1935, five emperors, eight monarchies and 18 minor dynasties disappeared (1983, p.145). The rush of construction in capital cities across Europe after 1918 left Britain's late-Victorian ensemble looking venerable and antique. This obscuring of the actual historical context of the site is then sustained in, for example, commemorative literature and the popular press: a 1952 souvenir History of the Coronation speaks of the 'threads by which the Abbey is entwined with the history of the nation' (Tanner, 1952, p.7). As we shall see, this rhetoric is also applied to events: 'the ceremonies and rites ... have a history which is older still, so old, indeed, that some at least of them have their origins lost in the past' (Tanner, 1952, p.16).

As Lefebvre has argued, space, or in this case 'site', does not exist outside the events and social practices which take place there. How, then, do events, performances, and counter-performances function in ceremonial space? Any royal or state-sponsored event – such as a coronation, state funeral, or commemoration event – works in tandem with the legible intentions of the ceremonial site: the performance reciprocally endows the site with formality, as the site lends antiquity and legitimacy to the performance. The myth of unbroken continuity of tradition, layered onto the specificity of site, works to legitimate both. The tropes of performance are, for example, very similar in the coronations of Elizabeth I, Victoria, and Elizabeth II. The contexts, however, are entirely different, in terms of the power relationships governing public society at any one time, the stages of development of popular democracy, and definitions of nation, identity, and community. But the real struggles inherent in this historical trajectory are overwritten by the invented 'timelessness' of the presentation. In one sense, this reverses the 'palimpsest' model at work in site-specific analysis. Here we have the performance re-inscribing the assumptions inherent in the constructed site: writing over their potential contradictions with a certainty that carries political and rhetorical force. The people stand on the sidelines, eagerly awaiting a glimpse of their rulers who sweep past them in gilded finery, gorgeous uniforms, and carriages. Any procession of course operates as a form of narrative or storytelling in its own right. The rigid operations of hierarchy in the strict rules of precedence that adhere to British ceremonies make even more legible the relations embedded in the court, and those it has negotiated over centuries with parliament. Politicians and royal personages appear fleetingly, moving between the great buildings of state in which they are engaged in their proper business: business which (we are encouraged to believe) would continue whether or not we were there to see it. The 'people' appear not as individuals, but as a collective, fulfilling our role in the stage management of state: we witness, we acknowledge, we assent.

But this, of course, is only one possible story, the one that chimes with the organization and intention of the architecture of the site. As we have seen, site is not stable, with a set of fixed meanings: it is provisional and shifting, built from the activities which take place there and sustained only as long as those activities lend their force to one particular iteration of social and political relations. And this is what makes the ceremonial spaces of a nation also the place where power can be called to account by the people, for, as we have noted, it is very difficult to create a space which asserts itself with such totalitarian force that it cannot be performatively challenged, undermined, and redirected. Ceremonial or monumental sites deal in the manifestation of abstract ideas, such as nation, power, and people. These are materialized in state performances that are designed for these sites, among other ways. Making a different performance in the site does not just haunt it; it turns it into something else. Whitehall, Parliament Square and, most notably, Trafalgar Square, have a long tradition of being the site of protest. The original Select Committee in charge of the designs for Trafalgar Square reported, '[i]t appears to us that other evils may be anticipated from leaving open so large a space in this particular quarter of the Metropolis' (Mace, 1976, p.87). The square was opened in 1843. By 1848, the Chartists were holding the first of hundreds of public demonstrations there.[1]

When the Stop the War demonstration, for example, made its way through the streets of Westminster, it staged a re-articulation of just 'who' the nation comprises, and in whose name (and with whose consent) power is exercised by parliament. Clearly, the occupation of space by the 'people' is very different in this kind of context than in the spectatorial relation that is established by the royal procession. Not least, the politics is participatory: it is impossible for any individual demonstrator to see the whole extent of a protest march. The 'felt' effect is more of a shared power, a transgression and reclaiming of site, towards a redefinition of the locus of authority itself.

The territory 'occupied' by the demonstration is an alternative space. It is no longer the space of power. Nor is it, of course, entirely appropriated by resistance. In this transitional, in-between moment, the provisionality at the heart of site is revealed. Protest does not just occupy the space, it reinvents it.

There remains a practical difficulty, however, and this lies in the mobilization of symbolic vocabularies and tropes of representation that are still being used in demonstrations of a formal kind. As Rory Rowan has noted:

The standard form for modern symbolic protests has been to gather a concentrated mass of people in a defined space to produce a spectacular opposition. Of course such protests work to disrupt the daily functioning of the streets and hence economic and other activity but the main aim is to produce a semblance of 'the people' visibly standing in opposition to the government or its policy. (2010)

Lefebvre warns of this problem in relation to practices of demonstration and resistance. As we have seen, he cites monumental space, a space designed to be read, as the most deceptive imaginable. This holds true of 'legible' opposition: he notes that '[t]he "real" appropriation of space [...] is incompatible with abstract *signs* of appropriation serving merely to mask domination' (Lefebvre, 1991, p.393; original emphasis).

It is not surprising that successive governments argue for the rights of people to 'lawful' demonstration and to be able to 'make their point'. Even Tony Blair, under whose leadership a series of draconian infringements of the right to demonstrate were passed by parliament, said in 2002, '[w]hen I pass protestors every day at Downing Street ... I may not like what they call me, but I thank God they can. That's called freedom' (cited in Kadri, 2007). Although there is certainly dramaturgical force in the assembly of thousands of people contesting the will of 'their' government, and a significant reproduction of the 'site' that articulates and determines nation, nevertheless demonstrations seldom result in significant changes in policy. What they produce is an exchange of symbolic performances: the presentation of an alternative 'version' of state, nation, and people, but one which can be absorbed, perhaps, into the dominant narrative of the site. And there are limits, here, to what a state can or will permit.

When we consider the possibilities for a more 'improvised' performance, for a protest or resistant act on the part of people who have not negotiated 'stage-time' with the authorities, and who have not undertaken to restrict their 'performance' to the accepted norms, it quickly becomes clear that questions of ownership of the space, and legal and juridical control of its management, are increasingly being invoked to restrict the gestural and symbolic actions which may take place there. Fear of public disorder has led to increasing legislative restrictions on the rights to protest and to assemble publicly. As Burns pointed out,

the planned demonstration is something very different from the riot, even if the riot should emerge from it [...]. A demonstration is what it says it is – a show, a gesture [...]. The containment of demonstrations by the police is one way in which the 'powers that be' can empty the gesture of real meaning [...]. The riot was traditionally the one means of political action open to the politically impotent: it has reappeared as a way of restoring meaning to demonstrations.

(1972, p.92)

In 2005, the Serious Organised Crime and Police Act legislated that no demonstration was allowed within a kilometre of the Houses of Parliament without the prior permission, in writing, of the Commissioner of the Metropolitan Police. Section 132 reads:

Any person who –

(a) organises a demonstration in a public place in the designated area, or
(b) takes part in a demonstration in a public place in the designated area, or
(c) carries on a demonstration by himself in a public place in the designated area,

is guilty of an offence if, when the demonstration starts, authorisation for the demonstration has not been given under section 134(2).

(National Archives, 2005)

This is punishable by up to 51 weeks in prison. It is strongly believed that the legislation was originally formulated in response to the ongoing demonstration by anti-war protestor Brian Haw, who set up camp in Parliament Square directly opposite the House of Commons in 2001. Legal challenges were made to his presence there (complicated by the fact that different civic authorities are responsible for the grass, the pavement, and the road). Haw's protest was removed on 23 May 2006, but was replaced after the courts found that the 2005 Act could not be applied retrospectively. This confusion has led to some interesting contradictions. Most notably, Mark Wallinger won the Turner Prize for his 2007 'State Britain', a recreation of Haw's 40-metre display of placards, banners, and posters in the Tate gallery, a few hundred yards along Millbank from Parliament Square. The kilometre exclusion zone neatly bisects the Tate and ran right through the centre of the piece, making half of it simply illegal (Higgins, 2007).

But the legislative control has led to other consequences. In 2005, Maya Evans was convicted for reading the names of Britons killed in the war in Iraq on the steps of the Cenotaph in Whitehall (Anon., 2005).

So-called 'illegal' demonstrations now run the risk of being subject to a new police tactic known as 'containment', or 'kettling', in which a group of people gathered to stage a collective opposition or protest are then surrounded by police, often dressed in riot gear, and held there until such time as the police deem that it is appropriate to allow them to leave. It was introduced in 1999 and 2000 during anti-capitalist protests in London as part of the international anti-globalization movement, and was most recently used in response to the student protests of 2010. The intention is to subdue the crowd, and thus limit any potential disruption to public order or public safety which they might be understood to represent, by exercise of sheer boredom. This has often meant people being restricted from exiting the 'kettle' for several hours, and on occasion being without access to water, toilet facilities, or food. As Rowan notes, however,

> Part of the problem of approaching police kettling is that the phenomenon has not been fully understood. Although it may at first seem the grossest form of numbskull territorialisation it is in fact a more complex spatial strategy that works precisely within the same logic of concentration and spectacle as symbolic protest. [...] As the kettle aims to restrain the crowd it simultaneously seeks to incite them. By making the kettle unpleasant and by limiting the protester's freedom of movement as such the police aim to provoke an angry and violent response from the crowd. [...] The aim here is to identify, isolate and arrest the 'trouble-makers' so that they are punished both making an example of them and putting them off further engagement in protest. But the crux I would argue is not to produce violence in order to produce arrests but to produce violence itself. By inciting the crowd the police guarantee a violent spectacle that will feed the media's addiction to violence, which always makes a news-worthy story. (2010)

The 'kettle' is, then, part of a direct conflict over the occupation of space, and the right to control definition of 'site' by determining what kind of performance might take place there. The autonomy of the demonstrators is entirely restricted, and, it might be argued, subject to direct manipulation, without the need to force them out of the space. They are simply cast in a different role: by surrounding them, the police re-frame the activity and reshape the performance. No longer readable as a popular occupation of civic space, that which, for the most part, is intended to be legitimate opposition (albeit without official 'permissions') is re-framed as violent disorder, which has required the intervention of the police to contain and control it.

The real tension at the heart of site and its relationship to the varied and various performances that take place there becomes visible. These are debates, conflicts, and struggles staged around significant political and civil questions: what is the relationship of the people to the state, to the law, and to the government? Who has the right to determine the meanings of a site, and decide what can and cannot take place there? Whose performances are legitimate, and whose are not? To fully understand the work of this site and its relationship to the performances which inhabit and produce it, we must recognize its provisionality. It is not a stable container, either for the events which work in tandem with its meanings, or for those which seek to challenge it. The site is built of concepts to do with power and authority: as these events succeed and follow one another, they bring different interpretations of those concepts into play, reshaping and reproducing the space as they do so. To arrive at a full sense of the work of this space, and the construction of this 'site', we must recognize that the whole sequence of events is implicated in its formation and evolution. This is not a single inscription onto a scraped-out parchment, but a larger narrative: a changing sequence of superimpositions, inscriptions, occupations, and clearances; not a single site-specific performance, but a dramaturgy of space. It is here that Lefebvre's idea of the 'horizon of meaning' becomes particularly useful.

In this, he argues, the layers of sedimentation of often opposing spatial practices and events which impose upon one another in a place form a *'horizon of meaning*: a specific or indefinite multiplicity of meanings, a shifting hierarchy in which now one, now another meaning comes momentarily to the fore, by means of – and for the sake of – a particular action' (Lefebvre, 1991, p.222; original emphasis). No site, then, can be 'fixed' in its meanings, nor, in this context, a 'host' into which performance comes to stage a temporary haunting. All actions which have gone into, and which continue to go into, the constitution of a space, remain in it as part of its specific horizon of meanings.

We also see here a re-temporalization of site. Although, of course, its work and the experience of its work is in the present, just as the 'horizon' of its meanings is perceived from the present, the echoes of previous performances remain in the resonances of the space rather than being erased or disappearing. With ceremonial site, this problematizes its pretended 'timelessness', situating this as merely one strategy among many, and as one moment in a narrative sequence that has seen the inauguration, alteration, and occupation of the site over many hundreds of years.

So what might this perspective offer to the field of site-specific theatre? Rather than site preceding performance, or performance animating or inscribing site, the site and the performance can be seen to be producing each other in a reciprocal exchange of nuanced and subtly shifting meanings.

Whitehall, during a coronation, becomes the space which speaks of the monarchical state: the mighty coronation procession sweeping through Horseguards and down Whitehall, with rows of brightly uniformed soldiers snapping to attention, and crowds ranged behind barriers waving flags and shouting. During a demonstration, it speaks of a popular democracy in which dissent is enabled and encouraged, and in which the 'people' can re-situate themselves in relation to their rulers and speak truth to power. Under occupation – in conditions of riot or containment – the actual material struggles which underpin these symbolic exchanges become visible, and are played out in real time. No space is timeless; all spaces are under production all the time – and so can be intervened in, disrupted, argued with, and reproduced. Performance, rather than being a temporary occupier of a found or reclaimed site, is able to shift the meanings of that site permanently. Space is material: by occupying space, one changes it. Scanning the horizon of meanings that have been produced by a sequence of activities restores historical narrative to a site, which reasserts and revises political possibility. This chapter has addressed sites which are particularly concerned with issues of nation, people, and politics, but the horizon of meaning is true of all sites. There is more at stake in a performative moment than a transient, fleeting 'ghosting', which will be lost to the memory of the site once it is over. The work of performance is not a haunting: it is a battle for the right to determine, inflect, and produce the site itself.

Note

1. Chartism was a working-class political movement in the UK between 1838 and 1859 that sought electoral and social reform (Chartism Ancestors, 2011).

Bibliography

Ahmed, S. (2004) *The Cultural Politics of Emotion* (Edinburgh: Edinburgh University Press).

Ahmed, S. (2006) *Queer Phenomenology: Orientations, Objects, Others* (Durham, NC and London: Duke University Press).

Aitch, I. (2006) 'Plagues of frogs and lice...', *The Guardian*, 26 September, p.22.

Anon. (2000) 'Would you know how to identify a refugee? Starting today: Asylum seekers in Thanet – the reality and the myths', *Isle of Thanet Gazette*, 21 April.

Anon. (2005) 'Activist convicted under demo law', *BBC News*, 7 December, http://news.bbc.co.uk/2/hi/uk_news/england/london/4507446.stm, date accessed 12 November 2011.

Anon. (2006a) 'Campaigners plan to exploit Margate movie', *Kent News*, 29 September, http://www.kentnews.co.uk/kent-news/Campaigners-plan-to-exploit-Margate-movie-newsinkent1638.aspx, date accessed 6 June 2007.

Anon. (2006b) 'Chance for all to shine with film project', *Isle of Thanet Gazette*, 16 June.

Anon. (2006c) 'Vogue loves', *Vogue*, September, p.122.

Anon. (2006d) 'Your chance to be a star', *Isle of Thanet Gazette*, 9 June, p.13.

Anon. (2006e) 'Your invitation to create an art legend', *Isle of Thanet Gazette*, 11 August.

Anon. (2007) 'The lasting legacy of Exodus', *TurneroundMargate.com*, 22 March, http://www.turneroundmargate.com/the-lasting-legacy-of-exodus/, date accessed 22 July 2011.

Artangel (2011) *About Artangel*, http://www.artangel.org.uk/about_us, date accessed July 2011.

Auslander, P. (1997) *From Acting to Performance: Essays in Modernism and Postmodernism* (London and New York: Routledge).

Auslander, P. (2008) *Liveness: Performance in a Mediatized Culture*, 2nd edn (Abingdon and New York: Routledge).

Babb, G. (2008) 'Center and edge of the world: Frontiers of site-specific performance in Alaska', *TDR: The Drama Review* 52(3), 61–78.

Bacon, H. (2009) 'Blendings of real, fictional, and other imaginary people', *Projections* 3(1), 77–99.

Bailes, K. (2006) 'Be a star in movie of town', *Isle of Thanet Gazette*, 12 May, p.10.

Ball, M. and D. Sunderland (2001) *An Economic History of London, 1800–1914* (London: Routledge).

Banes, S. and A. Lepecki (2007) *The Senses in Performance* (London: Routledge).

BarbaraKruger (2003) *Allegiance*, http://www.barbarakruger.com/art/allegience.jpg, date accessed 29 October 2010.

Barton, B. (2008) 'Devising the creative body', in Bruce Barton (ed.), *Collective Creation, Collaboration and Devising* (Toronto: Playwrights Canada Press), pp.vii–xxvii.

Becker, C. (2002) *Surpassing the Spectacle: Global Transformations and the Changing Politics of Art* (Lanham, MD: Rowman and Littlefield).

Behrendt, E. (2007) 'I HAVE TO LET IT OUT!', trans. Michael Roberts, *Rimini Protokoll*, http://www.rimini-protokoll.de/website/en/article_2787.html, date accessed 11 December 2010.

Benjamin, W. (1999) *The Arcades Project*, Rolf Tiedemann (ed.), trans. Howard Eiland and Kevin McLaughlin (Cambridge, MA: Belknap Press of Harvard University Press).

Bennett, M. (2008) 'Legion of memory: Performance at branch 51', *Theatre Research in Canada* 29(1), 129–35.

Bergeron, D. M. (1978) 'The wax figures in *The Duchess of Malfi*', *Studies in English Literature, 1500–1900, Elizabethan and Jacobean Drama* 18(2), 331–9.

Berlant, L. (2000) 'Intimacy: A special issue', in Lauren Berlant (ed.), *Intimacy* (Chicago, IL: Chicago University Press), pp.1–8.

Bevington, D. and P. Holbrook (eds) (1998) *The Politics of the Stuart Court Masque* (Cambridge: Cambridge University Press).

Birch, A. (2004) 'Staging and Citing Gendered Meanings: A practice-based study of representational strategies in live and mediated performance'. PhD Diss. The SMARTlab Centre, Central Saint Martins College of Art and Design, The University of the Arts, London.

Birch, A. (2006) 'Staging and citing gendered meanings: A practice-based study of representational strategies in live and mediated performance', in Birgit Haas (ed.), *Der postfeministische Diskurs* (Würzburg: Königshausen & Neumann), pp.79–100.

Birch, A. (2008) 'Sites of performance: The *Wollstonecraft Live Experience!*', in Alison Oddey and Christine White (ed.), *Modes of Spectating* (Bristol: Intellect), pp. 231–42.

Birch, A. (2009) 'Wollstonecraft Live!', in Ludivine Fuschini, Simon Jones, Baz Kershaw and Angela Piccini (eds), *Practice-as-Research in Performance and Screen Media* (London: Palgrave Macmillan) p.193.

Birch, A. (2011) 'Performing research, cite, sight, site', in Leora Farber (ed.), *On Making: Integrating Approaches to Practice-Led Research in Art and Design* (Johannesburg: University of Johannesburg Press) pp.127–36.

Birch, A. and T. Iohe (2010) *The Wollstonecraft Live Experience!* (London: Fragments & Monuments).

Bishop, C. (2002) 'As if I was lost and someone suddenly came to give me news about myself' in Gerrie van Noord (ed.), *Off Limits: 40 Artangel Projects* (London: Merrell), pp. 22–9.

Bishop, C. (2009) 'Outsourcing authenticity? Delegated performance in contemporary art', in Clare Bishop, et al. (eds), *The Double Agent* (London: ICA), pp.115–19.

Bishop, C., S. Jestrovic, N. Ridout, and S. Tramontana (eds) (2009) *The Double Agent* (London: ICA).

Blair, S. and M. Truscott (1989) 'Cultural landscapes: Their scope and their recognition', *Historic Environment* 7(2), 3–8.

Blau, H. (1990) *The Audience* (Baltimore, MD: Johns Hopkins University Press).

Bleeker, M. (2008) *Visuality in the Theatre: The Locus of Looking* (Houndmills: Palgrave Macmillan).

bluemouth inc. (2005) *American Standard* (unpublished performance text, original work 2001).

bluemouth inc. (2006) 'Please dress warmly and wear sensible shoes', in Andrew Houston (ed.), *Environmental and Site-Specific Theatre* (Toronto: Playwrights Canada Press), pp.160–8.

bluemouth inc. (2011) *bluemouth.com*, http://www.bluemouthinc.com/, date accessed 10 November 2011.

Blunt, C. (2006) 'Neither last resort nor promised land', *Street Signs*, Autumn, 28–9.

Boon, R. and J. Plastow (2004) 'Introduction', in Richard Boon and Jane Plastow (eds), *Theatre and Empowerment: Community Drama on the World Stage* (Cambridge: Cambridge University Press), pp.1–12.

Bosseur, M. (2011) Interview by Susan Haedicke (Brest, 15 February).

Braidotti, R. (1994) *Nomadic Subjects: Embodiment and Sexual Difference in Contemporary Feminist Theory* (New York: Columbia University Press).

Brandon, J., W. Malm, and D. Shively (1978) *Studies in Kabuki: Its Acting, Music, and Historical Context* (Hawaii: University of Hawaii Press).

Branigan, E. (2010) 'Soundtrack in mind', *Projections* 4(1), 41–67.

Brennan, E. M. (ed.) (1993) *The Duchess of Malfi*, by John Webster, 3rd edn (London: A & C Black), first published 1963.

Brown, C. (1977) 'The Chirk Castle entertainment of 1634', *Milton Quarterly* 11, 76–86.

Brown, C. (1985) *John Milton's Aristocratic Entertainments* (Cambridge: Cambridge University Press).

Brown, C. (1987) 'Presidential travels and instructive Augury in Milton's Ludlow Masque', *Milton Quarterly* 21, 1–12.

Brown, C. (1995) *John Milton: A Literary Life* (Basingstoke: Macmillan).

Brown, R. (2010) *Sound: A Reader in Theatre Practice* (Houndmills: Palgrave MacMillan).

Bryant-Bertail, S. (2000) 'Theatre as heterotopia: Lessing's "Nathan the Wise"', *Assaph: Studies in the Theatre* 16, 91–108.

Burns, E. (1972) *Theatricality: A Study of Convention in the Theatre and in Social Life* (London: Longman).

Butler, J. (2011) *Bodies That Matter: On the Discursive Limits of 'Sex'* (London: Routledge Classic), first published 1993.

Butler, M. (2008) *The Stuart Court Masque and Political Culture* (Cambridge: Cambridge University Press).

Cameron, A. (2006) 'Geographies of welfare and exclusion: Social inclusion and exception', *Progress in Human Geography* 30(3), 396–404.

Campbell, G. and T. N. Corns (2008) *John Milton: Life, Work, and Thought* (Oxford: Oxford University Press).

Cannadine, D. (1983) 'The context, performance and meaning of ritual: The British monarchy and the "Invention of Tradition," c. 1829–1977', in Eric J. Hobsbawm and Terrence O. Ranger (eds) *The Invention of Tradition* (Cambridge: Cambridge University Press).

Cardiff, J. and G. B. Miller (2001) 'Paradise Institute', http://www.cardiffmiller.com/artworks/inst/paradise_institute.html, date accessed 10 November 2011.

Carlson, M. (2001) *The Haunted Stage: The Theatre as Memory Machine* (Ann Arbor, MI: University of Michigan Press).

Carruthers, J. (2007) *An Uprooted Community*, http://humanitieslab.stanford.edu/ 132/80, date accessed 31 August 2010.

Casey, E. S. (2009) *Getting Back into Place: Toward a Renewed Understanding of the Place-world*, 2nd edn (Bloomington, IN: Indiana University Press).

Cavendish, D. (2009) 'Edinburgh Fringe 2009: Is increased intimacy the future of theatre?' *Telegraph*, 28 August.

Chamberlin, E. H. (1962) *The Theory of Monopolistic Competition: A Re-Orientation of the Theory of Value*, 8th edn (Cambridge, MA: Harvard University Press).

Chartist Ancestors (2011) *Chartist Ancestors*, http://www.chartists.net/, date accessed 15 November 2011.

Chater, D. (2006) 'TV choice', *The Times: The Knowledge*, 2 December, p.45.

Chaudhuri, U. (1994) ' "There must be a lot of fish in that lake": Toward an ecological theater', *Theater* 25(1): 23–31.

Chaudhuri, U. (2002) *Staging Place: The Geography of Modern Drama* (Ann Arbor, MI: University of Michigan Press).

Chion, M. (1994) *Audio-Vision: Sound on Screen* (New York: Columbia University Press).

Chion, M. (2009) *Film, A Sound Art*, trans. Claudia Gorbman (New York: Columbia University Press).

Cieri, M. (2009) 'Robbie McCauley's *Primary Sources*: Creating routes to an alternative public sphere' (unpublished manuscript).

Clapp, S. (2010) '*Ditch*; *Marine parade*', *The Observer*, 23 May, The New Review, p.39.

Collins, J. and A. Nisbet (2010) 'Looking: The experience of seeing', in Jane Collins and Andrew Nisbet (eds), *Theatre and Performance Design: A Reader in Scenography* (London: Routledge), pp.5–10.

Connected UK (2010) 'Join the conversation', http://www.connected-uk.org/ join-the-conversation/, date accessed 26 November 2010.

Corcoran, S. (2010) 'Introduction', in Jacques Rancière (ed.), *Dissensus: On Politics and Aesthetics*, trans. by Steven Corcoran (London and New York: Continuum), pp.1–24.

Costa, M. (2006) 'Reviews: Film sets and reality blur into one as Margate takes starring role', *The Guardian*, 2 October, p.36.

Cotton, G. (2006) 'Previews: The promised land beside the seaside', *The Independent*, 25 September, p.21.

Crawley, P. (2010) 'I think we're alone now', *Irish Times*, 7 August.

Creaser, J. (1984) ' "The present aid of this occasion": The setting of *Comus*' in David Lindley (ed.) *The Court Masque* (Manchester: Manchester University Press), pp.11–34.

Crick, F. and C. Koch (2003) 'A framework for consciousness', *Nature Neuroscience* 6(2), 119–26.

Crossfiring (2006) *Crossfiring: The Claybank Project*, http://crossfiring2006.ca/, date accessed 8 November 2011.

Csepregi, G. (2004) 'On sound atmospheres', in Jim Drobnick (ed.), *Aural Cultures* (Toronto: YYZ Books and Banff, AB: Walter Phillips Gallery Editions), pp.169–78.

Cutler, A. (2007) 'Towards a promised land', in David Butler and Viv Reiss (eds), *Art of Negotiation* (London and Manchester: Cornerhouse), pp.187–223.

Dance Current (2007–08) 'the ART of participation', Special Issue, 10(6), http://www.thedancecurrent.com/.

Davis, T. C. (2003) 'Theatricality and civil society', in Tracy C. Davis and Thomas Postlewait (eds), *Theatricality* (Cambridge: Cambridge University Press), pp.127–55.

DCMS (2003) *Culture at the Heart of Regeneration* (London: DCMS).

de Certeau, M. (1984) *The Practice of Everyday Life*, trans. Steven Rendall (Berkeley, CA: University of California Press).

Debord, G. (1994) *The Society of the Spectacle*, trans. Donald Nicholson-Smith (New York: Zone Books).

Deleuze, G. and F. Guattari (1987) *A Thousand Plateaus*, trans. Brian Massumi (Minneapolis, MN: University of Minnesota Press).

Demaray, J. (1968) *Milton and the Masque Tradition* (Cambridge, MA: Harvard University Press).

Denham, C. (2006) '*Margate Exodus* is more than a great arts event', *Thanet Extra*, 15 September.

Deutsche, R. (1996) *Evictions: Art and Spatial Politics* (Cambridge, MA: MIT Press).

Diamond, E. (1997) *Unmaking Mimesis: Essays on Feminism and Theater* (London: Routledge).

Diedrich, A. (2002) 'Talent is the ability to be in the present: Gestalt therapy and George Tabori's early theatre practice', *New Theatre Quarterly* 18, 375–91.

Dillon, B. (2006) 'The revelation of erasure', *TATE ETC,* 8, www.tate.org.uk/tateetc/issue8/erasurerevelation.htm, accessed 6 January 2011.

Downey, A. (2009) 'An ethics of engagement: Collaborative art practices and the return of the ethnographer', *Third Text* 23(5), 593–603.

Dreamland Trust (2011) 'Dreamland Margate', http://www.dreamlandmargate.com/, date accessed July 2011.

Dudai, Y. (2008) 'Enslaving central executives: Toward a brain theory of cinema', *Projections* 2(2), 21–42.

Duša, Z. (1991) '*You – The City*: Fiona Templeton confronts her audience one by one', *Euromaske: The European Theatre Quarterly*, 3(3): 64–5.

English Heritage (2011) 'Listed buildings', http://www.english-heritage.org.uk/caring/listing/listed-buildings/, date accessed 7 November 2011.

Escolme, B. (2000) 'Webster's women', (unpublished paper, Performance Studies International Conference, Phoenix, AZ).

Escolme, B. (2005) *Talking to the Audience: Shakespeare, Performance, Self* (London and New York: Routledge).

Escolme, B. (2008) 'Shakespeare, madness and theatricality: Distracted actors in recent productions' (unpublished paper delivered at Shakespeare's Globe, London).

Etchells, T. (1994) 'Diverse assembly: Some trends in recent performance', in Theodore Shank (ed.), *Contemporary British Theatre* (London: Macmillan), pp.107–22.

Evans, G. and P. Shaw (2004) *The Contribution of Culture to Regeneration in the UK: A Review of Evidence* (London: DCMS).

Ewald, W. and M. Morris (2006) 'Towards a promised land' in Louise Neri (ed.), *Towards a Promised Land* (Gottingen: Steidl), pp.141–52.

Eyre, H. (2005) 'Talk of the town', *Independent on Sunday*, 25 September, p.11.

Fahlenbrach, K. (2008) 'Emotions in sound: Audiovisual metaphors in the sound design of narrative films', *Projections* 2(2), 85–103.

Feld, S. (2005) 'Places sensed, senses placed: Towards a sensuous epistemology of space', in David Howes (ed.), *Empire of the Senses: The Sensual Culture Reader* (London: Berg Publishers).

Ferris, L. (2006) 'Fragments of a life: Performing history in Newington Green', *Theatre Forum* (28), 75–80.

Ferris, L. (2007) Interview with Anna Birch (Town Hall, London, 8 October).

Fine, K. (2005) *Wollstonecraft Live!* (Unpublished manuscript).

Fischer-Lichte, E. (2008) *The Transformative Power of Performance*, trans. Saskya Iris Jain (London: Routledge).

Foster, H. (1995) 'Artist as ethnographer?' in George E. Marcus and Fred R. Myers (eds), *The Traffic in Culture: Refiguring Art and Anthropology* (Berkeley, CA: University of California Press), pp.302–9.

Foster, S. (2008) 'Movement's contagion: The kinaesthetic impact of performance' in Tracy C. Davis (ed.), *The Cambridge Companion to Performance Studies* (Cambridge: Cambridge University Press), pp.46–59.

Foucault, M. (ed.) (1975) *Moi, Pierre Rivière ayant egorge ma mère, ma soeur et mon frère . . . : Un Cas de parricide au XIXe siecle présenté par Michel Foucault*, trans. Frank Jellinek (New York: Pantheon).

Foucault, M. (1986) 'Of other spaces', *Diacritics* 16(1), 22–7.

Fragments & Monuments (2005) Programme for *Wollstonecraft Live!* by Kaethe Fine, 21 and 24 September (London: Newington Green).

Fragments & Monuments (2007) *Wollstonecraft Live!,* http://wollstonecraftlive. com/fm/?page_id=9, date accessed 29 October 2010.

Freshwater, H. (2009) *Theatre & Audience* (Basingstoke and New York: Palgrave Macmillan).

Gabbatt, A. and P. Lewis (2010) 'Student protests: Video shows mounted police charging London crowd', *The Guardian*, 26 November, http://www.guardian. co.uk/uk/2010/nov/26/police-student-protests-horses-charge?intcmp=239, date accessed 15 November 2011.

Gardner, L. (2006) '*The Margate Exodus*, Margate', *The Guardian*, 30 September, p.38.

Gardner, L. (2009) 'How intimate theatre won our hearts', *Guardian*, G2, 12 August, p.22.

Garner Jr, S. B. (2002) 'Urban landscapes, theatrical encounters: Staging the city' in Elinor Fuchs and Una Chauduri (eds), *Land/Scape/Theater* (Ann Arbor, MI: University of Michigan Press), pp.94–120.

Giddens, A. (1992) *The Transformation of Intimacy: Sexuality, Love and Eroticism in Modern Societies* (Cambridge: Polity Press).

Gilroy, P. (2004) *After Empire: Melancholia or Convivial Culture?* (Abingdon: Routledge).

The Glasgow Story (2004) *The Glasgow Story*, http://www.theglasgowstory.com/ image.php?inum=TGSb00370, date accessed 10 November 2011.

Goethe, J. W. von (1993) 'Women's parts played by men in the Roman theater', trans. Isa Ragusa, in Lesley Ferris (ed.), *Crossing the Stage: Controversies on Cross-Dressing* (London: Routledge,), pp.47–51.

Guilding, R. (2006) 'Unforgettable fire', *The Spectator*, 7 October, p.56.

Gumbrecht, H. U. (2004) *Production of Presence* (Stanford, CA: Stanford University Press).

Halling, S. (2008) *Intimacy, Transcendence, and Psychology: Closeness and Openness in Everyday Life* (Basingstoke and New York: Palgrave Macmillan).

Harvey, D. (2000) *Spaces of Hope* (Berkeley, CA: University of California Press).

Harvey, D. (2001) *Spaces of Capital: Towards a Critical Geography* (Edinburgh: Edinburgh University Press).

Haurant, S. (2006) 'Average house price breaks £200,000 barrier', *The Guardian*, 8 November, http://www.guardian.co.uk/business/2006/nov/08/housingmarket.houseprices, date accessed 7 November 2011.

Hedges, J. B. (2008) *Building the Canadian West; The Land and Colonization Policies of the Canadian Pacific Railway* (London: Macmillan).

Herodotus (1998) *The Histories*, trans. Robin Waterfield, (Oxford: Oxford University Press).

Hetherington, K. (1997) *The Badlands of Modernity: Heterotopia and Social Ordering* (London: Routledge).

Higgins, C. (2007) 'Wallinger takes Turner prize with re-creation of parliament protest', *The Guardian*, 4 December, http://www.guardian.co.uk/uk/2007/dec/04/art.artnews, date accessed 12 November 2011.

Holland, T. (2005) *Persian Fire* (London: Abacus).

House of Commons Communities and Local Government Committee (2007) *Coastal Towns: Second Report of Session 2006–07* (London: Stationery Office).

House of Commons Information Office (2010) 'Factsheet M4 – Women in the House of Commons', http://www.parliament.uk/about/how/guides/factsheets/members-elections/m04/, date accessed 5 September 2011.

Houston, A. (2007a) 'Introduction: The *thirdspace* of environmental and site-specific theatre', in Andrew Houston (ed.), *Environmental and Site-Specific Theatre* (Toronto: Playwrights Canada Press), pp.vii-xix.

Houston, A. (ed.) (2007b) *Environmental and Site-specific Theatre* (Toronto: Playwrights Canada).

Houston, A. and L. Nanni (eds) (2006) 'Site-specific performance', Special Issue, *Canadian Theatre Review*, 126.

Howells, A. (2007) 'Artist's statement for AHRC creative fellowship', http://www.gla.ac.uk/departments/theatrefilm televisionstudies/ourstaff/howells/, date accessed 29 August 2010.

Howells, A. (2009) 'The burning question #3: What's it like washing feet every day?' http://fest.theskinny.co.uk/article/96651-the-burning-question-adrian-howells, date accessed 20 December 2010.

Hughes, H. (1998) *An Uprooted Community: A History of Epynt* (Llandysul, Wales: Gomer).

Hunter, V. (2005) 'Embodying the site: The here and now in site-specific dance performance', *New Theatre Quarterly* 21(4), 367–81.

Hunter, W. B. (1983) *Milton's 'Comus': Family Piece* (New York: Whitston).

Hurley, E. (2010) *Theatre & Feeling* (Houndmills: Palgrave Macmillan).

Islington Council (2011) 'Mary Wollstonecraft', http://www.islington.gov.uk/Search/results.asp?query=Newington+Green, date accessed 29 September 2011.

Islington Council Environment and Conservation Service (2001) *Census 2001 Mildmay*, http://www.islington.gov.uk/DownloadableDocuments/Environment/Pdf/keystatisticsmildmay.pdf, date accessed 29 October 2010.

Jasper, J. M. (1998) 'The emotions of protest: Affective and reactive emotions in and around social movements', *Sociological Forum* 13(3), 397–423.

Jaubert, C. (2010) Interview with Susan Haedicke, 12 March.

Joyce, P. and C. Sills (2009) *Skills in Gestalt Counselling and Psychotherapy*, 2nd edn (London: Sage).

Joyland Books (2011) 'Save Dreamland campaign', http://www.savedreamland.co.uk/, date accessed 7 November 2011.

Kadri, S. (2007) 'Changing the rules', *New Statesman*, 5 March, http://www.newstatesman.com/human-rights/2007/03/civil-liberties-london-expert, date accessed 7 November 2011.

Kahn, D. and G. Whitehead (1992) 'Preface', in Douglas Kahn and Gregory Whitehead (eds), *Wireless Imagination: Sound, Radio, and the Avant-Garde* (Cambridge, MA: MIT Press), pp.ix–xi.

Kahre, A. and H. Taylor (2008) 'The aesthetics of disappointment', in David Cecchetto, Nancy Cuthbert, Julie Lassonde, and Dylan Robinson (eds), *Collision: Interarts Practice and Research* (Newcastle upon Tyne: Cambridge Scholars Publishing), pp.299–314.

Kastner, J. and B. Wallis (1998) *Land and Environmental Art* (London: Phaidon).

Kaye, N. (2000) *Site-Specific Art: Performance, Place and Documentation* (London and New York: Routledge).

Kershaw, B. (1999) *The Radical in Performance: Between Brecht and Baudrillard.* (London and New York: Routledge).

Kershaw, B. (2007) *Theatre Ecology: Environments and Performance Events* (Cambridge: Cambridge University Press).

Kester, G. (1995) 'Aesthetic evangelists: Conversion and empowerment in contemporary community art', *Afterimage*, 22(6), 5–11.

Kester, G. (2004a) *Conversation Pieces: Community and Communication in Modern Art* (Berkeley, CA: University of California Press).

Kester, G. (2004b) 'Position paper presented at The Monongahela Conference on Post Industrial Community Development', (3 Rivers, 2nd Nature Studio for Creative Inquiry and Carnegie Mellon University), http://moncon.greenmuseum.org/papers/kester.pdf, date accessed 3 November 2011.

Kidd, B., S. Zahir, and S. Khan (2008) *Arts and Refugees: History, Impact and Future* (Birmingham: Hybrid), http://www.artscouncil.org.uk/media/uploads/artsandrefugees.pdf, date accessed 7 November 2011.

Kim-Cohen, S. (2009) *In the Blink of an Ear: Toward a Non-Cochlear Sonic Art* (New York and London: Continuum).

Klingmann, A. (2007) *Brandscapes: Architecture in the Experience Economy* (Boston, MA: MIT Press).

Kloetzel, M. (2010) 'Site-specific dance in a corporate landscape', *New Theatre Quarterly* 26(2), 133–44.

Kochhar-Lindgren, K. (2003) 'Di's midsummer night party: "On dramaturgy"', *Women & Performance: A Journal of Feminist Theory* 26, 176–9.

Konigsberg, I. (2007) 'Film studies and the new science', *Projections* 1(1), 1–24.

Kurosawa, A. (1957) *Throne of Blood* (Tokyo: Toho Company/Kurosawa Production Company).

Kwon, M. (2002) *One Place After Another: Site Specific Art and Locational Identity* (Cambridge, MA: MIT Press).

LaBelle, B. (2007) *Background Noise: Perspectives on Sound Art* (New York and London: Continuum).

Lavery, C. (2005) 'The Pepys of London E11: Graeme Miller and the politics of linked', *New Theatre Quarterly* 21(2), 148–60.

Lefebvre, H. (1991) *The Production of Space*, trans. Donald Nicholson-Smith (Cambridge, MA: Blackwell).

Levin, D. T. and C. Wang (2009) 'Spatial representation in cognitive science and film', *Projections* 3(1), 24–52.

Levin, L. (ed.) (2009) 'Performance art', Special Issue, *Canadian Theatre Review* 137.

Levin, L. and K. Solga (2009) 'Building utopia: Performance and the fantasy of urban renewal in contemporary Toronto', *TDR: The Drama Review* 53(3), 37–53.

Lewalski, B. (2000) *The Life of John Milton: A Critical Bibliography* (Oxford: Blackwells).

Lewis Jones, B. (1985) 'Cynefin – The word and the concept', *Nature in Wales*, 121–2.

Licht, A. (2007) *Sound Art: Between Music, Between Categories* (New York: Rizzoli).

Light Honthaner, E. (2010) *The Complete Film Production Handbook*, 4th edn (Oxford and Burlington, MA: Focal Press), first published 1993.

Lind, M. (2007) 'The collaborative turn', in Johanna Billing, Maria Lind, and Lars Nilsson (eds), *Taking the Matter into Common Hands: On Contemporary Art and Collaborative Practices* (London: Black Dog Publishing), pp.15–31.

Lingwood, J. (1995) 'Introduction', in James Lingwood (ed), *House* (London: Phaidon), pp.7–11.

Lycouris, S. (2001) '*Di's midsummer night party*', *Live Art* 36, 13.

Mace, R. (1976) *Trafalgar Square: Emblem of Empire* (London: Lawrence and Wishart).

Macfarlane, R. (2005a) 'Common ground', Series of essays, *The Guardian*, 26 March – 4 June, http://www.guardian.co.uk/books/series/commonground, date accessed 23 January 2011.

Macfarlane, R. (2005b) 'The burning question'. *The Guardian*, 24 September, http://www.guardian.co.uk/books/2005/sep/24/featuresreviews.guardian review29, date accessed 23 January 2011.

Mackey, S. (2007) 'Performance, place and allotments: Feast or famine?', *Contemporary Theatre Review* 17, 181–91.

Mansfield, S. (2010) 'Interview: Adrian Howells, theatrical producer', *Scotsman*, 18 May.

The Margate Exodus (2007) *The Margate Exodus Flyer* (Margate: Margate Exodus).

The Margate Exodus (2011) *The Margate Exodus*, http://www.themargateexodus. org.uk/about.html, date accessed 7 November 2011.

Marks, L. (2002) *Touch: Sensuous Theory and Multisensory Media* (Minneapolis, MN: University of Minnesota Press).

Marx, K. (1981) *Capital: A Critique of Political Economy*, vol. 3 (London: Penguin).

Mary on the Green (2011) *Mary on the Green*, www.maryonthegreen.org, date accessed 1 December 2010.

Massey, D. (1994) *Space, Place and Gender* (Minneapolis, MN: University of Minnesota Press).

Massey, D. (1997). 'Spatial disruptions', in Sue Golding (ed.), *The Eight Technologies of Otherness*. (London and New York: Routledge), pp.218–25.

Max Prior, D. (2006) Review of *Ten Thousand Several Doors*, *Total Theatre* 18(3), 24.

Mayor of London (2010) *Cultural Metropolis: The Mayor's Cultural Strategy 2012 and Beyond* (London: Greater London Authority).

McAuley, G. (ed.) (2006) *Unstable Ground: Performance and the Politics of Place* (Bruxelles: P.I.E. Lang).

McCauley, R. (1993) 'Mississippi freedom: South and north', *Theater* 24(2), 88–98.

McEvoy, W. (2006) 'Writing, texts and site-specific performance in the recent work of Deborah Warner', *Textual Practice* 20(4), 591.

McGinley, P. (2007) 'Floods of memory (A post-Katrina soundtrack)', *Performance Research* 12(2), 57–65.

McGrath, J. E. (2009) 'Rapid response', *New Welsh Review* 85, 9–14.

McKibben, B. (2005) 'Imagine that: What the warming world needs now is art, sweet art', *Grist Magazine*, 21 April, http://www.grist.org/article/mckibben-imagine, date accessed 23 January 2011.

McKibben, B. (2009) 'Oh, Here It Is! Four years after my pleading essay, climate art is hot', *Grist Magazine*, 5 August, http://www.grist.org/article/2009-08-05-essay-climate-art-update-bill-mckibben, date accessed 23 January 2011.

McKinnie, M. (2009) 'Performing the civic transnational: Cultural production, governance, and citizenship in contemporary London', in D. J. Hopkins, Shelley Orr, and Kim Solga (eds), *Performance and the City* (Basingstoke: Palgrave Macmillan), pp.110–27.

Meerzon, Y. (2007) 'An ideal city: Heterotopia or panopticon? On Joseph Brodsky's play *Marbles* and its fictional spaces', *Modern Drama* 50(2), 184–210.

Metis Arts. (2011) 'Third ring out: Rehearsing the future', http://www.3rdringout.com/, date accessed 15 September 2011.

Miles, S. and R. Paddison (2005) 'The rise and rise of culture-led urban regeneration', *Urban Studies* 42(5–6), 833–9.

Milton, J. (2000) '*A Masque Presented at Ludlow Castle, 1634 [Comus]*' in Robert Cummings (ed.), *Seventeenth-Century Poetry: An Annotated Anthology* (Oxford: Blackwells), pp.273–302, first published 1637.

Molotch, H. (2002) 'Place in product', *International Journal of Urban and Regional Research* 26(4), 665–88.

Möntmann, N. (ed.) (2009) 'New communities', Special Issue, *Public*, 39, http://www.publicjournal.ca/.

Moore, M. (2003) 'Poetry', *Poem Hunter*, http://www.poemhunter.com/poem/poetry/, date accessed 2 September 2011.

Morgan, R. (1995) *Y Llyfr Glas: Brith Gof 1988–95* (Cardiff: Brith Gof).

Morris, M. (2006a) 'G2: Yes, but...: Michael Morris, co-director of Artangel', *The Guardian*, 11 October, http://www.guardian.co.uk/theguardian/2006/oct/11/features11.g23, date accessed 7 November 2011.

Morris, M. (2006b) 'Prologue', in Louise Neri (ed.), *Towards a Promised Land* (Göttingen: Steidl), pp.15–17.

Motionhouse (2010) 'Cascade – Preview', *You Tube*, http://www.youtube.com/watch?v=RJhkvjQxvNE, date accessed 12 September 2011.

Motionhouse (2011) 'Cascade', http://www.motionhouse.co.uk/cascade.htm, date accessed 12 September 2011.

Mouffe, C. (1999) 'Deliberative democracy or agonistic pluralism?' *Social Research* 66(3), 745–58.

Mumford, L. (1961) *The City in History* (London: Pelican).

National Archives (2005) 'Serious organised crime and police act 2005', *Legislation.gov.uk*, http://www.opsi.gov.uk/acts/acts2005/ukpga_20050015_en_1, date accessed 15 November 2011.

National Theatre of Wales (2010) http://nationaltheatrewales.org, date accessed 31 August 2010.

Neri, L. (ed.) (2006) *Towards a Promised Land* (Gottingen: Steidl).

Ngugi, wa T. (1997) 'Enactments of power: The politics of performance space', *TDR: The Drama Review* 41(3), 11–30.

Nield, S. (2006) 'On the border as theatrical space: Appearance, dis-location and the production of the refugee', in Joe Kelleher and Nicholas Ridout (eds), *Contemporary Theatres in Europe: A Critical Companion* (Abingdon and New York: Routledge), pp.61–72.

Nightingale, The (2011) 'Welcome', *The Nightingale*, http://www.nightingale theatre.co.uk/, date accessed 27 October.

O'Callaghan, C. (2006) 'Shared content across perceptual modalities: Lessons from cross-modal illusions', *Electroneurobiologia* 14(2), 211–24, http://electroneubio.secyt.gov.ar/O%27Callaghan_Cross-Modal_Illusions.htm, date accessed 14 November 2011.

O'Connell, S. (2007) Workshop, Workshop leaders C. Adams, D. Pettrow, S. Reeves, L. Simic, R. Windeyer, Toronto.

O'Donnell, D. (2006a) 'Home Tours', *Canadian Theatre Review* 126, 62–3.

O'Donnell, D. (2006b) *Social Acupuncture: A Guide to Suicide, Performance, and Utopia* (Toronto: Coach House Books).

Opéra Pagaï (2011) '*Entreprise de Détournement*', http://www.operapagai.com/spectacle_entreprise.php?PHPSESSID=6c1333b4bb608f91f02071e263215ff3, date accessed 5 September 2011.

O'Reilly, K. (2010) *The Persians* (unpublished manuscript).

O'Shaughnessy, B. (2009) 'The location of a perceived sound', in Matthew Nudds and Casey O'Callaghan (eds) *Sounds and Perception: New Philosophical Essays* (Oxford: Oxford University Press), pp.111–25.

Oxford English Dictionary (2011) 'Scene', *OED Online*, http://www.oed.com/view/Entry/172219?redirectedFrom=scene#eid, date accessed 7 November 2011.

Palmer, A. (2007) 'The making of *Exodus*', DVD extra, *Exodus*, dir. by Penny Woolcock (London: Soda Pictures), DVD.

Parks, S.-L. (1995) 'Possession', in *The America Play and Other Works* (New York: Theatre Communications Group), pp.3–5.

Pearson, M. (1997) 'Special worlds, secret maps: A poetics of performance', in A.-M. Taylor (ed.), *Staging Welsh: Welsh Theatre 1979–1997* (Cardiff: University of Wales Press), pp.95–6.

Pearson, M. (2010) *Site-Specific Performance* (Houndmills: Palgrave Macmillan).

Pearson, M. and M. Shanks (2001) *Theatre/Archaeology* (London and New York: Routledge).

The Performance Kit (2010) 'The performance kit: A visual analysis and making kit', http://www.theperformancekit.com/, date accessed 29 October 2010.

Perls, F. S. (1969) *Gestalt Therapy Verbatim* (Moab: Real People Press).

Perls, F. S., R. Hefferline, and P. Goodman (1994) *Gestalt Therapy: Excitement and Growth in the Human Personality* (London: Pelican), first published 1951.

Petralia, P. S. (2010) 'Headspace: Architectural space in the brain', *Contemporary Theatre Review* 20(1), 96–108.

Piccini, A. and C. Rye (2009) 'Of fevered archives and the quest for total documentation', in Ludivine Fuschini, Simon Jones, Baz Kershaw and Angela Piccini (eds), *Practice-as-Research in Performance and Screen Media* (Basingstoke: Palgrave Macmillan), p.37.

Pimlott, J. A. R. (1947) *The Englishman's Holiday: A Social History* (London and Boston: Faber & Faber).

Podesva, K. L. (ed.) (2009) *Fillip*, 10, http://fillip.ca/.

Power, L. (2010) 'Performance Shopping', http://www.theage.com.au/news/entertainment/arts/articles/2010/03/14/1268501414488.html, date accessed 29 August 2010.

Prince's Regeneration Trust (2009) 'Dreamland, Margate: Conservation statement' (London: Margate Renewal Partnership and Prince's Regeneration Trust), http://www.dreamlandmargate.com/downloads/5_Dreamland_Margate_SC_Conservation_Statement_final_comp.pdf, date accessed 7 November 2011.

Prodigal Theatre (2011) *Prodigal Theatre*, www.prodigaltheatre.co.uk, date accessed 27 October.

Radix Theatre Society (2002) 'The Swedish Play', *Radix Theatre Society*, http://www.radixtheatre.org/past/#02, date accessed 5 March 2011.

Rancière, J. (2004) *The Politics of Aesthetics*, trans. Gabriel Rockhill (London and New York: Continuum).

Rancière, J. (2009a) 'The aesthetic dimension: Aesthetics, politics, knowledge', *Critical Inquiry*, 36, 1–19, http://www.scribd.com/doc/38406894/ranciere, date accessed 14 May 2011.

Rancière, J. (2009b) *The Emancipated Spectator,* trans. Gregory Elliot (London and New York: Verso).

Rancière, J. (2010) *Dissensus: On Politics and Aesthetics*, trans. by Steven Corcoran (London and New York: Continuum).

Ravelhofer, B. (1999) 'Bureaucrats and cross-courtly dressers in the Shrovetide Masque and *The Shepherds Paradise*', *English Literary Renaissance* 29, 75–96.

Ricardo, D. (1971) *On the Principles of Political Economy and Taxation* (Harmondsworth: Penguin).

Robinson, V., R. Andersson, and S. Musterd (2003) *Spreading the Burden?: A Review of Policies to Disperse Asylum Seekers and Refugees* (Bristol: Policy Press).

Roche, J. (2006) 'Socially engaged art, critics and discontents: An interview with Claire Bishop', *Community Arts Network Reading Room*, http://www.communityarts.net/readingroom/archivefiles/2006/07/socially_engage.php, date accessed 3 November 2011.

Rose, G. (1999) 'Performing space', in Doreen Massey, John Allen, and Phil Sarre (eds), *Human Geography Today* (Cambridge, UK: Polity Press).

Rotozaza (2008a) 'What is Rotozaza?', http://www.rotozaza.co.uk/ whatisrotozaza.html, date accessed 20 July 2010.

Rotozaza (2008b) 'Autoteatro', http://www.rotozaza.co.uk/autoteatro.html, date accessed 20 December 2010.

Rowan, R. (2010) 'Geographies of the kettle: Containment, spectacle & counter-strategy', *Critical Legal Thinking*, http://www.criticallegalthinking.com/?p=1180, date accessed 10 November 2011.

Said, E. (1993) *Culture and Imperialism* (New York: Knopf).

Samuel, R. (2010) 'Thanet', in John K. Walton and Patrick Browne (eds), *Coastal Regeneration in English Resorts – 2010* (Waterside South: Coastal Communities Alliance), pp.82–6.

Sanders, J. (2001) 'Ecocritical readings and the seventeenth-century woodland: Milton's *Comus* and the Forest of Dean', *English* 50, 1–18.

Sanders, J. (2011) *The Cultural Geography of Early Modern Drama, 1620–50* (Cambridge: Cambridge University Press).

Schafer, R. M. (1994) *Our Sonic Environment and the Soundscape: Tuning of the World* (Rochester, VT: Destiny Books).

Schechner, R. (1968) '6 axioms for environmental theatre', *TDR: The Drama Review* 12(3), 41–64.

Scott, A. J. (2008) *Social Economy of the Metropolis* (Oxford: Oxford University Press).

Sedgwick, E. K. (2003) *Touching Feeling: Affect, Pedagogy, Performativity* (Durham, NC and London: Duke University Press).

Shared Intelligence (2008) *Margate Renewal Study* (York: Shared Intelligence).

Sharp, B. (1980) *In Contempt of All Authority: Rural Artisans and Riot in the West of England, 1586–1660* (Berkeley, CA: University of California Press).

Shields, R. (1991) *Places on the Margin: Alternative Geographies of Modernity* (London and New York: Routledge).

Soja, E. (1989) *Postmodern Geographies: The Reassertion of Space in Critical Social Theory* (London and New York: Verso).

Somdahl-Sands, K. (2008) 'Citizenship, civic memory and urban performance: Mission Wall Dances', *Space and Polity* 12(3), 329.

Somerset, J. A. B. (ed.) (1994) *Records in Early English Drama: Shropshire*, vol. 1, (Toronto: University of Toronto Press).

Statistics Canada/Statistique Canada (2006) *2006 Census*, http://www12.statcan.ca/census-recensement/index-eng.cfm, date accessed 3 November 2011.

Steel, B. (2010) *Ditch* (London: Methuen).

Stephenson, J. (2010) 'Portrait of the artist as artist: The celebration of autobiography', *Canadian Theatre Review* 141, 49–53.

Stevens, J. O. (1971) *Awareness: Exploring, Experimenting, Experiencing* (London: Eden Grove).

Stevenson, J. (2003) *Dogme Uncut: Lars von Trier, Thomas Vinterberg and the Gang That Took on Hollywood* (Santa Monica: Santa Monica Press).

Styles, E. A. (2006) *The Psychology of Attention*, 2nd edn (Hove and New York: Taylor and Francis).

Tanner, L (1952) *The History of the Coronation* (London: Pitkin).

Taussig, M. (1993) *Mimesis and Alterity: A Particular History of the Senses* (New York: Routledge).

Taylor, Diana. (2003) *The Archive and the Repertoire: Performing Cultural Memory in the Americas* (Durham, NC: Duke UP).

Templeton, A. (2005) 'Radix: Individual & space, illusion & reality' (Talk presented on 31 May 2005 at the ACTR/ARTC Conference University of

Western Ontario, London, Ontario), *Radix Theatre*, http://www.radixtheatre. org/academic/, date accessed 5 March 2011.

Templeton, F. (1990) *YOU – The City* (New York: Roof Books).

Thanet Refugee Access (2007) 'Timeline of events', http://margate.pampa production.com/timelineofevents.html, date accessed 8 November 2007.

Thomas, N. (1973) *The Welsh Extremist* (Talybont, Wales: Y Lolfa).

Thompson, M. (2009) *Me* (London: Acumen).

Tinderbox Theatre Company (2009) 'Convictions', *Tinderbox Productions*, http://www.tinderbox.org.uk/productions/past-productions/convictions/, date accessed 10 November 2011.

Tompkins, J. (2009) 'Staging the imagined city in Australian theatre', in D. J. Hopkins, Shelley Orr and Kim Solga (eds), *Performance and the City* (Basingstoke: Palgrave Macmillan), pp.187–203.

Tornqvist, E. and B. Steene (2007) *Strindberg on Drama and Theatre* (Amsterdam: Amsterdam University Press).

Traub, P. (2007) 'Interview with Janet Cardiff and George Bures Miller', *Networked Music Review*, 20 September, http://turbulence.org/networked_music_review/ 2007/09/20/interview-janet-cardiff-and-george-bures-miller/, date accessed 25 August 2010.

Truax, B. (2001) *Acoustic Communication*, 2nd edn (Westport, CT: Ablex).

Trueman, M. (2009) 'Thoughts on implanted thoughts: Rotozaza at the Forest Fringe', http://carouseloffantasies.com/2009/09/thoughts-on-implanted-thoughts-rotozaza.html, date accessed 28 August 2010.

Tschumi, B. (1994) *The Manhattan Transcripts* (London: Academy Editions).

Tuan, Y. (1977). *Space and Place: The Perspective of Experience* (London: Arnold).

Turner, C. (2004) 'Palimpsest or potential space? Finding a vocabulary for site-specific performance', *New Theatre Quarterly* 20(4), 373–90.

Urry, J. (2002) *The Tourist Gaze*, 2nd edn (London: Thousand Oaks).

van Noord, G. (ed.) (2002) 'A conversation between Michael Craig-Martin, Lisa Jardine, James Lingwood and Michael Morris', in *Off Limits: 40 Artangel Projects* (London: Merrell), pp.10–20.

Viola, B. (2010) *Bill Viola*, http://www.billviola.com, date accessed 31 August 2010.

Voegelin, S. (2010) *Listening to Noise and Silence: Towards a Philosophy of Sound Art* (New York and London: Continuum).

Walton, J. K. (2010) 'Introduction', in J. K. Walton and P. Browne (eds), *Coastal Regeneration in English Resorts – 2010* (Waterside South: Coastal Communities Alliance), pp.1–11.

Warner, M. (1985) *Monuments & Maidens: The Allegory of the Female Form* (London: Weidenfeld and Nicholson).

Warren, R. M. (2008) *Auditory Perception: An Analysis and Synthesis*, 3rd edn (Cambridge: Cambridge University Press).

Western Economic Diversification Canada (2007) 'Canada's New Government invests $2 million in western Canadian Green Technologies', *News Release*, 23 March, http://www.wd.gc.ca/eng/77_7795.asp, date accessed 3 November 2011.

Westfall, S. (1997) ' "A commonty a christmas gambold or a tumbling trick": Household theater', in J. D. Cox and D. S. Kasten (eds), *A New History of Early English Drama* (New York: Columbia University Press).

Weyburn Project (2002) *The Weyburn Project: The Archaeology of Silence and the Discourse of Madness*, http://uregina.ca/weyburn_project/, date accessed 8 November 2011.

Widdis, R. W. (2006) 'Globalization, glocalization and the Canadian West as region: A geographer's view', *Acadiensis* 35(2), 129–37.

Wiles, D. (2000) *Greek Theatre Performance: An Introduction* (Cambridge: Cambridge University Press).

Wiles, D. (2003) *A Short History of Western Performance Space* (Cambridge: Cambridge University Press).

Wilkie, F. (2002a) 'Kinds of place at Bore Place: Site-specific performance and the rules of spatial behaviour', *New Theatre Quarterly* 18(3), 243–60.

Wilkie, F. (2002b) 'Mapping the terrain: A survey of site-specific performance in Britain', *New Theatre Quarterly* 18(2), 140–60.

Wilkie, F. (2008) 'The production of "site": Site-specific theatre', in Nadine Holdsworth and Mary Luckhurst (eds), *A Concise Companion to Contemporary British and Irish Drama* (Malden, MA: Blackwell), pp.87–106.

Wilson, C. (2007) 'The party line: Toronto's turn towards a participatory aesthetics', in Alana Wilcox, Christina Palassio, and John Dovercourt (eds), *uTOpia: The State of the Arts: Living with Culture in Toronto*, vol. 2 (Toronto: Coach House Books), pp.324–43.

Windblown/Rafales (2008) *Windblown/Rafales*, http://windblown2008.blogspot.com/, date accessed 8 November 2011.

Wollstonecraft, M. (1975) *Vindication of the Rights of Woman* (Harmondsworth: Penguin), first published 1792.

Woolcock, P. (2007) *Exodus*, dir. by Penny Woolcock (London: Soda Pictures), DVD.

Woolman, N. (2010) 'Creative partnerships cut', *The Stage*, 21 October, http://www.thestage.co.uk/news/newsstory.php/30043/creative-partnerships-cut, date accessed 7 November 2011.

Yarker, J. (2010) 'Remembering our humanity', http://www.iflair.biz/connected-uk/tag/james-yarker/, date accessed 26 November 2010.

YouTube (2007) 'Fragments & Monuments', http://www.youtube.com/watch?v=nDSlEmgryyA, date accessed 29 October 2010.

Zeitlin, F. I. (1990) 'Playing the other: Theater, theatricality, and the feminine in Greek drama', in John J. Winkler and Froma I. Zeitlin (eds), *Nothing to Do with Dionysos?: Athenian Drama in its Social Context* (Princeton, NJ: Princeton University Press), pp.63–96.

Zerihan, R. (2009) 'One-to-one theatre: A study room guide', http://www.thisisliveart. co.uk/resources/Study_Room/guides/Rachel_Zerihan.html, date accessed 26 November 2010.

Zinker, J. (1978) *Creative Process in Gestalt Therapy* (New York: Vintage).

Index